FENG-SHUI

FENG-SHUI

—

THE
ANCIENT WISDOM
OF HARMONIOUS LIVING
FOR MODERN TIMES

—

Eva Wong

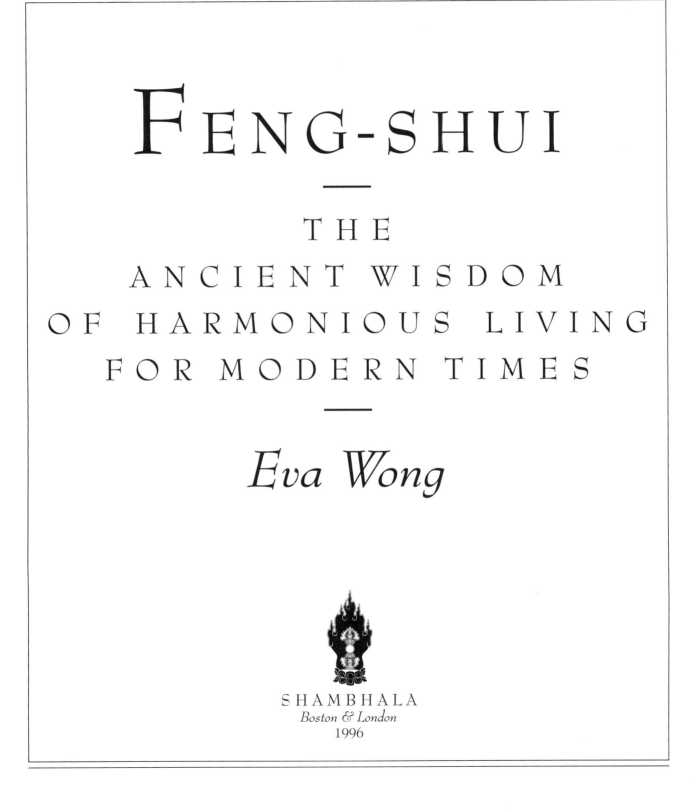

SHAMBHALA
Boston & London
1996

Shambhala Publications, Inc.
Horticultural Hall
300 Massachusetts Avenue
Boston, Massachusetts 02115
www.shambhala.com

Figures 12.1, 12.2, 12.4, 12.7, 12.8, 12.9, 12.10, and 12.11 are reprinted with permis-sion from New Compact House Designs: Twenty-seven Award-Winning Plans, 1,250 Square Feet or Less, *edited by Don Metz, published by Storey Publishing,* © 1991 *Storey Communications, Inc., Pownal, Vt. Figures 12.6, 12.12, and 12.14 are reprinted with permission from* The Compact House Book: Thirty-three Prize-Winning Designs, 1,000 Square Feet or Less, *edited by Don Metz, published by Garden Way Publishing,* © 1983 *by Storey Communications, Inc., Pownal, Vt.*

9   8   7   6   5

Printed in the United States of America

⊗ *This edition is printed on acid-free paper that meets the American National Standards Institute Z39.48 Standard.*

Distributed in the United States by Random House, Inc.,
and in Canada by Random House of Canada Ltd

Book Design by Ruth Kolbert

Library of Congress Cataloging-in-Publication Data

Wong, Eva, 1951–
Feng-shui: the ancient wisdom of harmonious living for modern
times / Eva Wong.—1st ed.
p.   cm.
ISBN 1-57062-100-4 (alk. paper)
1. Feng-shui.   I. Title.
BF1779.F4W66 1996   95-25356
133.3'33—dc20   CIP

Contents

To the memory of my granduncle.
Among the many gifts he gave me was
the Taoist art of feng-shui.

ACKNOWLEDGMENTS

I would like to thank all those who supported this project and my study of feng-shui. To my parents I owe much gratitude for their understanding and their support of my Taoist training. I also want to thank my husband, Charles Pearson, for computer work on the graphics of this book. Finally, I would like to thank Samuel Bercholz and Jonathan Green of Shambhala Publications for their patience. I hope that they have not waited in vain.

FENG-SHUI

Introduction

FENG-SHUI AS A TAOIST ART

Feng-shui (pronounced *fung-shway*), the pattern of wind and water, is the Taoist art and science of living in harmony with the environment. For centuries, the Chinese people have relied on feng-shui to design cities, build homes, and bury their dead. Today, in Hong Kong, Taiwan, Singapore, and many cities where there is a large Chinese population, feng-shui is a part of everyday living. The business community consults feng-shui masters in choosing offices and business locations. Homeowners rely on feng-shui to find or build a house that will give the family health and prosperity. Those who have the luxury of choosing their burial site will ask the feng-shui practitioner to select a location that will benefit their descendants. Recently, as more Westerners become familiar with the arts and sciences of China, feng-shui is no longer a practice valued by the Chinese alone. In North America, architects, real-estate agents, and even homeowners are beginning to be interested in feng-shui. However, despite its growing popularity, few people are aware that the art of feng-shui is Taoist in origin and that it is intimately tied to the practice of Taoism.

When I think about my own interest in feng-shui, the circumstances by which I became apprenticed in this art, and the eventual integration of this practice into my Taoist training, I cannot but attribute them to my childhood experiences in Hong Kong.

In Hong Kong, where I was born and raised, modernity and tradition existed comfortably side by side. While businesspeople make decisions that influence the world's economy, villagers in the rural areas farm the land with methods that have not changed for centuries. Even the streets and buildings exhibit this clash of tradition and modernism, for tucked between high-rise apartments are small temples, and in the midst of the noise of traffic, you can hear the melodious chant of the names of the Buddha. Streets that are crowded with trucks and minivans during the day are closed to traffic at night. In their place are makeshift tents where Chinese opera and traditional music are performed. The most popular radio and television plays are the ones that dramatize the legends of ancient Chinese heroes, mixing history with fantasy. And small bookstores stocked with cheap paperback martial arts novels and books on divination are always crowded with eager readers. This is the uniqueness of Hong Kong, more Western than many cities of North America and yet more Chinese than modern China.

My first exposure of feng-shui was from stories about the ancient sages of China. As a child I had always been fascinated by tales about Taoist immortals and magicians and the role they played in the rise and fall of the dynasties of China. I was a voracious reader then, and by nine I had read almost all the historical classics, including *Heroes of the Marsh, Investiture of the Gods, Journey to the West,* and others. I read about how the Yellow Emperor united China with the help of the Lady of the Nine Heavens, the patron deity of the divination arts. I read about how Kiang Shen, the advisor of King Wen of the Chou dynasty, used his knowledge of celestial divination to hasten the fall of the last emperor of the Shang, the tyrant Shang T'sou. But the story that made an impression on my young mind more than any other one was the story of the Taoist immortal Huang Shih-kung.

Huang Shih-kung and his student Chang Liang helped Liu Pang defeat the cruel emperor of Ch'in. In this story, it was said that the Lady of the Nine Heavens advised the ancestors of Liu Pang on the selection of a burial site that would produce in the descendants a future emperor. In the conflict between Liu Pang and a rival, two masters of feng-shui battled: the Taoist Huang Shih-kung on behalf of Liu Pang, and the evil magician Hui Jen for Liu Pang's rival. While Hui Jen sought to drain the energy in the land surrounding the burial site of Liu Pang's ancestor, Huang Shih-kung defended the integrity of the site's energy flow. In the end, the magic of Huang Shih-kung was stronger and the burial site of Liu Pang's ancestor was unharmed. Thus, Liu Pang's future was secured and he eventually became the emperor and the founder of the Han dynasty.

These stories greatly affected me. I wanted to know more about these mysterious landscapes and how their hidden power can determine the course of events. I also wanted to learn more about these sages who could interpret the phenomena of sky and earth, and who seemed to possess an understanding of the mysteries of nature. When you are twelve years old, nothing seems impossible. The only problem was that things weren't happening fast enough.

I started making plans on how I would learn feng-shui. The project had to be carried out discreetly, for I wasn't sure what my parents would think if they found out. This turned out to be an unwarranted fear, but I only realized it much later. My plan was divided into two parts. First, I took hikes around the rural areas in Hong Kong and made note of the locations of burial sites. There were plenty of those back then, for the rural region of Hong Kong, known as the New Territories, was not developed. Many grave sites dotted the hillsides, and on a good day I could spot and study five or six of them.

This part of the plan went smoothly, for I easily combined my geography and biology field trips with such a project. As far as everyone knew, I was doing "homework," for indeed I took extensive field notes, but among my notes of rocks, flora, and fauna were also details of landforms surrounding burial sites.

The second part of my plan involved finding biographies of the masters of feng-shui. I was hoping that these biographies would lead me to the works of the masters. This was where I got stuck. I realized that the wealth of written information lay in the histories of China, the classics known as the Twenty-four Histories. I dived into them and got as far as the biographies of the magicians and diviners (the *fang-shih*) section of Ssu-ma Ch'ien's and Pan-ku's works when I realized that my classical Chinese was not good enough. I was in the equivalent of seventh grade and had had only one year of classical Chinese. Either I had to give up or get help. Giving up meant defeat and getting help meant being exposed. I decided that being exposed was easier to deal with than admitting defeat. I was quite headstrong those days, and I would sooner endure a scolding than stop dead in the tracks of what I wanted to do.

Help came from unexpected circumstances: my grandmother died. In the conversations between my father and a granduncle, I heard something about "selecting a burial site that would benefit the descendants." When my father, uncles, and granduncle went around looking for a suitable burial site for my grandmother, I tagged along. I watched and listened carefully, mentally taking notes on what my granduncle had to say about the kinds of landforms that were most auspicious. I had finally met a feng-shui master. Moreover, my parents were actually quite interested in this art, and it looked as if I could pursue this interest without much trouble.

I began to ask my granduncle questions about feng-shui. I didn't know where to start, so I asked him to explain to me the difficult passages in the biographical histories of the diviners and magicians, for my granduncle was also very learned in the history and literature of China. When I saw that he was excited by my queries, I dropped all pretense and told him that what I really wanted to learn was feng-shui. Eagerly I showed him the notes I had collected and the books I had read. From that time on, my granduncle started to invite me on walks with him in the countryside. Occasionally, my parents would come along as well.

I looked forward to the weekends when we would have an early-morning breakfast of congee (rice porridge) and tea before setting out. As we walked, my granduncle would tell me about the flow of energies through nature and the changes that occurred with the cycles of the seasons. I began to appreciate what it means to live in harmony with the flow of the land and the waters.

When I was about fifteen or so, I asked my granduncle to accept me as an apprentice in the art of feng-shui. By then I had already accompanied him on many trips of "chasing the dragon"—that is, following the veins of energy. Thus, neither of us was surprised when I brought up the matter of apprenticeship.

My granduncle told me that learning feng-shui was a serious endeavor. First, he made sure that I was willing to commit time and effort. He likened the training to studying medicine. Acquisition of theoretical knowledge must be followed by practice. It would take years before one could become competent in this art. Even then, the practitioner of feng-shui would be learning all the time, always adding experience to his or her repertoire of knowledge. Second, he wanted me to understand that the practice of feng-shui involved more than theoretical knowledge. I would have to develop intuition and dissolve the barrier between myself and the universe. Only then could I be tuned to the energy that moves through nature. My granduncle then explained to me that the feng-shui masters were successors of the fang-shih tradition of Taoism. The fang-shih, or masters of the Taoist arts, were the doctors, diviners, magicians, and internal alchemists in the first and second centuries in China. Therefore, feng-shui is closely related to the other arts of Taoism such as internal alchemy and cultivating body and mind. Lastly, he told me that feng-shui readings should never be done in a casual manner. I must assume responsibility for every feng-shui reading I do and should do every reading as if it affected my own welfare.

After I received consent from my parents, my granduncle formally accepted me as an apprentice. In front of a figure of Fu Hsi, the patron of the divination arts of China, I took the oath that I would always use the art for good and never for unethical purposes.

My training began with the study of the I-ching and its various commentaries. I learned the science of the pa-k'ua (the eight trigrams), the five elements, and the intricacies of the Chinese calendar. Then I was introduced to the two techniques in feng-shui: the art of recognizing landforms and the science of the geomantic compass. As I continued to accompany my granduncle on his feng-shui trips, my theoretical knowledge was enriched by practical experience. He began to let me set up the geomantic charts to analyze the geomancy of burial sites. Later, I was allowed to lead in "chasing the veins of the dragon."

On one of our longer trips through a rugged area, I noticed that my granduncle walked with a gait that consistently outpaced me. I was fifteen and my granduncle was in his late seventies. I also noticed that while I needed to catch my breath after a long climb, he was not bothered at all by the terrain. He walked on the steep trails as if he were walking on level ground. When I commented on his relative ease in negotiating the difficult landscape, he told me that it was because his breathing was more effective than mine. He then added that if he had introduced me to the methods of controlling the breath, I would not have appreciated them, so he waited until I brought up the subject myself.

My granduncle never taught me "how" to control the breath. Instead, he made me do exercises that strengthened my constitution. He told me that he learned these exercises from a Taoist sage long ago when he was living in China. This Taoist also taught him meditation and herbal medicine. Later, my granduncle also taught me a form of "quiet sitting" to cultivate my sensitivity toward the natural order of things. I was delighted, for during that time I was beginning to develop a deep interest in Taoism and had just discovered the texts of the Taoist Canon. In the next few years my granduncle guided my study of the Taoist texts. He also told me that if I was serious about Taoist training, I should look for a Taoist master as he had done. I begged him to become my Taoist teacher, but he waved me off. He said that his time and his knowledge were limited, and that the Will of Heaven would determine whether I would find a master. Many years later, after my initiation into the Earlier Heaven sect, I realized that my granduncle practiced a form of meditation from the Wu-liu sect (a branch of the Lungmen sect of the Complete Reality School) and that the exercises that he taught me were called the Postures of the Immortals.

Selection of burial sites is only one aspect of feng-shui. It is actually called "feng-shui of the yin domain." There is also "feng-shui of the yang domain," which deals with residences and businesses. To study this aspect of feng-shui, my granduncle sent me to a friend of his. I soon found out that the feng-shui of the yang domain is quite different from the feng-shui of burial sites. Yang domain feng-shui relies heavily on the computation of the pa-k'ua positions and mapping these positions onto the floor plan of a building. However, it is also based on knowledge of the *I-ching* and the pa-k'ua, so my study of the theory of changes (*i-hsüeh*) in the early part of my apprenticeship paid off. I merely had to learn new ways of using what I already knew.

Learning residential feng-shui required me to walk around the city. I loved to hike around the countryside, but I had never liked to walk the busy streets of Hong Kong. However, my granduncle's friend was a great teacher, and his enthusiasm and approach to the subject more than made up for this less desirable part of the training.

On Sunday mornings, I would meet my teacher in a park. On the day of my first lesson, I arrived at the appointed area of the park at seven o'clock. My teacher was already there, going through what I thought then were strange patterns of walking. He was pacing around in a circle, sometimes slow, sometimes fast. Later I realized that this was *pak'ua chang,* an internal martial art. He told me that the "exercises" that he was doing helped him to clear his mind so that he could be more intuitive of the surroundings. Besides, he said that mental work should be balanced by physical activity. I took his advice immediately, and on the Sunday mornings I started arriving at the park at about six. While he did his pa-k'ua chang, I practiced my *t'ai-*

chi ch'uan. I was taking t'ai-chi ch'uan lessons from an uncle then and was interested primarily in the martial arts. However, I got fascinated by my feng-shui teacher's way of using these movements not for martial applications but for cultivating mind and body. It took me much longer to fully realize that feng-shui, and the cultivation of physical health and mental clarity, are all integral to the practice of Taoism.

My teacher said that each house, each building, has a "life." Depending on their compass bearing and the time they were built, some buildings are blessed by fortune, others cursed by misfortune. Surroundings also affect the "life" of a building. There are destructive forces and beneficial forces lurking around, and structures of neighboring buildings can direct, enhance, diminish, scatter, and gather these forces. As my lessons continued, I began to "see" streets and buildings differently. Indeed, they seemed to be alive. I could see that some houses are "healthy," some are "ill," and some are "dying." I began to cultivate an intuition for the flow of forces in an area, noticing details that normal perception would have missed. My awareness changed. I began to see not just streets, but the pattern of intersections; not just cars, but the flow of the traffic; not just single houses, but the relationship of buildings forming a larger structure.

It must have been a strange sight in the crowded streets of Hong Kong: a middle-aged man and a young person walking around with a geomantic compass, making notes, and talking about the fortunes of buildings. But in Hong Kong, where many strange things happen daily, people simply smiled at us. Some even asked us about our observations. Thus, throughout my high school years, I passed my Sundays either hiking around the countryside chasing the dragon with my granduncle or walking around the city streets evaluating the fortunes of buildings with my granduncle's friend. The most wonderful time was when both of them were together. I learned from them more than I could ever have imagined. They talked about everything in the world. The history of China came alive as they discussed the flow and ebb of the dynasties. They talked about their childhood experiences in China, and I caught a glimpse of how my grandfather's generation lived. They talked about their mutual acquaintances, the intrigues between the great families of South China, and my eyes were opened to a history that was never recorded in books. I followed the fortunes of my ancestors as they rose in power in Canton, only to flee communism and their ancestral lands to make a new home in a British colony. But, sooner or later in the conversation they would drift into discussing feng-shui, comparing this grave site to the other, this house to that, and the fortunes of one business to another.

I still remember the times when our large family got together for a birthday or wedding celebration. I loved to sit at a table with my granduncle and his friend. They would talk about feng-shui. In their usual enthusiasm, they would discuss the merit of one burial site over another or what was the best way to select an auspicious hour for burial—and all this at someone's birthday celebration or wedding! In Chinese culture, it was a no-no to talk about death during happy occasions. In fact, it would be considered downright malice. But no one seemed to care, for everyone knew that my granduncle and his friend lived and breathed feng-shui. To them, a burial site was a piece of art. They would discuss the feng-shui of a building or a grave site in the same manner that they would talk about the poetry of Wang Wei and Li Po. Like two immortals, they were not bound by rules and regulation, or pressured into the social roles that were demanded of them. They laughed and drank and enjoyed themselves, and were two very happy people.

My apprenticeship with my granduncle and his friend ended in my last year of high school. Both of them gave me tests to mark the occasion, although I did not know it then.

My granduncle tested me first. We were on one of our dragon-chasing trips. We had walked for several miles and had come to a heavily wooded slope on a hill called Kowloon Peak. The area is called the Wood of a Hundred Flowers. The wood has heavy undergrowth, and we had to push aside the tall grass with our umbrellas before we could walk through. My granduncle was in front, and I followed behind. Suddenly we emerged into an opening where the undergrowth thinned out and an opening in the dense wood revealed a view that was breathtaking. I had an instinctive liking for that place and sat down. My granduncle walked a few paces and beckoned me to follow him. When I went over, he pointed to a grave and told me to look over it carefully. The grave was old. The writings on the headstone were almost obliterated. I took the compass bearing of the grave and then examined the surrounding landscape. To its left was a high green mound with rocks that resembled the shape of a dragon. To its right was a lower hilltop, squat and strong. On its top were large granite rocks, white and polished by the sun and rain. They were a perfect pair of the landforms known as "green dragon" and "white tiger." The land behind the grave sloped gently back before ending against a vertical rock wall lined with green moss. It was as if the grave were cradled between the arms of a chair. And this was no ordinary chair, for it resembled the seat of an emperor as I had seen in pictures of the Imperial Palace in Beijing. In front, the openings in the trees revealed strands of waterfalls running down the slopes to collect in a pool that lay directly below the grave. When I matched the calculation of the pa-k'ua for the site with the surrounding landform, my mouth dropped open in disbelief. The grave in front of me was a "king-maker" site. In other words, a descendant of the person buried in that grave was destined to be a king or have the status of one. But which king's ancestor was buried on a hillside in Hong Kong?

When I told my granduncle the results of my observation and calculation, he agreed with me. Calmly, he told me that this was the grave of Sun Yat-sen's mother. Sun Yat-sen never became the emperor of China, although he could have if he had wanted to. Yet his status in the eyes of the Chinese people went beyond kingship. He is honored as the "father of the Republic of China" and remains the most respected figure in Chinese history.

The next weekend I met with my granduncle's friend. He led me to a busy street and stopped in front of a department store. This store had three stories and a basement. At the entrance was a spiral-like stairway leading downstairs and another one leading upstairs. On a Sunday afternoon, the store was crowded. My teacher told me to examine the building and evaluate the feng-shui of the business.

I obtained the readings off the geomantic compass and made a careful observation of the structures of the surrounding buildings. My teacher filled me in with information about when the building was erected and when the business moved in. I computed the pa-k'ua for the building and began to evaluate the fortunes of the business. The building itself was quite unusual for a department store. It had a small entrance. The stairways were right in the middle of the entranceway. One had to go under the spiral staircase to enter the ground floor of the store. Normally, this type of structure is considered very unsuitable for a business, as it forebodes misfortune and bankruptcy. However, the department store was always crowded with customers and certainly showed no sign of going under. I looked at the pa-k'ua again carefully and superimposed it onto the floor plan of the building. One feature caught my eye immediately. The position of fire lay right in the entranceway. In fact, the numbers of the pa-k'ua point to both "Earlier Heaven fire" and "Later Heaven fire." Earlier Heaven fire is fire that will occur regardless of the influence of human deeds. Later Heaven fire is fire that will occur as a result of human action. When both the pa-k'ua numbers for Earlier Heaven and Later Heaven fire are present, destruction by fire is inescapable. But as I examined the pa-k'ua more closely, I noticed another unusual thing. The pa-k'ua told me that the burnings would contribute to the prosperity of the business because fire would actually enhance the "stars" of prosperity for the business. I was both flabbergasted and curious. I did another detailed reading for the fortunes of the business for the year. The reading told me that the building would be damaged by fire before the year was over. When I told my teacher my conclusions, he did not seem surprised. He nodded in agreement with my readings and merely told me to see what would happen. Two months later, I read in the newspaper that a fire had broken out in the basement of that department store. Because of the narrow entrance, it was difficult for the firefighters to get inside to extinguish the flames, and so the entire store was destroyed by fire. I called my teacher immediately. He had seen the news too. We discussed the feng-shui of the department store for a while, and at the end of our conversation he told me that the feng-shui reading was a test to see if I had mastered the basics of the art. He seemed satisfied with my progress and told me that we need not meet again, for the formal lessons were over.

Thus, my apprenticeship with my grand-uncle and his friend ended. The next stage of my learning was going to be a long one, for it was time for me to gather experience through practice and cultivate intuition by stilling the mind.

I continued my practice and research in feng-shui after I moved to the United States. During my university years I returned to Hong Kong frequently, since my family still lived there. On these trips I studied other forms of divination, such as the powerful *chi-mun tun-chia* (theory of understanding the magical portals and hiding the heavenly stems) and the *t'ai-i-su* (numerical theory of great one) from other teachers. I began to use these various systems of divination to supplement each other and found that this approach provided me with different levels of understanding phenomena in nature that complemented feng-shui.

Since my initiation into the Earlier Heaven sect of Taoism in 1981, my practice of feng-shui has reached another dimension. I now study feng-shui not just for intellectual enjoyment or curiosity. It has become a Taoist art, an insight into the workings of the Way of Heaven. Manifested in phenomena in the sky and the earth, and hidden in the intricate flow of forces that could only be revealed through the knowledge of *chi-mun* divination, the Way of Heaven teaches us to be in harmony with its natural course. Feng-shui, as a Taoist art, is a method of helping ourselves and others to live according to the Way of Heaven so that universal harmony will be preserved.

HOW TO USE THIS BOOK

The study of feng-shui should start with its origins. Knowing the history of this discipline of knowledge will help you to understand its practice. Feng-shui has an illustrious history and is one of the oldest practical arts. Its origins can be traced back to the shamans of ancient China. Taoist magicians, diviners, and scholars all contributed to its popularity and its development into a systematic science. Today, feng-shui is considered one of the five great practical arts of Taoism.

You will find a brief history of feng-shui in Part One of this book. I have divided the history of feng-shui into four periods. The early period begins with the discovery of the pa-k'ua, the foundation of all Chinese divinational arts, and ends with the establishment of the Chinese calendar. The history of this period is based on legends and folklore, since many of these events occurred before there were written records of history. The next period saw the emergence of feng-shui and the divinational arts as a discipline of knowledge. These arts were practiced and developed by the fang-shih, the Taoist masters of magic, divination, and the arts of immortality. This period is documented well in the histories of the Warring States, the Ch'in, the Han, and the Chin dynasties (between the third century BCE and the fifth century CE).

The third period of feng-shui covers the T'ang, Sung, and Yüan dynasties (from the seventh to the fourteenth century), where we see the height of the development of feng-shui and other divinational arts. Texts and manuals on the "arts of the yin-yang and five elements" appeared, and feng-shui became a systematic science. The use of the *lo-p'an,* the geomancer's compass, probably dates from this era.

As China moved into the modern era, we enter the last period of the history of feng-shui. During this time the Taoist arts of divination, the martial arts, and the arts of longevity such as *ch'i-kung* began to be transmitted outside the Taoist communities. Social and political conditions contributed to the split between the lay and monastic traditions. The main difference between the two traditions is that the former isolates itself from Taoism, while the latter views the practice of Taoism as central to these disciplines. One of the Chinese proverbs that I learned when I was very young was "Know the source of the water you are drinking"; that is, respect the source that gave you what you have. I value the tradition and heritage of the Taoist arts that I practice. To me it is an honor and privilege to be part of that wisdom tradition, and I hope that you will share some of these feelings should you decide to learn and practice feng-shui.

In Part Two of the book you will begin your study of feng-shui by learning information basic to the divinational arts: the pa-k'ua (the eight trigrams), theory of changes (the *I-ching*), theory of yin and yang and the five elements, and the Chinese calendar. Then you will be introduced to the geomantic compass, the theory of the Nine Palaces, and the classi-

fication of landforms. Some writers consider the usage of the compass (the Compass School) and the evaluation of landforms (the Landform School) to be mutually exclusive because the former is said to be more computational and the latter more intuitive in its approach. This appears to be a modern and artificial division. In the traditional practice of feng-shui, both the compass approach and the evaluation of landforms are used jointly. They complement each other in the geomantic reading.

You will also find that I have put more emphasis on the feng-shui of residences and businesses than on burial sites. I think that most readers will have a greater chance to use their knowledge on the former than the latter.

Part Three takes you through the step-by-step process of doing a feng-shui reading. It assumes that you are already familiar with the information presented in Part Two. At this point you may find it useful to take field trips and begin to observe landforms and architecture. You will also want to start using the geomantic compass. You can purchase this kind of compass in bookstores in the larger Chinatowns. In Hong Kong, Singapore, or Taiwan, you can get the geomantic compass in bookstores specializing on divinational books and in Buddhist and Taoist temple supply stores. For those who cannot get hold of a geomantic compass, I have provided guidelines for converting the regular compass into a geomantic compass for the purpose of learning. However, if you want to be a serious practitioner, you will need a proper geomancer's compass.

Part Four puts feng-shui in perspective and relates it to similar practices found in other cultures. You will discover that feng-shui's understanding of the environment and its approach to environmental design are consistent with contemporary theories of urban design.

Finally, you will find in the appendixes some useful information and references. There is a list of the Chinese dynasties, a summary of steps in doing a feng-shui reading, page references to key information, and the Great Dharani, a chant used to sweep the karma of a building.

Feng-shui is both an art and a science. There are standard rules of thumb, and there are deductions and creative applications based on understanding the workings of the five elements, the movement of the Nine Palaces, the intricate relationships of yin and yang, and the general form of the landscape. This book gives you guidelines. They are by no means exhaustive. As I gained more experience in practicing feng-shui, I found that my observations became sharper and more discriminatory. My ability to choose artifacts and devise ways to enhance beneficial effects and counter or avoid harmful effects also increased. Probably the best way to learn feng-shui is to totally immerse yourself in it. Look at everything around you—landscape, architecture, the environment—with a geomancer's eye. Carry your compass around and take readings. Gradually, you will find that the landscape patterns and architectural features will become a part of your visual imagery. Only then will you be in tune with the surroundings.

Finally, there are ethics associated with feng-shui. These ethics underlie the practice of all Taoist divinational arts. The Taoist masters chose their students with care, making sure that those who learned the divinational arts do not use them to harm others. These ethics are best illustrated by an excerpt from a Taoist manual of the divinational and magical arts of the Kun-lun sect:

The divinational arts should only be taught to:

> those who are filial, upright, selfless, and dedicated in upholding the virtues:

> those who respect the teacher and the teachings of this art:

These persons may not be given the teachings:

> the person whose heart is not good and whose character is shallow;

> who has committed crimes against humanity;

> who has unhealthy habits and unethical intentions;

> who has an attachment to riches and material gains;

> who has a fierce and violent disposition;

> who desires comfort and craves sexual pleasure;

> who is aggressive and vengeful;

> who is not honorable and not honest in his or her dealings with fellow human beings.

—

PART ONE

KNOWING THE SOURCE

THE HISTORY OF FENG-SHUI

—

Observe the mountains and rivers to know the yin and the yang,
Observe the streams and springs to know the source of the waters.

—From the *Shih-ching* (Book of Poetry, c. 600–800 BCE)

1

Ancient Beginnings

To the early Chinese, wind and water (*feng* and *shui*) were important matters. Gentle winds meant good harvests and healthy livestock. Springs and rivers provide food and ensure the survival of a settlement against drought. On the other hand, harsh winds destroy crops, stagnant waters cause disease, and wild waters are a poor source for food. Wind, water, rain, fog, sun, and clouds were believed to be the energy of heaven and earth. Energy that moves is nourishing, and energy that is stagnant is destructive.

The early Chinese tribes were led by shaman-kings who knew the ways of the wind and water, and possessed power over the elements. One such shaman-king was the sage Fu Hsi, who is recognized as the patron of the divinational arts of China because of his discovery of the *Ho-t'u* (the pattern from the river Ho), the prototype of the Earlier Heaven pa-k'ua. However, Fu Hsi was also knowledgeable in the ways of animals. In paintings he is often shown wearing a tiger's skin and accompanied by animals such as the tortoise and the snake. It was probably Fu Hsi's mastery of animal lore that led him to the discovery of the Ho-t'u. The Earlier Heaven pa-k'ua was inscribed on a horse that rose from the depths of the river Ho to reveal itself to Fu Hsi. The Ho-t'u describes the underlying nature of all things. To understand the Ho-t'u is to understand the underlying structure of the universe and humanity.

Another such shaman-king was Yü. Legend said that Yü was ugly and crippled. When Shun, the aging leader, asked for a hero to drive back the floodwaters that threatened to wipe out the tribal villages, Yü was probably the most unlikely candidate. When several nobles, including Shun's own son, failed, Yü stepped forward. Yü was trained as a shaman and was designated by heaven to be the leader of his people. It was said that Yü received *The Book of Power over Waters* from an immor-

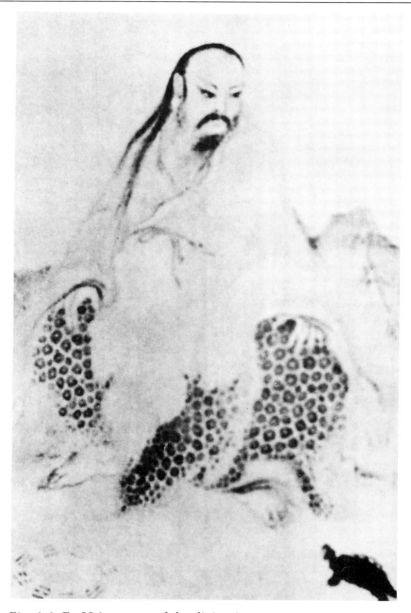

Fig. 1.1 Fu Hsi, patron of the divination arts.

tal. He quickly organized the villagers to build canals and dikes, and, aided by Yü's magical powers, the floodwaters subsided. As the rivers calmed down, Yü saw a tortoise emerge from the water. On the tortoise's shell was a pattern. This pattern was later known as the *Lo-shu,* the pattern from the River Lo, and it is the prototype of the Later Heaven pa-k'ua. Whereas the Ho-t'u's Earlier Heaven pa-k'ua described the ideal order of things (the permanent underlying reality), the Lo-shu's Later Heaven pa-k'ua was used to predict the phe-

Fig. 1.2 The Ho-t'u on a horse.

nomena of flux and change. Thus, when Yü became king after the death of Shun, he also had the power to understand changes in the skies and earth, the wind and water, and the cycle of the seasons.

Under the continuing guidance of the sha- man-kings, the Chinese gradually settled and built large cities. Yü founded the Hsia dy- nasty, and his descendants ruled for over four hundred years before they were overthrown by the family of Shang. The Shang dynasty, after six hundred years of rule, became cor- rupt and decadent. By then, the emperor had lost all connection with the rites and rituals of his ancestors. So arrogant was Shang Ts'ou, the last Shang emperor, that he considered

himself an equal of the gods and insulted and mocked the ancient deities. At that time there was a nobleman by the name of Ki Ch'ang. Ki Ch'ang would be later known as King Wen, who defeated the Shang and founded the Chou dynasty. Ki Ch'ang was adept at divina- tion. In his hands, the Ho-t'u and Lo-shu be- came powerful tools for predicting the course of events. Ki Ch'ang used his understanding of the cyclical nature of the universe to ex- pand the Lo-shu's pa-k'ua, the eight trigrams, into sixty-four hexagrams. It was said that Ki Ch'ang was able to predict his imprisonment, his son's death, his return to his homeland, and the eventual defeat of the man who im- prisoned him and killed his son. In Ki

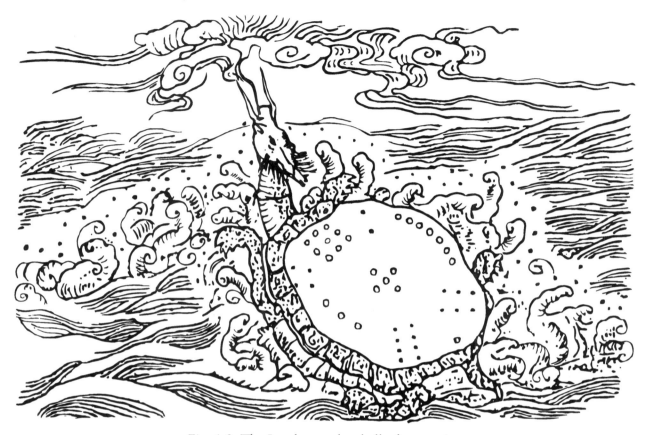

Fig. 1.3 The Lo-shu on the shell of a tortoise.

Ch'ang's efforts against the Shang tyrant, he was aided by his minister Kiang Sheng, a master of magic and divination who had powers over the sky and earth. It may have been owing to Kiang Sheng's influence over King Wen that the system of divination now recorded in the *I-ching* was developed.

Today there are three *I-ching*s documented by the Chinese historians. The *Lin-shan-i* of the Hsia dynasty was attributed to Yü. The *Kuei-chuang-i* was believed to be written by the first emperor of the Shang dynasty around 2200 BCE. Legend has it that in this effort he was aided by an advisor, the shaman I Wen. The *Chou-i* was written around 1100 BCE by King Wen, who was no doubt influenced by

his minister Kiang Sheng. The *I-ching* we have today are fragments of the *Chou-i* collected by Confucius in the sixth century BCE. Of the *Lin-shan-i* and the *Kuei-chuang-i,* the only knowledge is from references made by the historians of the Han and Chin dynasties.

The ancient shaman-kings' mastery of the elements can also be attributed to their knowledge of landforms and weather. Fog, cloud, mist, and rain are associated with certain geographical features, and the king was expected to lead his tribe safely through treacherous terrain. One legendary king who became a master of terrestrial features was Huang-ti, the Yellow Emperor. Legend says that Huang-ti lost his way when he was fighting a bandit

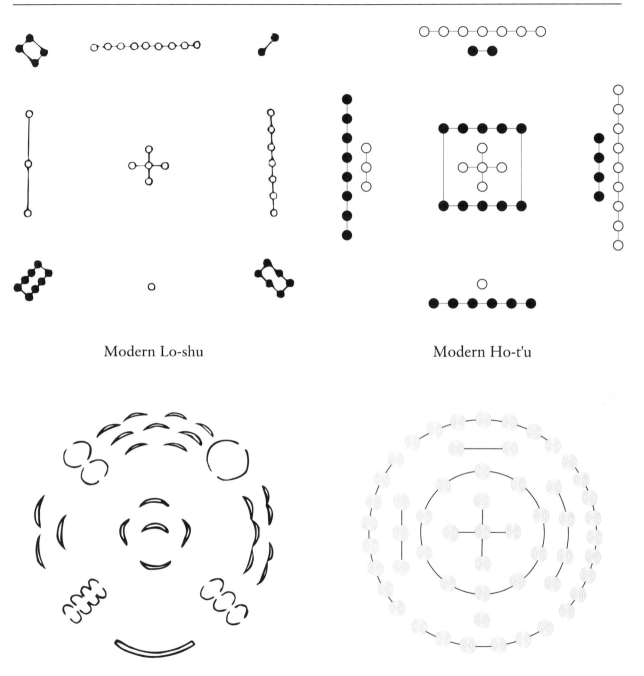

Modern Lo-shu   Modern Ho-t'u

Ancient Lo-shu   Ancient Ho-t'u

Fig. 1.4 Ancient and modern renditions of the Ho-t'u and Lo-shu.

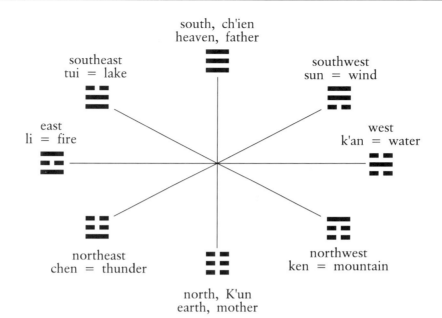

The Earlier Heaven Pa-k'ua

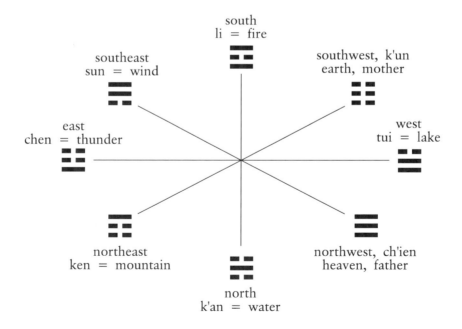

The Later Heaven Pa-k'ua

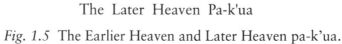

Fig. 1.5 The Earlier Heaven and Later Heaven pa-k'ua.

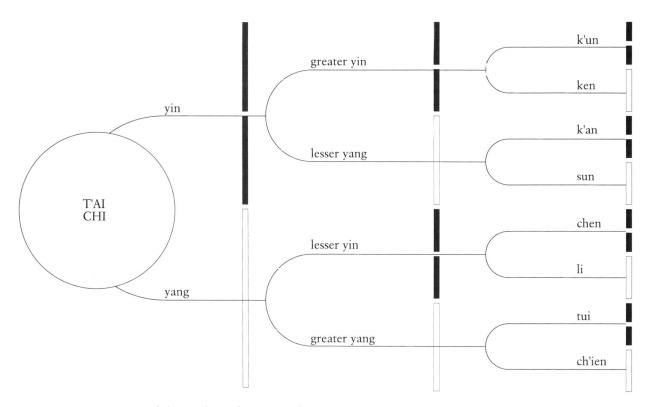

Fig. 1.6 Derivation of the pa-k'ua from t'ai-chi. T'ai-chi emerges from wu-chi, the Tao, when wu-chi differentiates within itself to form yin and yang. In the diagram, white bars indicate yang components and dark bars indicate yin components.

chief whose magical powers caused fog to envelop the mountain valleys. The Lady of the Nine Heavens came to his help and gave him the knowledge and technique of the compass. Using this device, Huang-ti outwitted the bandits and captured their leader.

The knowledge and technology of the compass were enhanced in the Chou dynasty by the emperor Shing, the grandson of King Wen. As a young man, he had seen the value of the compass when his uncle Chou Kung made a compass for tribute bearers from the south who were lost while journeying home. The emperor combined the knowledge of the compass with that of the *I-ching* and set up a theory of terrestrial and celestial divination. This

was the legendary *Lo-ching,* which is no longer extant. *Lo* means "encompassing all the knowledge of heaven and earth," and *ching* means "classic." Through the use of the compass and the Earlier Heaven pa-k'ua, ideal locations for building a city or a palace can be determined. With these divinational tools locations where "earth *ch'i*" (the vapor of life) is gathered can be identified and the path of the *sha-ch'i* (destructive energy) can be avoided. This is understanding the Way of Earlier Heaven. Using the knowledge of landforms, the movement of the stars, and the Later Heaven pa-k'ua, one can design countermeasures to combat adverse conditions. This is understanding the Way of Later

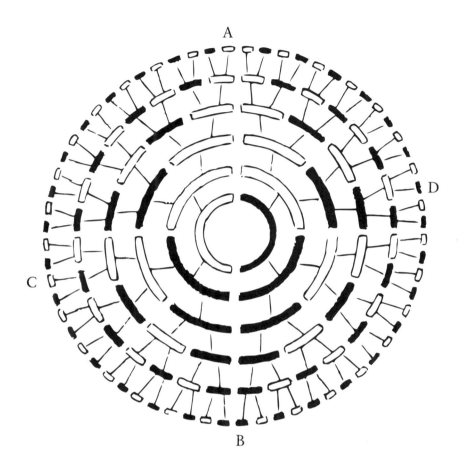

Fig. 1.7 Derivation of sixty-four hexagrams from t'ai-chi. White bars indicate yang components and dark bars indicate yin components. Each yin and yang component divides to give another pair of yin and yang. Thus, the yin and yang in t'ai-chi (the innermost ring) divide to give the four directions (second ring from center). Moving outward, the next ring is formed by the result of eight from each of the four directions dividing into two parts, and so on from eight to sixteen, from sixteen to thirty-two, and thirty-two to sixty-four. The six rings form the six components of the hexagrams. You can find out the components of a hexagram by tracing a line from a component in the outermost ring toward the center. For example, the hexagram Ch'ien is made of six yang components. You can identify the Ch'ien hexagram by tracing the line from position A to the center. You will see that this line connects all the yang components. Likewise, you can try this with the hexagram K'un, which is made of six yin components at position B. You will notice that K'un is directly opposite to Ch'ien. The hexagram Li, which is yang/yin/yang/yang/yin/yang (from bottom to top), can be found at position C, and K'an, which is yin/yang/yin/yin/yang/yin, can be found at position D.

Fig. 1.8 Huang-ti, the Yellow Emperor. In Chinese legend, he received the technology of the compass from the Lady of the Nine Heavens. In this picture, the Yellow Emperor is depicted as a student, bowing to the seated Taoist sage Kuang-shing Tzu.

TEN CELESTIAL STEMS	*TWELVE TERRESTRIAL BRANCHES*
chia	tzu
i	ch'ou
ping	yin
ting	mao
wu	ch'en
chi	ssu
keng	wu
hsin	wei
jen	shen
kuei	yu
	hsü
	hai

Fig. 1.9 The Ten Celestial Stems and Twelve Terrestrial Branches. If you pair a stem and a branch until the first stem and the first branch repeat, you get sixty pairs, which form the sixty years of the Sexagenary Cycle.

Heaven. Armed with the knowledge of the Ways of Earlier Heaven and Later Heaven, the kings knew the secrets of the designs of heaven. They recognized the locations favored by the deities and possessed knowledge to counteract destructive forces. They were indeed the masters of *I*, or change.

The early emperors of China were not only masters of earth lore. They also observed the skies, charted the course of the stars, and encoded this knowledge in the calendar system. Legend says that Huang-ti ordered his celestial ministers to study the stars. A primitive calendar system named *chia-tzu* was invented. Several hundred years later, during the Hsia dynasty, another, more sophisticated calculation of the sun, moon, and constellations was made and the calendar was revised. In the Shang period (between the eighteenth and twelfth centuries BCE), a sixty-day cycle was used. The movement of the constellations was now organized into the Ten Celestial Stems and the Twelve Terrestrial Branches. Each day was designated by a combination of one stem and one branch taken in serial order. The sixty-day cycle was then applied to the year, making six cycles per year of three hundred and sixty days.

In the Chou dynasty (twelfth–third centuries BCE) the Celestial Stems were matched to the five elements (metal, wood, water, fire, and earth), and the Twelve Terrestrial Branches were applied to the twelve solar months. By about 600 BCE (the time of Confucius and Lao-tzu), twelve animal symbols were attached to the Twelve Terrestrial Branches.

Thus, by the Spring and Autumn Period (eighth–fifth centuries BCE) the compass, the *I-ching,* and the calendar—the three building blocks of the divination arts—became a part of the Chinese science.

2

The Formative Period

The next several hundred years saw the emergence of the divinational arts into a branch of knowledge, the proponents of which were the *fang-shih*. *Fang* means formula, method, or technique, and *shih* means exponent or practitioner. Technically, the name means "those who are experts of the esoteric techniques." In other words, the fang-shih were the practitioners of the arts of divination, magic, healing, and longevity.

The fang-shih's predecessors were the wandering political and military advisors of the Warring States Period (fifth–third centuries BCE). They became a social and political force in the Han dynasty and the Era of the Three Kingdoms (third century BCE–third century CE), exerting their influence on the court, the nobility, and the common people. By the sixth century, during the Six Dynasties Period, the fang-shih became absorbed into the Taoist sects that began to flourish at that time.

One of the most colorful and shadowy figures who lived during the Warring States Period was named Kuei-ku Tzu. Even his name was a mystery. Some interpret his name as "The Master of Ghost Valley," after a place where he settled and taught. However, there is also a legend about his birth that sheds light on his name. Kuei-ku Tzu's father died before he was born. His mother wept bitterly at the grave and fell asleep by the tombstone. That night she had a dream in which her husband came to lie with her and told her that she would conceive a child with wondrous powers. When she found that she was pregnant, she named the child Kuei-ku Tzu, meaning "son of the seed of a ghost." In Chinese *Kuei* means ghost, *ku* can mean seed, and *tzu* is son. (The Chinese words for valley and seed are homonyms, and *tzu* can take on various meanings depending on the context.) So *Kuei-ku Tzu* can be construed as "Master of Ghost Valley" or "Son of the Seed of a Ghost."

Kuei-ku Tzu was a master of the arts of div-

Fig. 2.1 Kuei-ku Tzu, one of the most colorful persons of the Warring States Period (c. 200 BCE). Legend says that he lived in a place called Ghost Valley and taught some of the greatest statesmen of the Warring States.

ination, military strategy, and diplomacy. His expertise also encompassed astronomy (sky-lore), geography (earthlore), metallurgy, and military technology. Moreover, he was ru-mored to have practiced the arts of longevity and to possess magical powers. His students included Su Chin and Chang Yi, two great po-litical and military advisors of rival feudal fac-tions in the time of the Warring States. Su Chin advised the ruler of the Ch'i kingdom, and Chang Yi was minister to the ruler of Ch'in, who later united China after conquer-ing the other feudal states. Another of Kuei-ku Tzu's students was Sun Pin, the grandson of Sun Wu (Sun-tzu, the author of *The Art of War*). Although many of his students assumed positions of power in the various feudal courts, Kuei-ku Tzu himself remained a re-cluse all his life. Aside from the colorful sto-ries that were told around this semilegendary figure, the existence of the historical Kuei-ku Tzu was briefly documented by Ssu-ma Ch'ien, the Grand Historian, who lived dur-ing the Han dynasty (c. first century CE) and gave us the most definitive history of China up to that period. Ssu-ma Ch'ien wrote that "Su Chin learned from Kuei-ku. According to hearsay, Kuei-ku was an exponent of the ver-tical-horizontal philosophy and a master of the yin-yang school of thought. He left three treatises." The vertical-horizontal philosophy was a theory of diplomacy that advocated axes of alliance made orthogonal to each other. Thus, if a block of states was allied on a north-south axis, a rival alliance would be made among states on an east-west axis. In this way, a balance of power could be main-tained. The yin-yang school of thought as-serted that the notion of change and the inter-action of yin and yang are the basis of creation, and that t'ai-chi, the intertwining

yin and yang, is the origin of all things. The yin-yang school placed the *I-ching* above the other Confucian classics in its authority on the origin of things.

Kuei-ku Tzu can be considered the spiritual predecessor of the fang-shih, who emerged a hundred years later during the Ch'in, Han, and Era of the Three Kingdoms, because the fang-shih practiced and claimed expertise in the very same areas of knowledge that Kuei-ku Tzu had mastered. The biographies of the fang-shih of these periods allude to the fang-shih's broad spectrum of learning, including knowledge of the heavens, the earth, yin and yang and the five elements, and the esoteric arts of longevity and immortality.

The most famous of the earliest fang-shih was Chang Liang, who saw China through three dynasties. Born at the end of the War-ring States Period of the Chou dynasty, Chang Liang lived through the short but tyrannical rule of the Ch'in dynasty and helped Liu Pang to overthrow the Ch'in to found the Han dy-nasty. Legend has it that as a young man Chang apprenticed himself to Ch'ih-sun Tzu (Master Red Pine), also known as Huang Shih-kung, and learned military strategy, magic, and divination. It was said that a rea-son for Chang's continued military success was his skill in divining the right moment to make the right military maneuver. After the Han dynasty was established, Chang Liang wisely left the political arena and sought out Master Red Pine again, this time to study the arts of longevity and immortality.

In the Han dynasty, the fang-shih became a social, if not political, force. The imperial court retained many fang-shih for their knowledge and expertise in matters of astron-omy, geography, divination, medicine, and the arts of longevity.

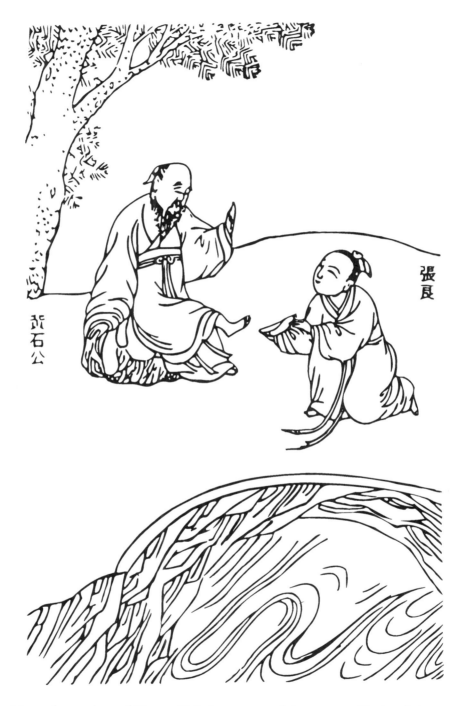

Fig. 2.2 Chang Liang the student of Huang Shih-kung, one of the greatest Taoist diviners, was responsible for the fall of the Ch'in dynasty. Chang Liang was statesman, military strategist, diviner, and magician. After his lord became emperor, Chang Liang withdrew from the political arena to lead the life of a recluse. This picture shows Chang Liang as a student (the younger man on the right) learning from the Taoist immortal Huang Shih-kung.

In the hands of the fang-shih the divinational arts became a branch of knowledge. The theory of yin and yang and the five elements formed the philosophical basis for divination. The trigrams and hexagrams of the *I-ching* provided a framework for the practice of divination. The theory and practice were backed by a sophisticated system of background references using the calendar, the compass, and the terrestrial and celestial records.

It was in the Han dynasty that feng-shui became a professional skill. In those times, feng-shui was known by its older name, *K'an-yu*. *K'an* means "land that rises." *Yu* means pattern. *K'an* is also interpreted as the Way of Heaven and *Yu* as the Way of Earth. Taken together, *K'an-yu* means the pattern of the land based on the understanding of the Way of Heaven and the Way of Earth.

We find K'an-yu mentioned in the *Huai-nan Tzu*, a sort of Taoist encyclopedia written in the early Han period, around the first century BCE. Its author, Huai-nan Tzu, was an exceptional figure. Born Liu An, he was the grandson of the first emperor of the Han dynasty, the man who overthrew the tyrannical Ch'in dynasty. His father was the lord of a feudal kingdom, but Liu An was not interested in the pastimes of the nobility, such as hunting, martial prowess, and politics. Instead, he wrote poetry, played music, and painted, and was attracted to the philosophy of Taoism. When Liu An inherited his father's title as lord of Huai-nan, he retained many fang-shih at his court. Even as a lord, Liu An lived a simple life. He mingled with the common people and spent much of his time learning from the Taoist sages. He was loved by his subjects and respected by his subordinates. Even today, in Anhwei Province, where Liu An once lived, there is a shrine dedicated to this sagely ruler. The book *Huai-nan Tzu* was the product of Liu An's lifetime collection of Taoist knowledge from the fang-shih.

The art of K'an-yu was practiced widely by the fang-shih of the Han dynasty. The books of K'an-yu written at that time were loosely collected into a section of the *Han-shu* (The History of the Han Dynasty) with the works of the theorists of the Five Elements and Yin-yang School of Thought. The most famous of the fang-shih was Master Ch'ing Hu, who wrote a treatise on the selection of burial sites.

Toward the end of the Han dynasty, China was divided into three warring factions. This was the Period of the Three Kingdoms (220–265 CE). The history of these times is not only documented in historical records but also immortalized in the novel *Romance of the Three Kingdoms*. One of the most colorful figures of this period is the Taoist magician Chu-kuo Liang, minister and advisor to Liu Pei, the lord of the Liu kingdom. It was said that Chu-kuo Liang could manipulate the wind and the elements and could conjure up mists and fog to hide the movement of Liu Pei's armies. A master of the divinational arts, Chu-kuo Liang was instrumental in introducing the *chi-mun tun-chia* system into both terrestrial and celestial divination. *Chi-mun* means "the mysterious openings," and *tun-chia* means "hiding movement." The system was originally designed to hide the movement of an army by manipulating mysterious portals of the earth that open and close at certain times of the year. Some portals are benevolent and some are destructive. Entering the wrong portals could mean death. Taoist magicians like Chu-kuo Liang knew where the portals were located and how to open and close them.

The chi-mun tun-chia combines the pa-k'ua with the Nine Palaces to determine which positions in a given area are the most auspicious

青
鳥
公

Fig. 2.3 Master Ch'ing Hu. The father of the science of kan-yu and the author of some of the earliest texts of the feng-shui of burial sites.

and which should be avoided. This system was to have enormous impact on the development of feng-shui in the next several hundred years.

The end of the Three Kingdoms brought unification of China under the Chin dynasty (third–fourth centuries CE). During this period lived a man who would singlehandedly make K'an-yu a recognized branch of knowledge in the Taoist arts. His name was Kuo-p'u, and he is acknowledged by many modern practitioners of feng-shui to be the Father of the geomantic arts. Legend says that Kuo-p'u was a scholar, poet, and master of the arcane arts. Kuo-p'u specialized in the selection of burial sites, and his expertise was sought by the emperor and the nobility as well as the common people. Kuo-p'u left geomantic treatises on se-

lecting burial sites (*Ch'uang-shu*) and evaluating landscape (*Ch'ing-lung Ching*). Historical records of the Chin dynasty tell us that these two classics enjoyed wide popularity at that time. Even the Chin emperor was familiar with these works and knew that burying an ancestor at the "horn of the dragon," a sharp outcrop of rock on a green hill, would lead to the destruction of the family clan.

The fall of the Chin dynasty in 420 CE plunged China into social chaos. For the next one hundred years, short-lived dynasties with limited control of the country came and went. Unification came in 589 CE when the Sui dynasty was established. However, it fell after a mere twenty-nine years of rule and was replaced by the T'ang dynasty.

3

The Rise of Feng-shui as a Science

The T'ang dynasty (618–960 CE) brought three hundred years of political stability that allowed the arts and sciences to flourish. During this period, the Taoist arts reached their height of development. K'an-yu became a science, and the divinational arts were brought to a sophistication never seen before. Since K'an-yu involves the understanding of the flow of the earth's energy, which is affected by the positions of the sun and moon, it is logical that a geomancer's knowledge should include the sciences of astronomy, geography, surveying, numerology, and architecture.

It was also during this time that use of the geomancer's compass, the lo-p'an, was incorporated into K'an-yu. (See fig. 7.1 on page 52). This device had seventeen rings and was partitioned into Twenty-four Directions. Only a few minor modifications separate the l'o-p'an of the T'ang dynasty from the one used by feng-shui practitioners today.

The name of Yang K'un-sun is synonymous with the development of K'an-yu as a branch of Taoist knowledge in the T'ang dynasty. History tells us that Yang was a philanthropist. This earned him his nickname, "Yang who helps the poor." Adept at all the divinational arts, Yang was especially fond of K'an-yu and spent considerable efforts developing and researching methods of using the geomancer's compass, evaluating landscapes, and selecting burial sites. Yang saw the divinational arts as ways of helping people by delivering them from disasters that they might otherwise walk into unknowingly. Thus, this great forefather of Chinese geomancy emphasized the role of virtue and compassion in the practice of feng-shui.

During the T'ang period, different schools of thought in K'an-yu emerged. Some, like Yang K'un-sun, used landforms, (such as dragon veins) as the focus of the geomantic divination. Others focused on an interaction between the position of the heavenly bodies and direction. Yet others used the pa-k'ua to aid in knowing the patterns of energy that flow in the landscape. The extent to which K'an-yu became a popular and influential science in the T'ang era can be seen in the fact that the emperor appointed geomancers as advisers in his court.

The T'ang dynasty fell after three hundred years of rule. Political intrigue among eunuchs, corruption, weakening of control over feudal lords, and peasant unrest all contributed to the end of one of China's most prosperous and cultured eras. When the T'ang ended, there was no strong successor. For the next fifty years China was divided into many small kingdoms that warred against each other. It was not until 960 CE that China was finally united under the Sung dynasty.

The first emperor of Sung, Ch'u K'ang-yin attempted to consolidate his realm by building fortresses in strategic locations throughout China. One such strategic area was in today's Shensi Province near the city of Sian. In this region, dramatic granite cliffs of over three thousand feet (called Hua-shan, the Grand Mountains) rise abruptly from the surrounding plains of the Yellow River. It was an ideal site for building a garrison.

For centuries, Hua-shan had been the sacred mountain of the Taoists, who had built monasteries, shrines, and temples throughout the inaccessible slopes. The most famous of the Taoist sages who lived as a hermit in Hua-shan at that time was Chen Tuan. When the Sung emperor approached the Taoist patriarch to discuss the building of forts on Huashan, Chen Tuan knew exactly how to deal with the emperor. The Taoist patriarch had to preserve the integrity of Hua-shan as a sacred Taoist mountain and yet could not afford to anger the emperor. Chen Tuan knew that the emperor could

not be dissuaded by arguments alone. However, the emperor was an honorable man and would stand by his word if a promise was made. Moreover, to gain the respect of the emperor, he needed to best the emperor in a skill that the emperor excelled in.

Chen Tuan knew that the Sung emperor was an expert chess player and respected those who were masters at the game. Therefore, the Taoist sage made a bold gesture. He invited the emperor to a game of chess and proposed that if the emperor won, the Taoists would leave the mountain. If Chen Tuan won, however, the emperor would promise that no troops would be garrisoned on the mountain.

The Sung emperor was an expert player, but Chen Tuan was always one step ahead of him, for as a master of divination, Chen Tuan was able to predict the emperor's moves. In the end, the emperor conceded defeat, and Hua-shan remained a Taoist refuge. The emperor was so impressed by Chen Tuan's vast learning and wisdom that he invited the Taoist to be his spiritual advisor. However, Chen Tuan politely declined, saying that he preferred the simplicity of life on the mountain. The emperor's admiration of Chen Tuan was so great that he conferred on him the title Hsi-i, *hsi* meaning rare or unfathomable, and *i* meaning mysterious. Thus, Chen Tuan became Chen Hsi-i, the master of the unfathomable and mysterious knowledge.

Divination arts today would not be where they are without Chen Hsi-i's contribution to the understanding of the *I-ching*. He wrote many treatises on understanding the cycles of changes in the universe and was the founder of the celestial divination system *tzu-wei tu-su*, which is still widely used today. Legend says that Chen Hsi-i's teachers included the Taoist immortals Lü Tung-pin and Chang Tzu-yang, through whom he learned the intricacies of the pattern of changes. His treatise on "things coming into being and returning to the void (wu-chi)" became the inspiration of Chou Tun-i's classic T'ai-chi t'u-shuo (Treatise on the T'ai-chi) and Chu Hsi's commentary on that treatise. These works by the two great neo-Confucianist scholars made the I-ching the foremost of all classics and raised the status of the divination arts to the highest level of scholarship and practice.

Another famous master of divination in the Sung era was Shao Yung, also known as Shao K'ang-chieh. His biography (in the Sung-yüan hsüeh-an, Chronicles of the Scholars of the Sung and Yüan Dynasties) describes him as one of the greatest sages and scholars of his time. Shao Yung was an expert in all the arts and sciences before he was twenty. Not interested in pursuing a career in the civil service, he chose to live in the mountains. He wore a single robe whether it was cold or hot. In winter he needed no woodstove; in summer he did not use a fan. He was humble, sincere, friendly, and kind. He was befriended by some of the greatest scholars of his time, like Ssu-ma Kuang, Ch'eng Hao, and Ch'eng I, and yet he was equally at home with farmers, woodcutters, and fisherfolk.

There are many stories about Shao Yung, but the best-known ones tell of his skill at divination. In one story, Shao Yung was walking in the woods with a friend and heard a raven's cry. Shao Yung sighed and said, "Within two years, the north will be in chaos." His friend asked, "How were you able to divine that?" Shao Yung explained, "When vapor flows from north to south, the country is stable. When vapor flows from south to north, there will be chaos. The raven is a bird of the south. Its cry is the breath of the south. This means that the vapor of the south will determine the course of events and the people who live in

the north will suffer, for the fires of the south will quench the waters of the north." Not long afterward, Wang An-shih, the minister and advisor to the emperor, introduced a series of reforms that resulted in a disaster for both the government and the people. The people in North China bore the brunt of the reforms and suffered most.

When Shao Yung was about to die, he was attended by his friends Ch'eng Hao, Ch'eng I, and Ssu-ma Kuang. The friends had wanted to bury him near his cottage so that he could be in his own surroundings. Shao Yung divined their thoughts and told them that he did not want to be buried near his home, for the grave would disrupt the energy of the area. This showed that Shao Yung not only was knowledgeable in the feng-shui of burial sites, but was also sensitive to preserving the harmony of the land.

Chu Hsi, the great neo-Confucianist scholar of that time, had this to say of Shao Yung:

> Heaven created him to be a man above humanity.
> On earth his talent and learning were without comparison.
> He rode with the wind and straddled the clouds.
> His vision was limitless and his insight knew no boundaries.
> His hands reached the moon's zenith,
> His feet touched the roots of heaven,
> He wandered leisurely among the past and present.
> Truly he has drunk the mysteries of the universe.
> —from Chu Hsi's introduction in Shao Yung's Wang-chi ching

Figure 3.2 shows the lineage of the transmission of divination arts in the Sung dynasty

陳希夷

Fig. 3.1 Chen Tuan. This Taoist patriarch of Hua-shan singlehandedly saved Hua-shan from military occupation. A master of the divination arts, he was the inventor of one of the most widely used system of celestial divination (*tzu-wei tu-su*) and was also responsible for reviving the study of the *I-ching* in the Sung dynasty.

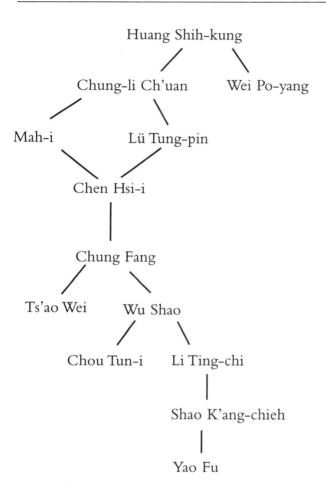

based on the *Sung-yüan hsüeh-an*. One can see the relationship of Shao Yung to Chen Hsi-yi, and the source of their teachings that traced back to the Taoist immortals Lü Tung-pin, Chung-li Ch'uan, and Huang Shih-kung.

With the scholarship of Chen Hsi-yi, Shao Yung, Chou Tun-i, Ch'eng Hao, Ch'eng I, and Chu Hsi, divination became intimately tied to the theory of changes (*I-hsüeh*). The study of the numerology and symbology of the pa-k'ua became a science, complete with a mathematics of change. Cycles and changes could be "computed," and the order and flux of the universe could be uncovered by a set of rules of transformation. By the time of the Southern Sung (the latter part of the Sung dynasty), feng-shui was practiced by Taoists, Buddhists, and neo-Confucianists alike.

The rise of feng-shui as a systematic science in the Sung dynasty can be seen in the publication of many works on the subject. Where there had been a handful of works on K'an-yu in the Han and Chin dynasties, there are some fifty or so books on the subject of feng-shui collected in the *Sung-shi* (History of the Sung).

Fig. 3.2 Lineage of transmission of the divination arts from the *Sung-yüan hseüh-an* (Chronicles of the Scholars of the Sung and Yüan Dynasties).

4

Decline and Resurgence

The Sung dynasty finally fell in 1279 when the Mongols under Kublai Khan invaded the central plains of China and established the Yüan dynasty. Less than one hundred years later, the Mongol dynasty also fell, to be replaced by the Ming dynasty. The Ming (1368–1644 CE) was founded by a leader of a peasant rebellion, Chu Yüan-chang. In this endeavor, Chu had the help of a Taoist master of divination by the name of Liu Po-hun. In the tradition of Chu-kuo Liang of the Three Kingdoms, Liu Po-hun was also adept at military strategy, logistics, and the use of divinational magic. Stories were told of how Chu was able to defeat the Mongols by ingenious movement of armies coupled with observation of celestial phenomena and terrestrial features. Therefore, the rebel peasant armies of Chu Yüan-chang could anticipate the moves of the Mongols and surprised them time after time.

After Chu Yüan-chang became emperor, he began to murder his former subordinates, especially those who had ability and military power. Despite his secrecy in carrying out his actions, Chu's plot was discovered by Liu Po-hun, who saw in the celestial signs that there would be death and murder in the court. He also knew that he would be one of the targets of Chu's political purge. Just before Chu Yüan-chang's assassins reached Liu Po-hun's home, Liu fled.

Chu Yüan-chang was so desperate to kill his former advisor that he ordered that anyone resembling a Taoist practitioner of the divination arts be executed without questioning. This had a disastrous effect on the Taoist community. The Taoists could no longer practice divination openly, and those who continued to do so could not claim to be Taoist.

After fifty years of persecution of Taoist diviners under Ming rule, Taoist practitioners of divination disappeared. A new crop of diviners appeared—lay practitioners of the Taoist

35

divination arts. They were not affiliated with Taoist sects or temples, and they viewed divination purely as a skill. Divination became a profession, and the Taoist roots of the art were slowly forgotten.

Feng-shui in the Ming dynasty took a turn and developed different orientations and methods. First, the classification of mountains was simplified into five major types and valleys into eleven types. Second, only the mountain immediately behind a burial site mattered in determining the auspiciousness of the spot. In pre-Ming times, several layers of ranges surrounding the site had to be considered. Third, the system of the Three Eras (*san-yüan*) and Nine Cycles (*chiu-hun*) was adopted. Each era consists of sixty years, or three cycles of twenty years each. Small changes occur between cycles, and large changes occur between each era. From the Ming dynasty onward, the Three Eras and Nine Cycles became important considerations in both yin and yang feng-shui. Finally, the lo-p'an, the geomancer's compass, was expanded from seventeen to thirty-six rings.

A feng-shui classic written in the Ming dynasty had a wide influence on the practice of the art and was to direct the development of feng-shui through the Ming and Ch'ing dynasties. Titled *Ti-li yin-tzu shiu-chih* (Essentials of Recognition of Landforms), this reference work gives examples of grave sites and their surrounding landforms taken from case studies of ancestral burial grounds of prosperous families and famous people. The book started a trend of feng-shui works that compile examples of "successful" burial sites.

In the latter part of the Ming dynasty, books on feng-shui multiplied. Anyone could get hold of the feng-shui classics or their popular imitators. As a result, many people claimed to be feng-shui masters after studying these texts. The practice of feng-shui was abused, as more people decided to make fast money by taking advantage of a superstitious and illiterate populace. In fact, feng-shui got such a bad image that we now have the saying "Feng-shui masters can fool you for eight or ten years," meaning that you will have to wait a long time before you know that you were cheated.

In many ways, feng-shui in the Ch'ing dynasty (1644–1911) was a reaction to that of the late Ming. In addition, the rise of literary criticism in the humanities also affected the feng-shui literature. The most prominent feng-shui texts were all criticisms of the Ming texts. Yeh Chiu-hsing's *P'ing-yang ch'üan-shu* is an example. Yeh regarded feng-shui practitioners in the Ming dynasty as frauds who had no understanding of the theory of changes (i-hsüeh) and lacked the sophistication of the Sung theorists. Even the *Yu-lin wai-shi* (Stories of the Scholastic Community) poked fun at feng-shui, saying that the function of the feng-shui masters was to fool fathers and sons.

Not all feng-shui texts of the Ch'ing dynasty were criticisms of Ming practice. There were also constructive contributions to feng-shui. Foremost among them is the *Lo-ching t'ao-chieh* (Complete Understanding of the Geomantic Compass). This book is a definitive study of the lo-p'an, the geomancer's compass, with detailed explanations of the thirty-six rings.

Another Ch'ing contribution to the art of feng-shui is the addition of an individual's karma (*ming-hun*) in evaluating the feng-shui of a location. An individual's karma is dependent on his or her birth star (called Earlier Heaven karma) and actions (Later Heaven karma). Birth stars of individuals interact with the pa-k'ua positions of a given location

圖詳

羅經透解

秘笈中的祕笈

山西 王道亨編

Fig. 4.1 An illustration from the Ch'ing-dynasty feng-shui classic *Complete Understanding of the Geomantic Compass.*

to decide whether a site is suitable or not for the individual or the family members.

The importance of selecting the "right" times for groundbreaking for a building, moving into a house, renovating, lowering a casket into the ground, and erecting a headstone was also an innovation of the Ch'ing period. For example, choosing the auspicious hour for groundbreaking is an important part of the feng-shui of residences and commercial buildings. Finding an appropriate time for lowering a casket into the ground became an important part of feng-shui of the yin domain.

Feng-shui as practiced today is quite similar to that of the Ch'ing dynasty. Most feng-shui masters see themselves as professionals and make their living as consultants to businesses and families. Some also combine their feng-shui practice with other divination arts such as physiognomy, palmistry, and various forms of celestial divination. A few are truly trained in the theory of changes and see feng-shui as a Taoist art. My granduncle and his friend are Taoists, although unlike my *sifu* and myself, they are not members of any Taoist sect. However, they practiced feng-shui as a Taoist art, and like Shao Yung, Yang K'un-sun, and Huang Shih-kung, they saw feng-shui as a way of understanding the workings of the Tao and in it a way of helping us to live closer to the natural way of the Tao.

PART TWO

ENTERING THE GATE

LEARNING THE BASICS

—

The subtlest of subtleties, this is the gateway to all mysteries.
—Lao-tzu, *Tao-te Ching*

5

Taoist Cosmology

The study of feng-shui begins with understanding the presence of the Tao in nature and in humanity. Through this understanding, humanity can follow the way of the Tao and be in harmony with the universe.

People often believe that divination is simply predicting the future, or events that are bound to happen. Because of this misunderstanding, many people resign themselves to fate or destiny and do not see themselves as participants in the creation and dissolution of things. In Taoist thinking, divination is the art of reading the patterns of the universe, so that the flux and permanence of the Tao can be admired and the interdependency between all things can be intuited.

The true learning of feng-shui begins when we acknowledge our place in the universe, not necessarily a dominant place, but one that has its role in the scheme of things. This recognition and acceptance allow us to perceive and work with the energies present in the environ-

ment. We have often been taught that we live in a hostile world, or that the world is there for us to conquer or dominate. In the practice of feng-shui, we need to adopt a different worldview, one that recognizes us as co-workers with nature rather than its master. We also need to understand that knowledge is the power to cooperate rather than to manipulate.

Our relationship with the Tao forms the foundation of the practice of feng-shui. To strengthen this relationship we need to understand that the primordial energy of the Tao is the essence of life in all creation. The human form is simply a shell, an impermanent structure. When the shell is old and fragile, it disintegrates, and the energy encased in the shell is released back into the universe. What makes us human, animal, plant, or stone is the difference in the shell, the part of us that is impermanent. The permanent part of us, which is the primordial energy of the Tao shared by all creation, is never born nor extinguished. This primordial energy gives life to a form and is released back into the cosmos when the form dissolves, only to give life again to another form. We do not see this endless cycle of coming and going because we focus on the difference between things. If we are less attached to our impermanent shell, we will understand that it is the primordial energy in us that links us with everything in the universe. The closer we are to the Tao, the more we can see the flow of energy in all things, and the more we are prepared to enter into a cooperative union with them.

Feng-shui masters know that all things come from the Tao and return to the Tao, and that change, or transformation, is that which sets in motion the coming and going of things. The most famous of the treatises on change include Kuo-p'u's *Ch'ing-lung ching* (Treatise on the Patterns of Green Mountains), written around the third century, and Chen Hsi-i's treatise on wu-chi, Chou Tun-i's *T'ai-chi t'u-shuo* (Treatise on the T'ai-chi), Chu Hsi's commentary on that classic, and Shao K'ang-chieh's *Wang-chi ching* (Treatise on the Grand Limit), the last four all written during the Sung dynasty between the tenth and thirteenth centuries.

Of all the treatises on change, Chou Tun-i's *T'ai-chi t'u-shuo* is the best known. It describes the process by which things are created from the Tao and how they eventually return to the Source. Read from top to bottom, Figure 5.1 is about creation and coming into being. At the top of the diagram is wu-chi, symbolized by a circle. This is the Tao, the primordial vapor, and the source of all things. It is also a state of stillness when all things are undifferentiated from the Tao. The Taoists call this "being embraced by the Tao."

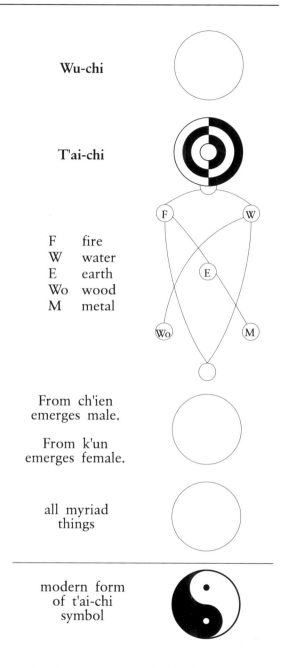

Wu-chi

T'ai-chi

F   fire
W   water
E   earth
Wo   wood
M   metal

From ch'ien emerges male.

From k'un emerges female.

all myriad things

modern form of t'ai-chi symbol

Fig. 5.1 Chou Tun-i's T'ai-chi diagram. Compare the older form of the T'ai-chi, shown in the upper part of the picture, and the more modern rendition, shown at the bottom.

The next symbol in the diagram is the t'ai-chi. Most people are probably more familiar with the t'ai-chi as two interlocking swirling patterns (shown at the bottom of fig. 5.1 for comparison). However, the one from Chou Tun-i's treatise is an older representation, and I think it tells us more about the nature of t'ai-chi. Where wu-chi is stillness, t'ai-chi is change. The concentric circles are one half yin and one half yang. Each circle describes a "moment" of change, and each moment of change is the transition from yin to yang (creation) and yang to yin (return). The three concentric circles describe the interplay of yin and yang in their three manifestations. The innermost circle is ancient yang and ancient yin (*lao-yang* and *lao-yin*). The next circle is greater yang and greater yin (*t'ai-yang* and *t'ai-yin*). The outermost circle is lesser yang and lesser yin (*shao-yang* and *shao-yin*). Taoists describe the t'ai-chi as "yang and yin embracing." If you draw a cross-section of the t'ai-chi, you will notice that in the left half of the picture, you get white-black-white (yang-yin-yang). In the right half of the picture you get black-white-black (yin-yang-yin). This is the same in the more modern rendition of the t'ai-chi, except that the cross-section must be made through the white and black dots.

To go from t'ai-chi to the five elements and the pa-k'ua, we need to understand how ancient yang and ancient yin, greater yang and greater yin, and lesser yang and lesser yin interact to generate the eight components of the pa-k'ua. This process is illustrated in figure 5.2 (page 44).

The five elements—metal, wood, water, fire, and earth—are associated with the four cardinal directions of the pa-k'ua (see fig. 5.3). Thus, when heaven (ch'ien) and earth (k'un) emerge, the elements fire and water are created. The numbers 1 and 6 (of the pa-k'ua, or eight trigrams) occupy the position of earth (north) and are associated with water. The numbers 2 and 7 occupy the position of heaven (south) and are associated with fire. When fire (li) and water (k'an) emerge, the elements wood and metal are created. The numbers 3 and 8 occupy the position of wood (east), and 4 and 9 occupy the position of metal (west). Odd numbers are associated with creation and initiation (yang) and even numbers with nourishing and completion (yin). Each component of the four cardinal directions of the pa-k'ua requires a pair of yang and yin before it can be completed. In the center of the pa-k'ua, which is the meeting point of all the directions, is the element earth. Its numbers are 5 (yang) and 10 (yin).

The pa-k'ua and the five elements are the building blocks of all things, for the *T'ai-chi t'u-shuo* says: "From the way of ch'ien comes the male; from the way of k'un comes the female," and "from there come the ten thousand myriad things." Thus, from wu-chi to the ten thousand myriad things is a process of continuous creation and differentiation through change.

When Chou Tun-i's diagram (fig. 5.1) is read from the bottom up, it describes the process of returning to the Tao. In the path of return, things become progressively less differentiated, and names lose their meaning. Commonality rather than individuality directs the course of change. All the myriad things can be categorized into eight basic substances: heaven, earth, fire, water, mountain, lake, thunder, and wind. In essence, these eight substances are nothing but metal, wood, water, fire, and earth. Finally, even those five elements are simply emanations of yin and yang. Eventually, as all duality between the

Wu-chi	in movement generates yang in wang-chi in stillness generates yin in wang-chi
Wang-chi	in movement generates yang in t'ai-chi in stillness generates yin in t'ai-chi
T'ai-chi	in movement generates the ancient yang in stillness generates the ancient yin
Ancient yang Ancient yin	in movement generates the greater yang in stillness generates the greater yin
Ancient yang Ancient yin	in stillness generates the lesser yin in movement generates the lesser yang
Greater yang Greater yin	in movement generates ch'ien in stillness generates k'un
Greater yang Greater yin	in stillness generates tui in movement generates ken
Lesser yang Lesser yin	in stillness generates k'an in movement generates li
Lesser yang Lesser yin	in movement generates chen in stillness generates sun

Fig. 5.2 The creation of the pa-k'ua from the interaction of yang and yin. In Taoism, the process by which movement and stillness, yin and yang, interact to create the pa-k'ua from wu-chi (the Tao) is called the Sacred Path.

object and object and between subject and object are dissolved, entities are merged with the Tao again, as they were before they came into being.

In the *T'ai-chi t'u-shuo,* we hear Chou Tun-i speak as a scholar of I. Now listen to what Kuo-p'u, the great feng-shui master, had to say in his classic *Ch'ing-lung ching.* Although Kuo-p'u lived some eight hundred years before Chou Tun-i, before the commentaries of the *I-ching* carried the notion of change to high levels of logical precision, Kuo-p'u's view of the universe is essentially the same as that of the Sung scholars. It is a view that was handed down from the time of Fu Hsi and is shared by all practitioners and theorists of the divination arts.

In the beginning was darkness, for the Great Void is not visible. It is also called the dark side of the yellow disk. The Great Void is Nothingness. This is what Lao-tzu meant when he said that the Nameless is the beginning of heaven and earth, for the undifferenti-

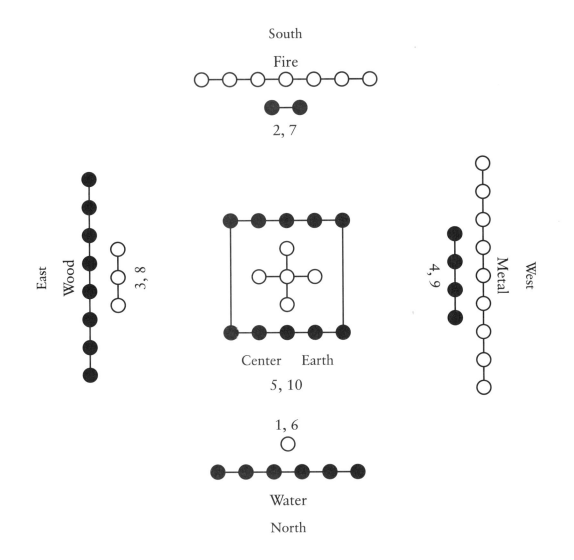

Fig. 5.3 The four cardinal directions of the pa-k'ua, and the five elements and numbers associated with each direction. Note that on the Chinese compass, south is at the top and north at the bottom.

ated vapor of the Three Existences cannot be grasped.

A point of pure yang hides in the middle of darkness and shines out. In dark there is light, in yin there is yang. The Great Named is not named. This is what Lao-tzu meant when he said that the Named is the mother of all things. If all things do not have a void in the center, if they do not have form as substance, if yin does not have yang, how can they come into existence? Know the light and hold on to the dark. This is the secret of being. Those who know this intuitively know the wondrous way of the Tao.

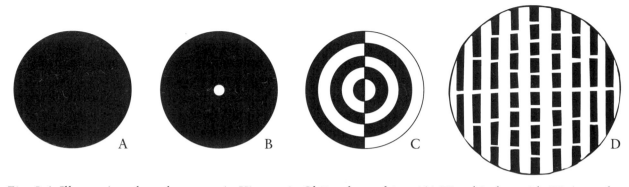

Fig. 5.4 Illustrations based on ones in K'uo-pu's *Ch'ing-lung ching*. (A) Wu-chi, the void. (B) A spark of movement emerging from the stillness of wu-chi. (C) T'ai-chi. (D) The creation of all things from wu-chi (edge of the circle). Moving from the edge of the circle to the center, 2 is created from nothingness, 4 from 2, 6 from 4, 8 from 6, 10 from 8, and so on, to the 10,000 myriad things.

Heaven and earth have their places. Yin and yang complement each other. The sun and moon run their course, determining winter and summer. This is what is meant by the interaction of the named and nameless giving birth to the ten thousand things. Movement and stillness have their times. Waning and waxing have their numbers. The eight trigrams (pa-k'ua) can be generated. The calendar can be set. The four seasons follow their course. *Tzu,* the essence of north, and *wu,* the essence of south, determine the change. Yang is born at tzu, and yin is born at wu. The waning and waxing of yin and yang lead to the birth and growth of the ten thousand things.

The One is the beginning. In waning and waxing, transformations occur, yielding the five elements. From yin and yang to the number ten is the complete transformation. Five and ten are the complete numbers of transformation. Odd numbers are yang, and even numbers are yin. Yang gives birth and yin nourishes.

Appearing and disappearing, coming and going, phenomena are but ripples of the Tao in movement. When water on a lake is stirred, waves and ripples are created, but the waves are patterns of water in movement, just as the glassy surface of the same lake is water in stillness. Feng-shui is the art of seeing the pattern of movement and stillness in the land. Just as we sail a boat according to the direction of the wind and the flow of the water, feng-shui teaches us how to live by watching the wind (feng) and water (shui) of the land. And, just as we need to trim the sail and move the rudder to navigate through favorable or treacherous waters, we need to know how to balance the elements and harmonize yin and yang to live through cycles of changes that are sometimes auspicious and sometimes malignant. In feng-shui, seeing the patterns of the land is the art of choosing a place to live. Balancing and harmonizing elements is the art of selecting countermeasures to deal with adverse conditions. Feng-shui, like the other divination arts, does not tell us to cast ourselves adrift at the mercy of whatever conditions may come. Rather, it allows us to navigate our lives through the ups and downs of the cycles of change.

6

The Chinese Calendar

We are used to seeing time as a line, flowing from past to present and from present to future. To the feng-shui practitioner, time is not linear but cyclical. The flow of energy in the universe changes with the years and seasons. When time is experienced as a cycle, there is no beginning and no end. Events come and go, and come again, when one cycle ends and another begins.

The Chinese calendar is designed to chart the cycles of time and the changes that accompany each cycle. There are four major cycles: the Sexagenary Cycle of sixty years; the Three Eras, with sixty years to an era; the Nine Cycles, with twenty years to a cycle; and the twenty-four seasonal markers, two markers for each of the twelve months of the year.

THE SEXAGENARY CYCLE

Sixty years make up the Sexagenary Cycle. This number is obtained from pairing the Ten Celestial Stems with the Twelve Terrestrial Branches. (See page 48. Note that the *wu* in the celestial stem is different from the *wu* in the terrestrial branch.)

Each year in the Chinese calendar is identified by the combination of a stem and a branch. For example, the year 1996 of the Western calendar is the year ping-tzu, the next year is ting-ch'ou, and so on. Lining up the Ten Celestial Stems and Twelve Terrestrial Branches until the first pair is repeated will result in sixty pairs, making the sixty years of

TEN CELESTIAL STEMS	TWELVE TERRESTRIAL BRANCHES
chia	tzu
i	ch'ou
ping	yin
ting	mao
wu	ch'en
chi	ssu
keng	wu
hsin	wei
jen	shen
kuei	yu
	hsü
	hai

the Sexagenary Cycle. Figure 6.1 lists the combinations of stems and branches that produce the names of the years. All this may sound very technical and difficult to understand at first, but as you start to think about time in a cyclical rather than linear manner, everything will become clearer.

The sixty-year cycle is used in all divination arts. It is also the basis of the Chinese calendar. The twelve animals that are attached to the years came much later (as mentioned in chapter 1). This animal scheme is more of a popular amusement than a serious consideration in the divination arts, which rarely make use of the animal scheme because it is less accurate. Let me illustrate with an example. The Western calendar year 1996 in the animal scheme is the year of the rat and in the sixty-year cycle is ping-tzu. (The Chinese year follows the moon and therefore does not completely overlap with the Western calendar year. Normally, the lunar new year starts sometime between January and March. The cross-reference between the Western calendar year and the Chinese lunar calendar is purely for convenience.) In the year 2008 it will be the year of the rat again, but in the sixty-year cycle it will be wu-tzu. The flow of energy for ping-tzu and wu-tzu are very different, although they are both the year of the rat. If you use the animal scheme rather than the sixty-year cycle in divination, this difference will not be appreciated.

chia-tzu	ping-tzu	wu-tzu	keng-tzu	jen-tzu
i-ch'ou	ting-ch'ou	chi-ch'ou	hsin-ch'ou	kuei-ch'ou
ping-yin	wu-yin	keng-yin	jen-yin	chia-yin
ting-mao	chi-mao	hsin-mao	kuei-mao	i-mao
wu-ch'en	keng-ch'en	jen-ch'en	chia-ch'en	ping-ch'en
chi-ssu	hsin-ssu	kuei-ssu	i-ssu	ting-ssu
keng-wu	jen-wu	chia-wu	ping-wu	wu-wu
hsin-wei	kuei-wei	i-wei	ting-wei	chi-wei
jen-shen	chia-shen	ping-shen	wu-shen	keng-shen
kuei-yu	i-yu	ting-yu	chi-yu	hsin-yu
chia-hsü	ping-hsü	wu-hsü	keng-hsü	jen-hsü
i-hai	ting-hai	chi-hai	hsin-hai	kuei-hai

Fig. 6.1. Pairing of the Ten Celestial Stems and Twelve Terrestrial Branches to give the sixty years of the Sexagenary Cycle.

THE THREE ERAS

Each sixty-year cycle is an era. Each era begins with year chia-tzu and ends with kuei-hai. There are three eras: upper, middle, and lower. Different patterns of energy accompany each era. Therefore, in feng-shui, it is very important to know which era a particular year falls into. The year 1996 falls in the Lower Era, for the Lower Era started in 1984.

THE NINE CYCLES

The Three Eras are subdivided into nine twenty-year segments. Thus, in one hundred and eighty years there are three sixty-year periods (the Three Eras) and nine twenty-year segments (the Nine Cycles). Figure 6.2 shows the Three Eras and Nine Cycles and their respective starting years.

To go back before 1864, subtract twenty years for each cycle. To go beyond 2024, add twenty years to each cycle. The Nine Cycles are very important in feng-shui because they determine the layout of the geomantic chart for a building or a burial site. Chapter 14 will go into these details. For the time being, keep in mind that the flow of energy in the universe changes with each era and each cycle. This is why the year in which a house was built is critical information in the practice of feng-shui.

Era	Cycle	Starting Year
Upper Era	first cycle	1864
	second cycle	1884
	third cycle	1904
Middle Era	fourth cycle	1924
	fifth cycle	1944
	sixth cycle	1964
Lower Era	seventh cycle	1984
	eighth cycle	2004
	ninth cycle	2024

Fig. 6.2 The Three Eras, Nine Cycles, and their starting years.

THE TWENTY-FOUR SEASONAL MARKERS

Each year is divided into twenty-four seasonal markers. There are two markers each month. These seasonal markers come from the Chinese almanac and were traditionally used for agricultural planning.

The Chinese calendar is based on the cycles of the sun and moon, so the seasonal markers will fall on different days but within the same month each year. The calendar reflects a sensitivity to the natural world and could only have come from a people who were observant of changes in nature through the seasons.

The seasonal markers that are important to feng-shui are Coming of Spring and Summer Solstice. It is the Coming of Spring that marks the change of the energy cycle for the year rather than lunar new year's day. After the Summer Solstice, the movement of energy

Month	Seasonal Markers	
1st	Coming of Spring	Coming of Rains
2nd	Insects Waken	Spring Equinox
3rd	Time of Bright and Clear	Rains for Growth
4th	Coming of Summer	Stalks Appear
5th	Grains Appear on Stalks	Summer Solstice
6th	Little Heat	Great Heat
7th	Coming of Autumn	End of Heat
8th	Dew Turns White	Autumn Equinox
9th	Cold Dew	Coming of Frost
10th	Coming of Winter	Light Snow
11th	Heavy Snow	Winter Solstice
12th	Light Freeze	Deep Freeze

Fig. 6.3 The twenty-four seasonal markers for the twelve lunar months of the Chinese calendar.

changes again because from then on, the yang (light) wanes and yin (darkness) waxes. These changes are associated with the positions of the pa-k'ua in the Nine Palaces and will be discussed in chapter 15.

Calendars with lunar months and the twenty-four seasonal markers can be bought at Chinese bookstores and grocery stores. If you read some Chinese, then I would suggest that you get a Chinese calendar every year. Don't necessarily look for the costliest version, because, oddly enough, the cheaper the calendar is, the more information it contains! There is also a book called the *Wan-nien li* that cross-references the Western and Chinese calendar. This book is revised regularly. The current edition starts at the year 1903 and ends at 2021. If you do not read Chinese, you can still learn the basics of feng-shui and prac-

tice the materials covered in the present book. You can pinpoint the day of the Summer Solstice in most Western calendars. As for the Coming of Spring, you can always ask at a Chinese restaurant. I have not seen a Chinese restaurant in North America that does not have a Chinese calendar or does not have access to one. The Chinese term for Coming of Spring is 立春. Show these two words to the restaurant owner and ask which date on the Western calendar this day falls on.

All the information you need concerning the Chinese calendar is contained in this book. Of course, the Chinese calendar is much more complex than what is covered in this chapter, but the goal here is not to discuss the intricacies of the Chinese calendar system, but rather to give you enough information to learn the basics of feng-shui.

7

The Geomantic Compass

The geomantic compass is called the lo-p'an. *Lo* means "everything," and *p'an* means "bowl." Indeed, the lo-p'an is a circular bowl that holds all the mysteries of the earth. It is used to determine the orientation of a site, the information that forms the basis of "computing" the geomantic chart (see chapters 9, 13, and 14). The geomantic compass has concentric rings and twenty-four points. Each ring is used to determine an aspect of feng-shui. (See fig. 7.1.)

The full geomantic compass comes with thirty-six rings, but very few feng-shui practitioners use all the rings for a reading. Most geomantic compasses today are simplified versions of the full compass. The smallest model I have seen has four rings, and the ones used by feng-shui practitioners in Hong Kong vary between nine and twenty-two rings. In most of my readings, I use the eighteen-ring compass and find it more than adequate. In any case, the rings are primarily used for eval-uating burial sites. In residential feng-shui, the ring of twenty-four directions should be sufficient most of the time. Therefore, you need not have a geomantic compass to learn the basics of feng-shui.

The geomantic compass is not only a tool for obtaining information needed for a feng-shui reading. It also contains the knowledge of the structure of the universe. This knowledge is encoded in three important rings in the compass; the Twenty-four Directions Circle, the Earlier Heaven Circle, and the Later Heaven Circle.

The Twenty-four Directions Circle describes the realm of the earth and the energy that flows in it. It is the world of mountains, lakes, valleys, rivers, wind, trees, streets, buildings, and other physical features that make up the immediate reality that we live in. Energy in this domain can be directed, dispersed, enhanced, and gathered.

The Earlier Heaven Circle describes the

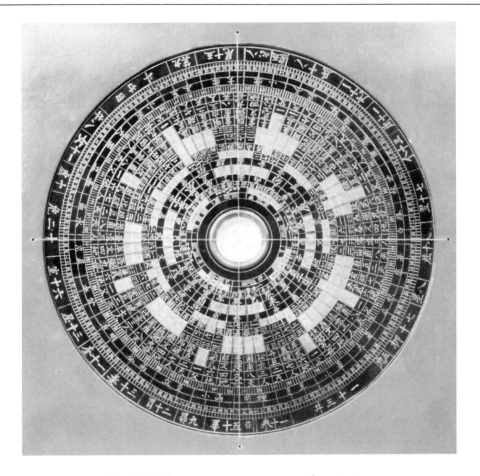

Fig. 7.1 The geomantic compass (lo-p'an).

realm of the underlying permanence of the Tao, the principles or laws of existence that do not change. Formless and timeless, energy in this realm is ambient in all things, animate and inanimate. This intrinsic energy can be tapped and used to influence the flow of energy in the land.

The Later Heaven Circle describes the realm of the flux of things. In this domain, energy changes with time and space but cannot be directed or used. Rather, like a visitor, it can only be interacted with or avoided, given the appropriate means.

THE TWENTY-FOUR DIRECTIONS CIRCLE

The Twenty-four Directions Circle (Fig. 7.2) is sometimes called the Mountain Circle. It is used to determine where the flow of land energy enters a given site. Feng-shui readings begin with taking the direction of the front and back of a site. In the lo-p'an, each of the eight compass directions is subdivided into three partitions, giving a total of twenty-four directions. Each partition is associated with either yin or yang.

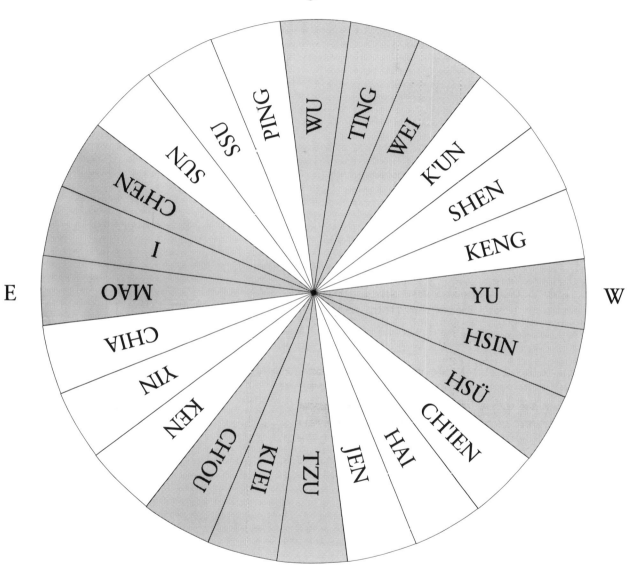

Fig. 7.2 The Twenty-four Directions Circle from the geomantic compass. Yin segments are shaded, gray, and yang segments are unshaded.

Direction	Components	Name in Twenty-four Directions Scheme
north	yang/yin/yin	jen, tzu, kuei
northeast	yin/yang/yang	ch'ou, ken, yin
east	yang/yin/yin	chia, mao, i
southeast	yin/yang/yang	ch'en, sun, ssu
south	yang/yin/yin	ping, wu, ting
southwest	yin/yang/yang	wei, k'un, shen
west	yang/yin/yin	keng, yu, hsin
northwest	yin/yang/yang	hsü, ch'ien, hai

Fig. 7.3 The Twenty-four Directions, their yin and yang components, and their geomantic names.

The direction of a location is designated by a pair of names. The first of the pair denotes the back facing, and the second name denotes the front facing. In feng-shui terminology, they are called the Mountain Direction and the Facing Direction, respectively. If you know the front orientation, the back is determined. Thus, the geomantic direction of a location facing due south will be designated by the pair tzu-wu, while one facing due west will be mao-yu.

Energy entering from the front is more influential than energy entering from the back. Energy entering a place can be beneficial, neutral, or malevolent, depending on the direction of entrance. Chapter 14 explains how to distinguish the nourishing energies from the destructive energies.

THE EARLIER HEAVEN CIRCLE

The Earlier Heaven Circle is the Ho-t'u, or the eight directions of the Earlier Heaven pa-k'ua (see Fig. 7.4). The Earlier Heaven pa-k'ua describes the order of the universe. The *Lo-ching t'ao-chieh* (Complete Understanding of the Geomantic Compass) states, "The pa-k'ua determines fortune or misfortune, and fortune and misfortune affect the success or failure of great endeavors."

In the Earlier Heaven pa-k'ua, ch'ien (heaven) is located in the south, k'un (earth) in the north, li (fire) in the east, and k'an (water) in the west. Chen (thunder) is in the northeast, ken (mountain) in the northwest, tui (lake) in the southeast, and sun (wind) is in the southwest. The *I-ching*, describing the layout of the Earlier Heaven pa-k'ua says: "Heaven and earth [north-south axis] anchor the positions [of the pa-k'ua]. Vapor flows between mountain and lake [northwest-southeast axis]. Thunder and wind nourish each other [northeast-southwest axis]. Fire and water do not conflict [east-west axis]." This is harmony and balance of yin and yang, for in

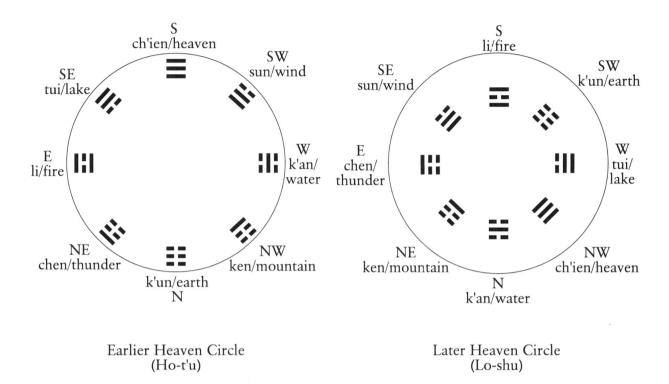

Earlier Heaven Circle
(Ho-t'u)

Later Heaven Circle
(Lo-shu)

Fig. 7.4 The Earlier Heaven Circle and the Later Heaven Circle of the Geomantic Compass. In a typical compass, the Later Heaven Circle is closer to the center of the compass. The trigrams are read from the outside in. Solid lines represent yang, and broken lines represent yin. The line nearest to the circumference corresponds to the top line of the trigram. Thus, the trigram ken has a yin line on the top and in the middle, and a yang line at the bottom.

all these axes, there are three parts yang (unbroken lines) and three parts yin (broken lines).

The order of the universe can be seen by setting the Earlier Heaven Circle in motion. Going clockwise from chen (thunder) to ch'ien (heaven), the locations of the trigrams in the Earlier Heaven pa-k'ua follow the principle of the waxing and waning of yang and yin. Yang is born at the north and reaches its height at the south. Therefore, ch'ien is located in the south, because south is where yang is at its height. It is represented by the three solid lines ☰, symbolizing the height

of yang. When yang reaches its extreme, yin is born. Sun (wind) in the southwest is the birth of the first yin. The trigram for sun is ☴, where the bottom line is yin. Waxing or growth starts at the bottom of the trigram. Therefore, the trigram for sun is called the birth of yin. When yin gets strong, it can envelop yang. This takes us to the next position, west, of which the trigram is k'an (water) ☵. As yin continues to wax and grow, yang wanes, so that in the next position (northwest), the trigram ken (mountain) is yin in its foundation, as represented by the two yin lines occupying the base of the trigram ☷. Yin approaches its height of development in the north. The trigram k'un (earth) is entirely yin ☷. It is also the position of north, the opposite of south. When yin reaches it zenith, yang is born. As we move to the northeast position, the trigram for chen (thunder) is the birth of the first yang ☳. The solid line forms the bottom component of the trigram, symbolizing the growth of yang from the ground up. When yang grows, yin wanes. In the next position, east, yang is strong enough to envelop yin. This is the trigram li (fire) ☲, opposite the trigram k'an (water). As yang grows stronger, it will push away yin. In the next position, southeast, two yang lines at the bottom of the tui (lake) tri-

gram symbolize the thrusting away of yin ☱. And, we are at ch'ien (heaven), the height of yang again. Hence the saying "When ch'ien meets sun, the new moon appears; when k'un meets chen, we see the root of heaven." This cryptic statement refers to the birth of yang and yin when their opposites have reached the extreme.

The Earlier Heaven pa-k'ua tells us about the cyclical nature of events. When something reaches its extreme, the opposite will appear. As day and night, summer and winter follow each other, so will benevolent and malevolent forces, nourishment and destruction, come and go.

THE LATER HEAVEN CIRCLE

The Later Heaven Circle is the *Lo-shu*, which is the eight directions of the Later Heaven pa-k'ua (see Fig. 7.4). While the Earlier Heaven pa-k'ua represents the underlying reality, the Later Heaven pa-k'ua represents change and movement. In the Later Heaven pa-k'ua, li (fire), not ch'ien (heaven), is in the south. Going clockwise from li (fire), k'un (earth) is in the southwest, tui (lake) in the west, ch'ien (heaven) in the northwest, k'an (water) in the north, ken (mountain) in the northeast, chen (thunder) in the east, and sun (wind) in the southeast.

In the Later Heaven pa-k'ua, each trigram is associated with a number and a color. Thus, k'an (water) is one-white, k'un (earth) is two-black, chen (thunder) is three-jade, sun (wind) is four-green, ch'ien (heaven) is six-white, tui

(lake) is seven-red, ken (mountain) is eight-white, and li (fire) is nine-purple. With the addition of the center (five-yellow) to the eight directions, the pa-k'ua has now expanded to nine positions. These are the Nine Palaces discussed in more detail in the next chapter.

The transformation of the Later Heaven pa-k'ua into the Nine Palaces is the key to understanding how and why the Lo-shu, not the Ho-t'u, is the vehicle of divination. With the Nine Palaces, the trigrams are no longer tied to a direction. Their positions will move according to the year, month, and the Nine Cycles. It is the movement of the trigrams in the Nine Palaces that reveals the cycle of changes, allowing us to observe the changes in energy that swirl in the universe.

8

The Nine Palaces

The flow of forces, benevolent and malevolent, is revealed in the movement of the pa-k'ua through the Nine Palaces. The Nine Palaces are the eight directions of the compass plus the center. The eight positions are filled by the eight trigrams. Each palace is identified by a number-color pair, also called a "star" (see fig. 8.1).

Figure 8.2 shows the "root structure" of the Nine Palaces. The root arrangement is also known as the Magic Circle, because the numbers are arranged such that the rows, columns, and diagonals all add up to fifteen. In the root structure of the Nine Palaces, five is always located in the center, and the eight directions are associated with the eight-point compass. Note that in the Chinese compass, south is on top and north is at the bottom. In the Taoist universe, yang embraces yin. Therefore, yang is on top and yin is at the bottom. South is considered yang because southern slopes receive more sunlight. North is yin be-

cause northern slopes are usually in the shade. In the same manner, south is associated with fire, or yang energy, and north is associated with water, or yin energy. Therefore, the number one (water) is located in the north, and nine (fire) is in the south.

Some of the "stars" in the Nine Palaces are benevolent and some are malevolent. Five-yellow and two-black are malevolent stars. One-white, four-green, six-white, and eight-white, are benevolent stars. Three-jade and seven-red can be benevolent, malevolent, or neutral depending on other factors. Nine-purple is a powerful star that can be malevolent or benevolent but not neutral.

On the diagram of the root structure of the Nine Palaces, you can trace two paths through the nine positions, or "squares," following the sequence of the numbers (see fig. 8.2). These paths are the movement of energies: one forward (from 1 to 9) and one reverse (from 9 to 1). Yang energy follows a for-

Direction	Trigram/Palace	Number & Color (Star)	Element
north	k'an (water)	one-white	water
southwest	k'un (earth)	two-black	earth
east	chen (thunder)	three-jade	wood
southeast	sun (wind)	four-green	wood
center		five-yellow	earth
northwest	ch'ien (heaven)	six-white	metal
west	tui (lake)	seven-red	metal
northeast	ken (mountain)	eight-white	earth
south	li (fire)	nine-purple	fire

Fig. 8.1 The Eight Directions (plus the center), the Nine Palaces, the pa-k'ua, and the elements.

ward movement and yin energy flows backward. Whether these two energies are beneficial or malevolent will depend on other factors such as the orientation of a site and the year the place was occupied (see chapter 14).

The Nine Palaces are a powerful configuration that is used in many aspects of feng-shui reading. In fact, in the divination arts, it is said that if you understand the pa-k'ua and the Nine Palaces, "you will uncover the mystery of the universe." The many uses of the Nine Palaces in feng-shui are discussed in chapters 14, 15, and 16.

Each of the Nine Palaces is associated with one of the five elements—metal, wood, water, fire, or earth. Contact with the elements is a major part of feng-shui, and the interactive nature of the five elements is used extensively in enhancing benevolent energies and dissolving malevolent energies. The feng-shui practitioner is fully aware of the power of the elements and seeks their cooperation in building a harmonious relationship with the world we

live in. In working with the elements, the practitioner sets himself or herself in an intimate relationship with the underlying structure of the natural world.

Each of the five elements is related to the others in a cycle of creation and a cycle of destruction. When the elements are used to enhance each other, they follow the creation cycle. In the creation cycle, metal in the veins of the earth nourishes the underground waters. Water gives life to vegetation and creates wood. Wood feeds fire, and fire creates ashes, forming earth. The creation cycle is completed when metal is formed in the bowels of the earth. When used to counter each other, the elements follow the destructive cycle. The destructive cycle begins with metal destroying wood. Wood chokes earth as the roots of the trees dig into the ground. Earth has mastery over water and prevents the flow of rivers and seas. Water extinguishes fire, and finally fire melts metals.

Knowing how and when to use the elements in the creative or destructive cycle is an

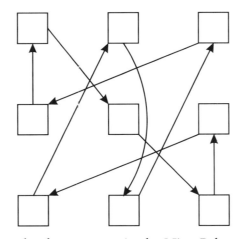

path of movement in the Nine Palaces

4   9   2

3   5   7

8   1   6

clockwise
sequence

6   1   8

7   5   3

2   9   4

counter-
clockwise
sequence

Fig. 8.2 The root structure of the Nine Palaces and the numbers of the Nine Palaces in clockwise and counterclockwise sequence. The diagram at top shows the path of movement in the Nine Palaces. Regardless of what number occupies the center, the square in the center is filled first, then the square in the lower right corner, then the one above it, and so on. The grid of numbers at the lower left shows an example of the clockwise sequence, and the grid at the lower right shows the counterclockwise sequence. When yin conditions dominate, energy flow in the Nine Palaces is counterclockwise. When yang conditions dominate, energy flow in the Nine Palaces is clockwise. The two grids of numbers also illustrate the root structure of the Nine Palaces. This is the condition in which the number 5 occupies the center and all axes add up to fifteen.

important skill in feng-shui. Power in itself is neither good nor bad. What matters is the way we use it. In feng-shui we use powers resident in the universe to help avoid malevolent energy and enhance benevolent energy for the good of all. Because the feng-shui practitioner understands the delicate process of balancing the powers of nature and has an intimate communion with the land, methods that involve excessive human interference in the natural state of things are never used. On the other hand, methods that involve restoring the environment to a more natural and harmonious state are encouraged.

The feng-shui practitioner therefore has access to a universe of mystery and wonder. The gateway to these mysteries is opened when you develop an affinity with the environment. As you work with the elements and familiarize yourself with the path of the magic circle, you will learn to sense the infinitesimal changes that occur around you. In time you will appreciate what it means to merge with the elements, move with the energy of the Nine Palaces, and wander in the realm of the infinite.

9

The Geomantic Chart

The geomantic chart both orders and reveals the coherence of the universe. It shows us how energy moves in the land and in the environment around it. It is a tool that makes the invisible visible.

The structure of the geomantic chart is derived from the Nine Palaces. The specific layout consists of three numbers in each of the nine positions. What numbers go into which position is determined by three factors. In residential feng-shui, the factors are (1) the year the house was built, (2) the front orientation, and (3) the back orientation of the building. In the feng-shui of burial sites, they are the year that the site was purchased (not when the casket was interred) and the front and back orientations of the headstone or marker. These three pieces of information generate the three components of the geomantic chart: the Earth Base, the Facing Star, and the Mountain Star. Each of the three components is a dimension of influence, and all three dimensions interact to determine the nature of energy that flows in that space.

In the geomantic chart the Earth Base is denoted by the large number in each of the Nine Palaces. The Earth Base is energy that is gathered at a place when the site is acquired by an owner. It is the resident energy of the place.

The front orientation of the site or building determines the Facing Star. The Facing Star is energy that enters a site. Incoming energy, like inhalation, is expansive energy. When this energy enters each of the nine positions, it has the property of interacting with the Earth Base or resident energy and multiplying the effects of the interaction. The number denoting energy of the Facing Star is usually placed to the upper right of the large number.

The back orientation determines the Mountain Star. The Mountain Star is energy that forms the ambient or background influence. Less intense than the energy of the Facing Star, energy from the Mountain Star has

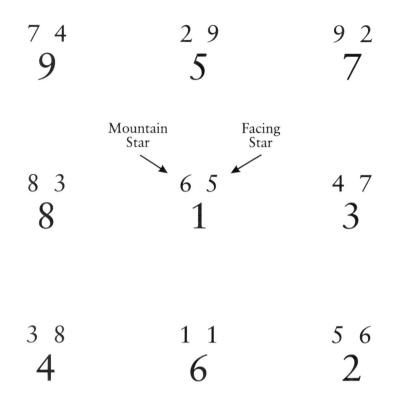

Fig. 9.1 The geomantic chart. The large numbers denote the Earth Base. The number in the center of the Earth Base is determined by which year in the Nine Cycles a site was purchased or occupied. The smaller numbers on the upper right of the large numbers denote the Facing Star and the numbers on the upper left of the large numbers denote the Mountain Star. The numbers in the facing stars and mountain stars are obtained with information from the geomantic compass. See chapter 14 for instructions on how to find the facing and mountain stars of a site.

Notice also that the numbers in all three components of the geomantic chart (the Earth Base, the Facing Stars, and the Mountain Stars) all follow the sequence specified by the structure of the Nine Palaces (see figs. 8.1 and 8.2).

"retaining" power. This power holds the energy from the Facing Star. The number denoting the Mountain Star is placed to the upper left of the large number. The Mountain Star and Facing Star are sometimes called the moving stars because they change with the orientation of the building or burial site. The procedure for setting up the geomantic chart is described in chapter 14.

10

Landforms

Feng-shui is first and foremost a tradition tied to the land. The relationship of the feng-shui practitioner with the land is the expression of a bond, of understanding the flow of energy in the earth and cooperating with it.

By listening to the earth, we become attuned to the energy of the universe, for this energy is manifested in the air as wind, on the earth as water and land, and in the sky as stars. In the world of the feng-shui practitioner, the earth is an entity animated by energy. Energy flows in it, through it, and around it. Energy in flat open spaces is different from energy in mountainous areas. Energy in a valley is different from energy on a plateau. Each type of landform has a particular kind of energy associated with it, and becoming aware of the primeval energy of the land and the power of place requires opening yourself to the natural world.

Landscapes can speak to you if you listen. They can reveal their moods if you feel them. They can show you their true nature if you learn to see and experience them directly.

MOUNTAIN AND WATER

Land can be yang or yin, hard or soft, dynamic or still. Yin is the quality of containment and gathering. Yang is the quality of expansion and dispersion. In feng-shui, all land can be described as mountain or water. Mountains are still and yin. Waters are dynamic and yang. Terrestrial harmony is the balance of yang and yin, of mountain and water. That is why the best feng-shui locations are found in places where there are both mountains and water. In a place where there are only mountains and no water, energy flow will normally be diminished. If there is only water and no mountains, it will be difficult to contain energy. For a place to have power, energy must not be stagnant, yet it must not dissipate.

Mountains are still by nature. When mountains move, things out of the ordinary appear. Thus, it is said, "When mountains appear as if they are dancing and swirling, dragons [the power of the land] are born." The nature of water is dynamic. When waters become still and appear endless and calm, power is accumulated. Mountains that move indicate the presence of yang in yin, and calm waters show the presence of yin in yang. The spark of yang in yin and the spark of yin in yang attract the opposite energies to each, and so power is gathered.

Although mountains in general are considered yin in nature, relative to each other they can be subdivided further as yang or yin. High mountains are yin, and low mountains are yang. Mountains with sharp peaks are yin, and flat-topped mountains are yang. The side of the mountain facing you is yang, and the side of the mountain away from you is yin. Mountains that have steep slopes or cliff edges are yin, and mountains with gentle slopes are yang. In general, yang mountains are associated with beneficial energy, and yin mountains have destructive energy.

Mountains can also be hard or soft. Rocky mountains are hard. Mountains covered with greenery are soft. Land that has a stony surface is hard, and land that has a sandy or muddy surface is soft. Mountain ranges that are long and have many branches are hard, and mountains ranges that are short are soft. Mountains with knife-edge ridges are hard, and mountains with gentle ridges are soft. However, in hardness there is softness, and in softness there is hardness. You can find short ranges with knife-edge ridges and long ranges that are rolling and gentle. In general, hard mountains contain malevolent energy, and soft mountains contain nourishing energy.

Although water is still and yang in nature, it also can be classified further as yang or yin. Water that drops from great heights, as in waterfalls, is yin. Water that gathers in a pool is yang. If the course of the waterway meanders sharply or changes its course suddenly, it is yin. Watercourses that wind around gently are yang. Water that runs rapidly, like whitewater, is yin, and calm waters are yang. Water that rises, like surf or breakers, is yin. Water that drains into the earth, like water flowing into sink holes, is yang. In general, yin waters are destructive, and yang waters are beneficial. Interestingly, springs are considered similar to sinkholes and are thus yang.

PROTECTOR ANIMALS: GREEN DRAGON, WHITE TIGER, RED RAVEN, BLACK TORTOISE

Landforms surrounding a location are guardians of the place. Depending on their formation, some guardians are more effective than others. These features are called Green Dragon, White Tiger, Red Raven, and Black Tortoise, named after the four animal protector spirits recognized by the ancient shamans. Protectors can contain beneficial energy and prevent destructive energy from entering an area.

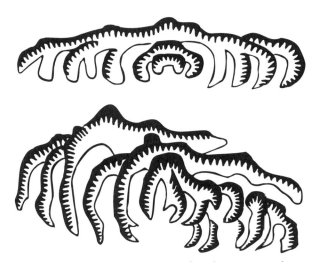

The Green Dragon and White Tiger are high ground to the left and right of a location (fig. 10.1). The Red Raven and Black Tortoise are high ground to the front and back of the site. The Green Dragon and White Tiger are arms protecting the left and right side of the site, and the Red Raven and Black Tortoise are protectors of the front and back of a site. The effectiveness of these protectors will depend on their shape and their relationship to one another. In the next chapter we will look at the kinds of landforms that make effective protectors.

Fig. 10.1 Green Dragon and White Tiger formations as protectors of a site. This drawing is a stylized representation of high land formations surrounding a site. If you face the site, the Green Dragon is to the left and the White Tiger is to the right. Ideally, both formations should be like arms cradling a site. The more layers of arms, the better the protection.

Dragon Veins

The dragon vein is a path of concentrated earth energy. Usually found in mountain ranges, dragon veins are said to emanate the breath of the dragon, the force of earth currents that move through the land. Mountains with dragon veins also contain magnetic fields, and many veins follow a magnetic direction. In feng-shui, "chasing the dragon" is walking the path of the dragon vein.

Dragon veins can be classified as kingly or ordinary, coherent or scattered. Veins in mountain ranges with many branches, numerous peaks, ridges, cols, and valleys are kingly. Veins in small mountain ranges are ordinary. Coherent veins follow a continuous path and are organized in a pattern. Scattered veins are discontinuous and appear as a random pattern.

The starting and ending points of dragon veins can be classified as gradual or abrupt. A gradual starting point of a vein consists of branches of the range coming together and then continuing like the spine of a dragon. The height of the range also gradually builds up as the vein "matures" along its path. An abrupt starting point of a vein begins with a few solitary peaks having steep slopes. The peaks of the range also rise abruptly along the vein with little space and time for the dragon to develop. A gradual terminus of a vein is one that ends with branches spreading out and gradually losing height. It is as if the

Fig. 10.2 (left) An example of coherent dragon veins (after A Ch'ing-dynasty feng-shui manual). Notice how the ranges, or arms of the mountains form a coherent pattern surrounding the site, marked by the ellipse in the center.

Fig. 10.3 An example of scattered dragon veins (after a Ch'ing-dynasty feng-shui manual). Notice that the ranges have no systematic pattern, as compared to the pattern shown in fig. 10.2.

Fig. 10.4 (above) Abrupt start and end points of veins (after a Ch'ing-dynasty feng-shui manual). The sharp points indicate hanging cliffs.

Fig. 10.5 A mature dragon vein (after a Ch'ing-dynasty feng-shui manual). The system of the vein is marked by the dotted lines. Small circles indicate locations in the system that will benefit from the energy of the vein. This dragon vein formation is called the Journeying Dragon.

Fig. 10.6 Absorbing the energy of the dragon. The horseshoe-like formation in the center of the picture indicates the location where all breaths of dragons (energy from surrounding veins) converge.

mountains have run their course and are willing to merge with flat land. An abrupt terminus of a vein is one that ends in a few solitary peaks with steep slopes. It is as if the vein is being forced to end without a chance of winding down. This kind of terminus, also called the "sudden death" of a vein, can be ex-tremely disastrous for cities located at this point.

A place is said to swallow the life-giving energy of the dragon when a vein terminates gently into it. The more veins terminate gradually on a location, the more energy that location will absorb, and the more powerful it is.

CLASSIFICATION OF MOUNTAIN LANDFORMS

The feng-shui of landforms requires the use of our visual imagination. The land is alive, and to be tuned to this animation we need to lay aside our view that rocks, trees, and water are inanimate. To understand mountain landscapes, we must be willing to grant them qualities of sentience. Thus, mountains become sen-tient beings that can stand, sit, run, fly, burrow, feed, devour, consume, or lie in repose.

Five-Element Classification

In feng-shui, mountains are classified according to the shape of the peaks and the

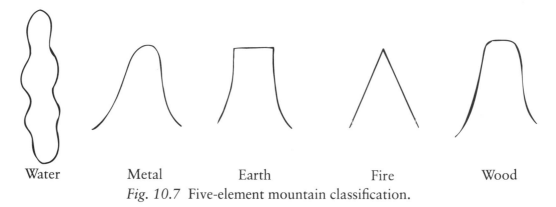

| Water | Metal | Earth | Fire | Wood |

Fig. 10.7 Five-element mountain classification.

shape of the range. Five-element classification is the most elementary way of looking at different types of mountainous landforms. A mountain can be categorized as metal, wood, water, fire, or earth according to its shape. (See figs. 10.7 and 10.8 A–D.)

Metal-type mountains have rounded peaks with gentle slopes. Wood-type mountains have flat tops that slope gently down. Water-type mountains have uneven slopes and round tops. Fire-type mountains are triangular in shape with a sharp peak. Earth-type mountains have a flat top whose sides drop suddenly and steeply.

Often, mountains are part of a range and are not isolated peaks, so that the five-element classification may be too simple to be useful. Feng-shui masters have therefore identified more complex formations made up of a combination of some or all of the five elements.

Complex Five-Element Mountainscapes

Twenty-four combinations of the five elements have been recognized as places of power. They can be divided into five classes, each class having a dominant element being transformed by the influence of others. These mountainous landforms contain dragon veins and have stored in them the primordial energy of the universe. A house or a grave located in such areas will absorb the nourishing energy of the land.

The twenty-four mountainscapes formed by a combination of the five elements are all mountain systems with dragon formations (see figs. 10.9–10.13). Therefore, they describe ranges where there is a concentrated pathway of energy. To appreciate the combined effects of the elements, you need to have an intuitive feel of the nourishing and destructive cycle of the five elements (see chapter 8). At this point, you may wish to review this information before reading the next section.

TRANSFORMATION OF WATER ELEMENT

1. Water meets wood and nourishes it. In figure 10.9A, this is where the zigzag (water) section in the center merges into the round-topped structure (wood) above it. Wood merges into earth as the foundation of a house digs deep into the earth, or a casket in the ground. This particular formation is called "roots dig deep into firm foundations." The rounded formation terminates into the flat-topped structure at the top of the drawing (earth). This site produces prosperity and wealth.

2. Water falls from the earth-shaped

A

B

C

D

Fig. 10.8 Mountainscapes classified by element. (A) Fire. (B) Wood. (C) Metal. (D) Earth. The Water formation describes the shape of a mountain chain rather than the shape of a mountain. (See fig. 10.7.)

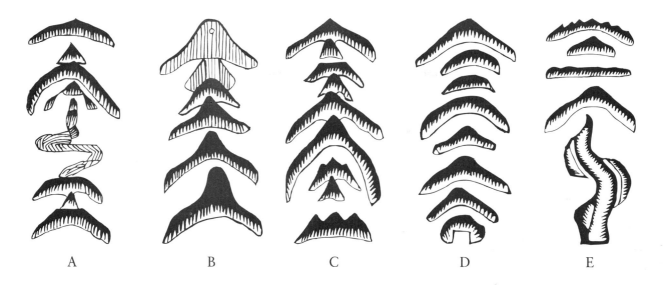

Fig. 10.9 Transformations of the Water-type landform.

mountain (top part of fig. 10.9B) and gives nourishment to various layers of earth. Earth absorbs water and regenerates continuously. Wood is the element of the scholar. This site will produce a person who will be successful in scholastic endeavors as well as wealthy and prosperous.

3. Water connects two wood formations. This refers to the upper part of fig. 10.9C, where there is a segment connecting the two round-shaped mountains. The range continues and blends into a fire formation (the group of peaks in the center and the range in the bottom of the picture).

The mountain range begins with a water formation, and water is a symbol of procreative strength in the male. Wood is born of earth and therefore is the product of female fertility. When male procreative strength meets female fertility, there will be many descendants. Fire is a tempering process. This means that the descendants will have virtue and strength of character. This is a site that

will produce many descendants who will be filial. Wealth will be preserved in the family.

4. Water falls to blend into fire (fig. 10.9D). The entire shape of the mountain system is like a cascading waterfall. It terminates into fire-type mountains at the bottom. Out of the interaction of fire and water comes a powerful combination of two opposing forces. This formation is also called "ascending the spine of the dragon." Although water quenches fire and heat evaporates water, the immersion of water into fire is needed to produce dramatic transformations. In the encounter of water and fire, the opposites will be dissolved and transformed into extraordinary products. This site will produce a person who will be equally adept as a scholar or warrior.

5. In this transformation water dominates, as shown at the bottom of fig. 10.9E. However, its flow is reversed, as indicated by the upward flow, and is blocked by metal and wood. This kind of water will not be enriched

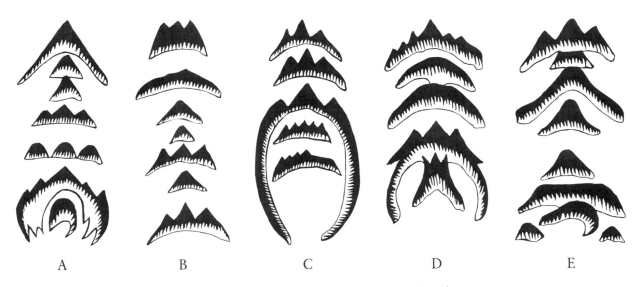

A   B   C   D   E

Fig. 10.10 Transformations of the Fire-type landform.

by wood and metal, although the strength of water is tremendous. This site will produce someone with extraordinary abilities, but he or she will not make these skills known to the world. In other words, the person will have much talent but will prefer to be a hermit.

TRANSFORMATION OF FIRE ELEMENT

1. Fire descends and is fed by wood to create earth (fig. 10.10A). The earth layer is thick, suggesting that energy accumulated from the consumption of wood by fire is plenty. The strength of fire is enhanced by the wood, but the strength of wood is partially used in binding earth together. This makes the amount of wood just enough to feed fire without taxing the energy of fire. The thickness of the earth layer of the range indicates accumulation of earth energy. This site rapidly produces prosperity.

2. Fire descends to be fed by wood but meets water as the mountain range continues (fig. 10.10B). The strength of fire is enhanced by wood, and when it meets water, the im-

mersion of fire in water will produce nobility.

3. Two layers of fire receive energy from wood to produce greater fire (fig. 10.10C). This formation is also known as "the three altar fires." The three altars are the Three Altar Stars, which form a companion constellation to the Dipper. The Dipper is the imperial seat. The Altar Stars are like ministers, second only to the highest seat of power. Therefore, this site produces great nobility or leaders.

4. Metal emerges out of fire (fig. 10.10D). Metal is tempered in fire again to produce the legs of two blades.

Metal gleams as it emerges from fire. This high-quality metal is transformed again by a second process through fire to produce an artifact. The blades represent the power to change events by force. This site will produce a person who will be a mover of great events, but who will use force in doing so.

5. Fire burns to produce ashes, or earth (fig. 10.10E). Wood is fed into fire to strengthen the flames, which in turn produces

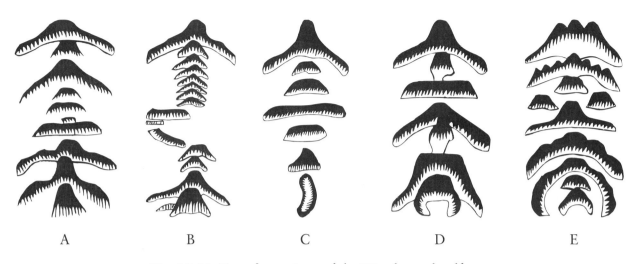

A   B   C   D   E

Fig. 10.11 Transformations of the Wood-type landform.

more earth. The moundlike structures at the bottom of the drawing indicate accumulation of wealth and prosperity through a series of good investments.

TRANSFORMATION OF WOOD ELEMENT

1. Wood enters the earth and fire shoots up (fig. 10.11A). Earth is created by fire and then nourished by water. Wood is born from this encounter. The strength of this site lies in the presence of earth. It provides a shelter for wood so that it can mature in strength. Wood is the symbol of the scholar, just as metal is the symbol of the warrior. The scholar needs to be protected and nurtured to allow talent to be developed. Without the protection of earth, wood will be destroyed by the trials of fire and never get a chance to be nourished by water. This site produces a person who will be successful in scholastic endeavors.

2. Wood pierces through many layers of earth to emerge as water (fig. 10.11B). This stretch of water forms a bridge and connects to another layer of earth with wood reclining against it. Wood is buried in layers of earth until the time is ready for it to emerge. Wood is the symbol of the scholar. The more layers of earth it passes through, the more developed it will be. Water is the symbol of wealth. When wood finally emerges as water out of the earth, scholastic achievements will result in wealth. This site produces a person whose success in the humanities will bring great wealth and prosperity.

3. Wood digs into earth, and out of the earth emerges metal (fig. 10.11C). At the end of the range, a wood-shaped mound is situated orthogonally to the vertical axis of the range. The merit of this site lies in the orientation of the wood-shaped mountain at the bottom of the picture. This extraordinary arrangement of wood will produce an extraordinary person of virtue. This site will produce a philosopher who will win the respect of others through virtue and strength of character.

4. Two tiers of wood connected by water are contained in earth (fig. 10.11D). Wood symbolizes scholarship. Water symbolizes

prosperity. When wood is contained in earth and nourished by underground water, scholastic achievements will bring wealth. This site will produce a person with high scholastic attainment that brings wealth and prosperity.

5. Wood forms three altars at the top (fig. 10.11E). The abundance of wood feeds fire, which breaks a path through a barrier. From the destruction of the barrier, wood emerges to meet three earth-shaped peaks. At the end of the range two branches of water flow out. Three altars of wood symbolize attainment in government service to the point of influencing world affairs. Fire breaks the wood barrier, meaning that sometime in midlife, there will be change in career toward the humanities and with it success in this field. This site will produce a person who will excel first in politics and then in scholarship.

TRANSFORMATION OF METAL ELEMENT

1. Metal descends to meet water and is carried into earth (fig. 10.12A). Metal is the element of the warrior. Water is the symbol of wealth. When metal meets water, the result is

an adventurous spirit in business pursuits. Earth is containment and gathering. This means that business enterprises will accumulate wealth. This site will produce a person who is successful in adventurous business enterprises.

2. Metal is tempered by fire (fig. 10.12B). Out of fire emerges water. When metal is tempered by fire, it matures. Water is the symbol of wealth. This site will produce a person who will slowly build up a career in the military, and with it comes wealth and prosperity.

3. Three layers of metal are shaped and transformed by fire into water (fig. 10.12C). When metal accumulates, it becomes old. If it is not renewed by fire, it will be useless. The strength of this site lies in the presence of fire that tempers the metal and renews it. Metal is the element of the warrior and, when sharpened, will be effective in the military and political arena. This site will produce a person who will become involved in high levels of government, especially in the military, and will make decisions that will have a wide influence in politics.

4. Fire approaches metal, and vapor is

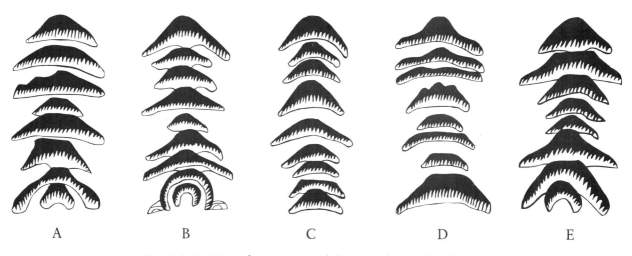

A   B   C   D   E

Fig. 10.12 Transformations of the Metal-type landform.

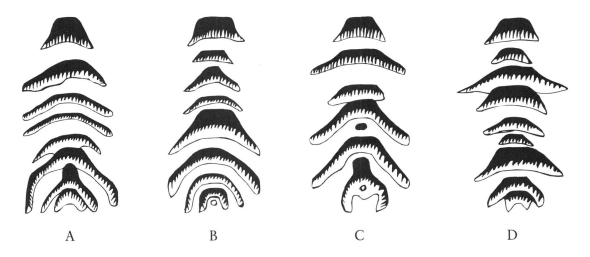

Fig. 10.13 Transformations of the Earth-type landform.

given out as water descends (fig. 10.12D). Three layers of wood build a good barrier to contain water. The strength of this site is in the presence of wood and metal together. Although wood is cut by metal, without wood, metal cannot be tested; and without metal, wood cannot be carved into a useful object. Water and fire add strength to the tempering process of metal before it is tested on wood. This site produces several generations of successful scholars and politicians.

5. Metal descends into earth and is born again, to be once more buried by a thick layer of earth (fig. 10.12E). Metal is the element of the warrior. When it is nourished by the earth and emerges again, there will be great achievements. However, because wood is absent, the warrior spirit will not be complemented by scholarship. As a result, the site will produce a militaristic person with little culture.

TRANSFORMATION OF EARTH ELEMENT

1. Earth descends to cover water (fig. 10.13A). Water blends into earth to nourish it. Out of this process wood emerges. Earth is the symbol of prosperity. Water is the symbol of wealth. The interaction of wood and water means that wealth and prosperity will enhance each other. Wood is the symbol of the arts and humanities. In this formation water and earth both feed wood, indicating that the site will produce a prosperous person who will expend his or her wealth on cultural and artistic pursuits.

2. Earth covers fire and continues as water (fig. 10.13B). In the middle of the formation, earth receives the nourishment of water and contains it. In this system, the smaller earth formation is at the top, and the larger earth formation is lower down. This indicates that the growth of prosperity is balanced and stable. Moreover, prosperity will increase from the first generation to the next.

3. The element earth is associated with the number five (fig. 10.13C). When there are five earth-type mountains in a range, the system is said to be naturally complete. Wood emerges

out of the five layers of earth and receives the greatest nourishment that any earth formation can give. This site will produce a person of great wealth and a patron of the arts.

4. Earth covers as metal rises (fig. 10.13D). The range continues with five layers of earth. Five is the number of earth and symbolizes completeness. Metal is the element of the warrior. Fire is absent in this formation. Therefore, metal cannot be tempered. However, the completeness of earth provides tremendous strength to metal. This site will benefit business ventures that require risk. The path to success will not be smooth, but the results will be great.

In addition to the above twenty-four forms, there are some special formations that are also derived from the five elements. They all have dragon veins, are very rare, and contain energy that can produce persons and events out of the ordinary.

Special Formations of Five-Element Mountainscapes

Dragon Chariot (fig. 10.14A). Earth-shaped mountains in a range form the Chinese character for "jade." On the highest peak (top of drawing) there is a mound that resembles a bubble. This is a king-maker site.

Nine Steps of Jade Palace (fig. 10.14B). Nine horizontal ranges parallel each other, resembling a series of steps. The number nine and jade palace are symbols of royalty. This is another king-maker site.

Ascending Ladder to the Sky (fig. 10.14C). In this formation, a series of wood-shaped peaks are arranged in ascending order of height like a ladder. (The lowest peak is at the bottom of the drawing.) The number of peaks must be seven or more. The entire group is

surrounded by a protective range with an opening aligned with the ladder formation. This is a king-maker site.

Golden Bull Pulls Chariot (fig. 10.14D). This is a transformation of a fire-type formation. The dragon vein emerges out of the heart of the mountain at the start of the range and circles around. In the circular section of the range are pointed peaks (the fire formation). This is a very powerful site and will produce extreme wealth and prosperity.

Golden Chain and Lock (fig. 10.14E). This dragon vein is made of tiers of metal-type peaks arranged in an interlocking pattern. They are all connected to a larger metal-type mountain at the end of the system. This site also produces tremendous wealth and prosperity.

Snake Crossing Stream (fig. 10.14F). The snake is the formation in the center, and the stream is the surrounding range. This site will produce a child prodigy or a genius.

Nine-Star Classification

The Nine Stars are the stars in the Constellation of the Dipper plus two neighboring stars. In Taoism the Nine Stars are the home of deities that control the destiny of humanity. Their names are Guardian or Virtue, The Scholar, Great Gate, The Warrior, Left Guardian, Craving Wolf, Destroyer of Armies, Right Guardian, and Prosperity. In feng-shui, the Nine Stars are used to describe the shape of mountains.

One or two isolated peaks is called a "star." Like the complex five-element classification, a range with multiple peaks (or stars) is a "formation." A range that has a combination of Craving Wolf, Great Gate, Warrior, Destroyer of Armies, and Prosperity is said to have a "dragon formation." If the peaks of

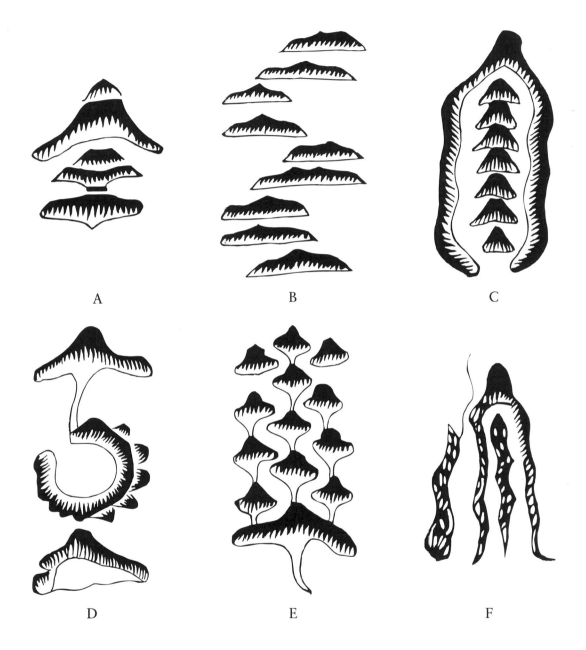

Fig. 10.14 SPECIAL TYPES OF TRANSFORMATIONS OF THE FIVE-ELEMENT MOUNTAINS

A. Dragon chariot.   C. Ascending ladder to the sky.   E. Golden chain and lock.
B. Nine steps of Jade Palace.   D. Golden bull pulls chariot.   F. Snake crossing stream.

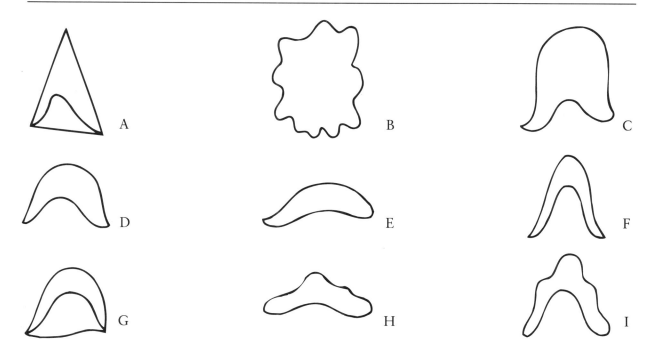

Fig. 10.15 NINE-STAR FORMATIONS. THESE ARE ALSO FORMATIONS WITH NOURISHING ENERGY

A. Guardian of Virtue.
B. The Scholar.
C. Great Gate.
D. The Warrior.
E. Left Guardian.
F. Craving Wolf.
G. Destroyer of Armies.
H. Right Guardian.
I. Prosperity.

that range are interlaced with dips and valleys, the area is said to resemble the earth inhaling and exhaling energy. Such a landscape is filled with the breath of the dragon and is a place of tremendous power.

Complex Mountain Landforms

Some mountain landforms have configurations that appear like animals, people, or natural phenomena. These mountains are animated by energy and are the most powerful types of landforms. It is said that such land has absorbed the essence of the sun and moon, and it is the copulation of the yang and yin energy at these places that gave birth to such animated landforms.

ANIMAL FORMATIONS

Landforms that resemble an animal are said to have animal form. There are three kinds of these formations. In order of power, they are: the basic or passive form, the dynamic form, and the magical form.

Basic animal formations. Any land that has a basic animal form can gather and store energy. Energy stored in such landforms is limited and will not regenerate once it is absorbed by a house or a burial site. Such a landform will only benefit one generation or one (the first) owner. These landforms are also passive in nature and are poor in spreading or enhancing energy. Their passivity is seen in their shape and the names given to

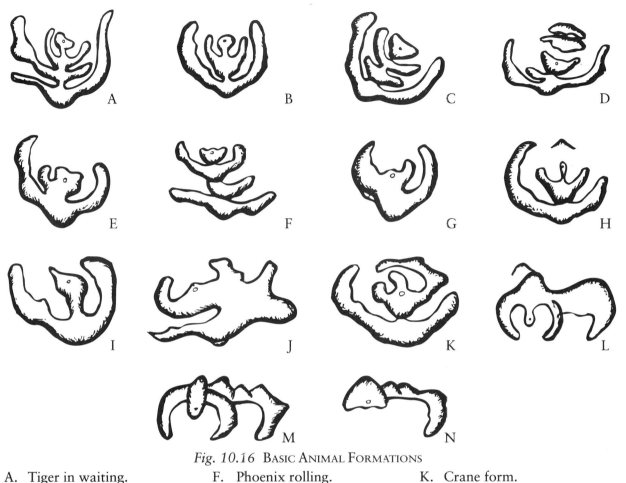

Fig. 10.16 BASIC ANIMAL FORMATIONS

A. Tiger in waiting.
B. Angry tiger.
C. Tiger feeding.
D. Dragon and tiger.
E. Phoenix stretching.

F. Phoenix rolling.
G. Phoenix form.
H. Bird in hiding.
I. Swan form.
J. Crane form.

K. Crane form.
L. Camel form.
M. Horse form.
N. Bear form.

them. Compare them with the next category of animal formations and you will appreciate the difference between basic animal forms and the dynamic animal forms.

Dynamic animal formations. Any land that resembles an animal in motion is land that has dynamic energy. This land is active and is capable not only of storing and gathering energy but also of spreading and enhancing energy. Energy in these places also regenerates and therefore can support successive owners of the site.

Nine groups of dynamic animal formations have been identified by feng-shui masters. In order of their degree of power they are the dragon, tortoise, snake, phoenix and eagle, tiger, elephant, bull, sea animals, and insects.

A   B   C   D   E

F   G   H   I   J

K   L   M   N   O

P   Q   R   S   T

U   V   W

Fig. 10.17 DYNAMIC DRAGON FORMATIONS

A. Dragon coiled clockwise.
B. Golden dragon coiled around flower.
C. Flying dragon.
D. Golden dragon in the ocean waves.
E. Brown dragon drinking from spring.
F. A gathering of dragons.
G. Dragon coiled counterclockwise.
H. Dragon standing erect.
I. Dragon walking.
J. Five dragons gathering.
K. Baby dragon looking at its mother.
L. Two dragons fighting over the pearl.
M. Green dragon.
N. Green dragon catches pearl.
O. Green dragon crossing the river.
P. Baby dragon feeding.
Q. Dragon turning around to look at its young.
R. Dragon ascends to heaven.
S. Brown dragon spits water.
T. Baby dragon enters river.
U. Dragon bringing rain.
V. Flying dragon leaves cave.
W. Caged dragon guarding the pearl.

The dragon, tortoise, snake, phoenix, and eagle are recognized by the Chinese as having magical qualities, and these have the greatest chance of becoming "immortal" by absorbing the yin and yang energies of the earth and sky. Therefore, land having these dynamic animal formations contains more power than landforms that resemble the other animals.

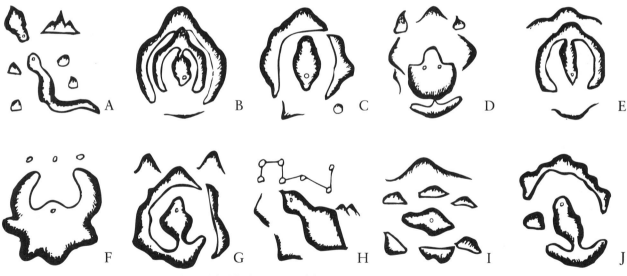

Fig. 10.18 DYNAMIC TORTOISE FORMATIONS

A. Tortoise meets snake.
B. Tortoise hiding in sand.
C. Golden tortoise on the water.
D. Tortoise swimming.
E. Golden tortoise leaving gorge.
F. Tortoise form.
G. Tortoise in hiding leaves cave.
H. Tortoise gazing at the seven stars.
I. Tortoise watching the young.
J. Lotus leaf covering golden tortoise.

Fig. 10.19 DYNAMIC SNAKE FORMATIONS

A. Yellow snake chasing toad.
B. Snake in panic amid grass.
C. Yellow snake.
D. Yellow snake listening to toad's call.
E. Bamboo stick hitting snake.
F. Yellow snake coming out of hole.
G. Yellow snake leaves cave.
H. Snake burrowing into sand.
I. Snake descending mountain.
J. Snake in coil.
K. Snake hanging in tree.
L. Yellow snake spitting breath.

Fig. 10.20 DYNAMIC BIRD FORMATIONS

A. Phoenix flies over fence.
B. Flying swan dives into water.
C. Golden cocks fighting.
D. Pair of phoenix presenting imperial summons.

E. Phoenix and dragon copulating.
F. Phoenix in flight.
G. Eagle descends toward field.
H. Lonely eagle penetrates the clouds.

I. Eagle spreads wings.
J. Pair of phoenix gazing at each other.
K. Phoenix spreads wings.
L. Phoenix in nest.

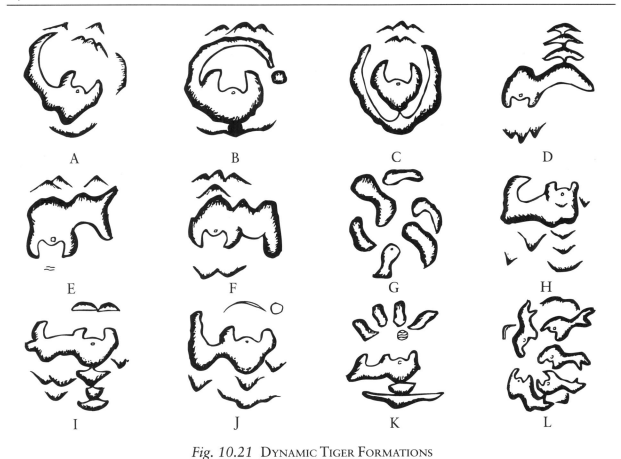

Fig. 10.21 DYNAMIC TIGER FORMATIONS

A. White tiger lying on the ground.
B. Sleeping tiger.
C. Brave tiger leaves forest.
D. Angry tiger jumps over a stream.

E. Thirsty tiger drinks from a spring.
F. Hungry tiger opens its mouth.
G. Five tigers capturing a sheep.
H. Tiger crossing a river.

I. Tiger licking its fur.
J. Tiger roaming in the mountains.
K. Hungry tiger chases boar.
L. Five tigers gathering.

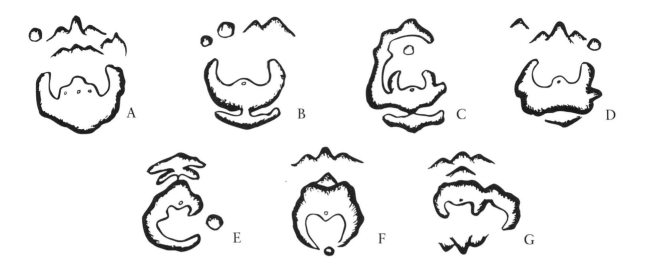

Fig. 10.22 DYNAMIC LION FORMATIONS

A. Lion form.
B. Lion holding ball.
C. Lion playing with ball.

D. Lion laughing at the sky.
E. Lion sitting on mountain.

F. Lion sniffing at food.
G. Lion crossing river.

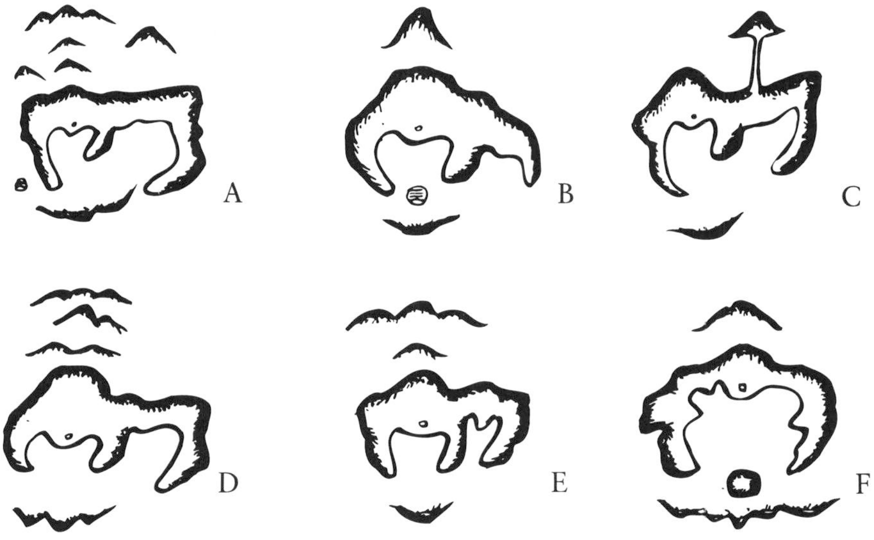

Fig. 10.23 DYNAMIC ELEPHANT FORMATIONS

A. Elephant hiding its tusks.
B. Sleeping elephant laughing at the sky.

C. Immortal riding on elephant.
D. Golden Elephant walking in the mountains.

E. Elephant rolling in mud.
F. White elephant stirring lake.

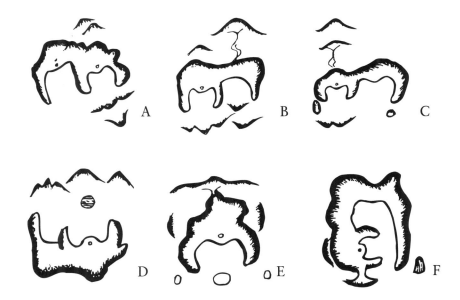

Fig. 10.24 DYNAMIC BULL FORMATIONS

A. Sleeping bull.
B. Bull in hibernation.
C. Yellow bull pulling cart.
D. Horned bull (rhinoceros) looks at moon.
E. Thirsty bull drinking.
F. Golden bull tied by iron chain.

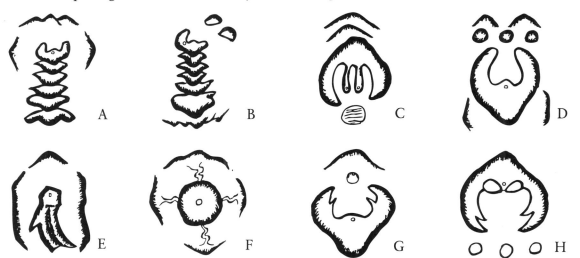

Fig. 10.25 DYNAMIC CREEPING AND CRAWLING ANIMAL FORMATIONS

A. Centipede swimming.
B. Centipede with broken horns.
C. Two worms at water's edge.
D. Prawn playing with pearl.
E. Carp swimming upstream.
F. Spider weaves web.
G. Clam form.
H. Crab crawling at night.

Magical animal forms. These are landforms that resemble animals with magical qualities. A look at these formations will show that sometimes the animals have qualities out of the ordinary. For example, an animal that normally crawls has the ability to fly ("centipede flies across the sky"), or an animal is in the process of absorbing energy from a source of power ("giant worm drinks from magic spring"), or it is identified as an immortal animal ("immortal eagles in embrace"). They not only gather, store, spread, and enhance energy but have in them a concentration of spirit energy (*ling-ch'i*). These are "immortal-maker" sites, producing persons who will have high spiritual attainment.

HUMAN FORMATIONS

Landforms that resemble humans in action are dynamic and can store, gather, spread, and enhance energy.

FORMATIONS
THAT RESEMBLE IMMORTALS

These landforms have tremendous power, for their configurations resemble activities of immortals. They have special inherent energy and contain the primordial vapor of the universe. These are also "immortal-maker" sites.

NATURAL PHENOMENA FORMATIONS

All landscapes with formations that resemble natural phenomena have absorbed the essence of heaven and earth, and have gathered power from the stars and stones for millennia. They are the most powerful of all landscapes in all aspects. Absorb energy from these places and you will be "born with heaven and earth" and "age with the sun and moon." In other words, these places contain the primordial energy of the Tao in the purest form. These are also immortal-maker sites.

Water Patterns. Mountains are the bone of the land and water is the blood. Mountain is yin and water is yang. The copulation of yin and yang generates all things. Therefore a land with mountains but no water is not balanced and not fertile. A land with water but no mountains cannot gather energy. Water that flows toward mountains feeds the energy of the mountains and enhances their power. Water that flows away from mountains dissipates energy. Mountains help water to gather energy, and water helps mountains to direct and spread energy. Mountain and water complement each other in giving power to a place.

In feng-shui, we evaluate water by the shape of the body of water and its surface patterns. The shape of a river is defined by its course. Coastal water is defined by land around it. The shape of lakes is the drainage area that is covered by water, including any swamps and river channels that are next to the lake. Surface patterns in water are formed by the flow of currents, wind, and differences in coloration in the water.

Bodies of water that have animated and coherent flow patterns are said to have water dragon formations. Water dragons are paths of energy in water, just as dragon veins are paths of energy in mountains. A region with water dragons is a place of power. Water that has no coherent surface patterns cannot collect and spread energy, and water that has no surface pattern at all is "dead" water, devoid of energy.

River Patterns. In rivers with water dragon formations, the tail of the dragon is toward the source and the head is toward the mouth of the river. Generally, rivers that run toward a place carry energy to the site and rivers that run away from a site carry energy away.

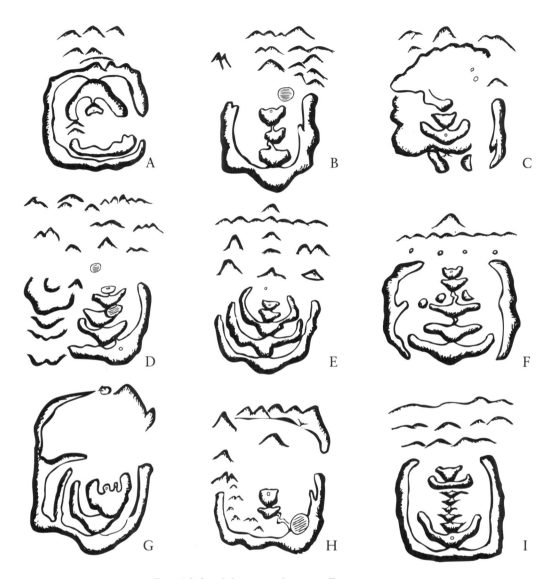

Fig. 10.26 MAGICAL ANIMAL FORMATIONS

A. Young dragon watching its mother.
B. Yellow dragon drinks from magic well.
C. Baby dragon nursed by mother dragon.
D. Magic frog spits out pearl.
E. Dragon of many colors rise to heaven.
F. Ascending dragon transforms its bones.

G. Playful lion tossing ball.
H. Mother dragon watching baby dragon.
I. Dragon spreads wings in flight.
J. Magical snake emerges from river gorge.
K. Magical centipede skims over land.
L. Giant worm gazes at the sky.

M. Immortal eagles in embrace.
N. Heavenly tortoise approaches Milky Way.
O. Giant worm drinks from magic spring.
P. Centipede flies across the sky.
Q. Magical tortoise watching its young.

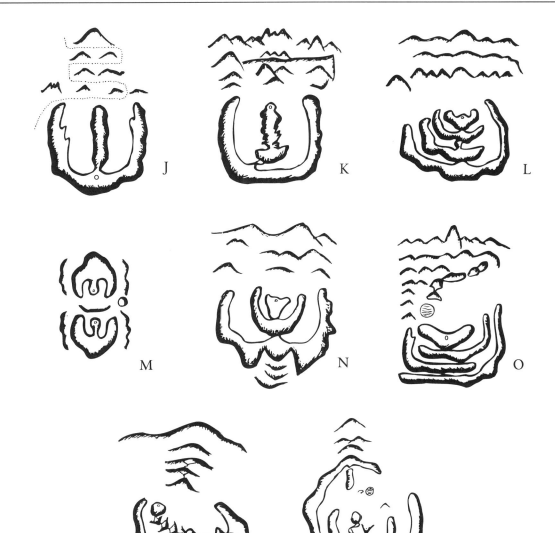

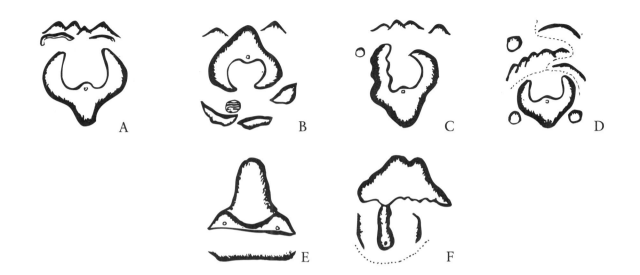

Fig. 10.27 DYNAMIC HUMAN FORMATIONS

A. True warrior gazes at sky.
B. Warrior sits under canopy.

C. Dancer waving her sleeves in the wind.
D. Lady works at the loom.

E. Nobleman pulls bow.
F. Warrior holds banner.

Fig. 10.28 IMMORTAL FORMATIONS

A. Immortal descending pagoda.
B. Heroic archer pulls bow.
C. Comet flies through the constellations.
D. Immortal casts hook into stream.

E. Immortal in meditation.
F. Lotus form.
G. Golden needle pierces pearl.
H. Immortal stretches leg.
I. Immortal ties on sash.

J. Immortal holds harp.
K. Immortal's footstep.
L. Magical warrior holds sword.
M. Persian warrior offers treasure.

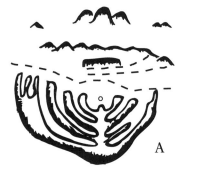

A

B

C

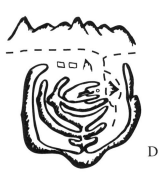

D

E

F

G

H

I

J

K

L

M

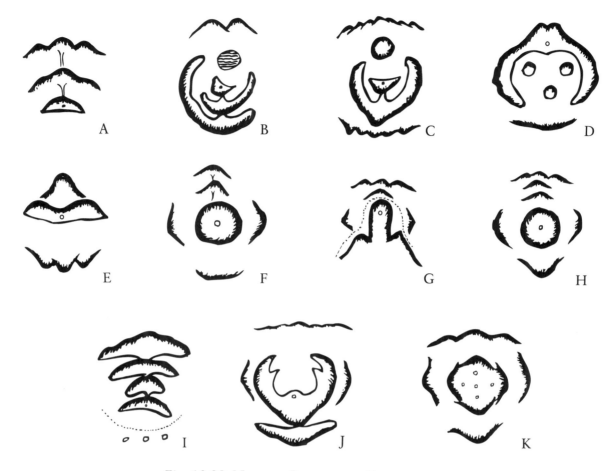

Fig. 10.29 NATURAL PHENOMENA FORMATIONS

A. Half moon.
B. Lonely moon sinks into the river.
C. Wispy clouds hold up the moon.
D. Three stars in gateway.
E. Gold coin.
F. Jade pendant.
G. Candle rising up to the sky.
H. Golden coins on a ledge.
I. Half moon rises in the east.
J. Lotus emerging from water.
K. Lotus bends down to touch the ground.

Fig. 10.30 WATER PATTERNS

A. Five dragons fighting for pearl.
B. Funnel of water rises to the clouds.
C. Mandarin ducks in embrace.
D. Submerged dragon swirls tail.
E. Moon hangs on golden hook.
F. Yellow snake spits out breath.
G. Coiled dragon stirring water.
H. Dragon plays with pearl.
I. Frog spits magic pearl.
J. Flowers floating on a spring river.
K. Golden star acompanying moon.
L. All the stars greeting the dawn.
M. Magical tortoise carrying young.
N. Golden tortoise prostrating before the North Star.
O. Clouds circle around the moon.
P. Six yin prostrates before yang.

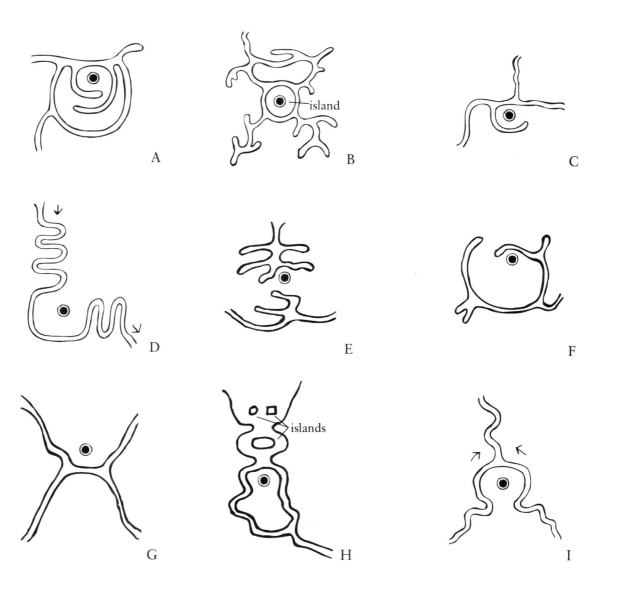

Fig. 10.31 WATER DRAGON FORMATIONS IN RIVERS

A. Crossed swords.
B. Four dragons playing with pearl.
C. Nobleman ascending dais.
D. Coiled dragon.
E. Male and female dragon playing.
F. Warrior pulls bow.
G. Water leaps over palace.
H. Running water collects spirit.

I. Twin rivers in embrace.
J. Welcoming beautiful maiden from afar.
K. Winding waters gather in front of palace.
L. Golden hook.
M. Rainbow swallowing azure clouds.
N. Double hook.
O. Dragon turning back.
P. Wind blows gently at sash.

Q. Flowers standing on stems.
R. Golden carp hides under lotus.
S. Sun and moon embracing.
T. Flags and banners flying in the wind.
U. Boat sails with wind.
V. Immortal hands playing on harp.
W. Phoenix in flight.

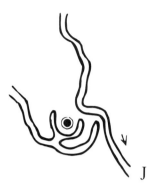

J

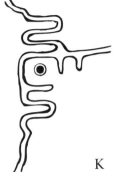

K

L

M

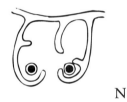

N

O

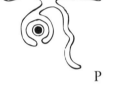

P

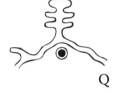

Q

R

S

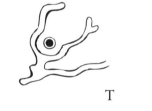

T

U

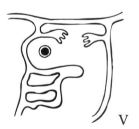

V

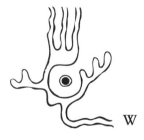

W

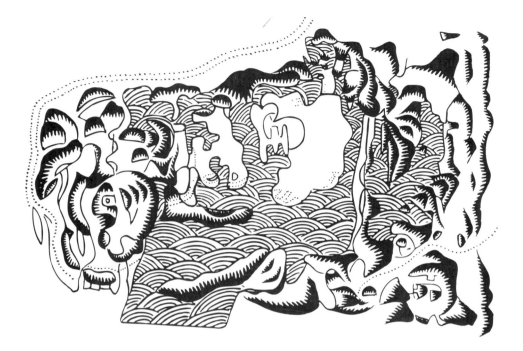

Fig. 10.32 COASTAL WATER FORMATIONS

This image (after an illustration in a Ch'ing-dynasty feng-shui manual) shows an inlet with mountains gradually sloping into the sea. The surface patterns on the water are also shown. The area covered by the wavy lines has a different coloration than the unmarked white area. Lines in the white area also indicate the pattern of the current in that area of the sea. The site that gathers the energy of both the mountain and water dragons is marked by a small circle at the left part of the drawing. Notice how it faces a cove with alternating colorations in the water. The original illustrator of this picture also wanted to show that the waters gather energy toward the site, as indicated by several arm-like sections (in white).

Road as Waterways. Sometimes roads and pathways can function as waterways where there are no rivers. Here, the flow of traffic defines the direction of the flow of energy. However, as conductors of energy, roads are not so effective as natural waterways.

Water Surface Patterns and Drainage Patterns. Surface patterns can be found in larger bodies of water, especially in wide rivers, lakes, and coastal waters. Prevailing winds create surface currents, and different depths in the water create differences in coloration. If a region is drained by several rivers (as in deltas) and lakes, the entire pattern of the drainage pattern is considered a surface pattern.

Coastal Water Formations. Coastal water formations are closely tied to the surrounding land. Dragon formations in coastal waters are usually created by gentle winds over water and the absence of sea cliffs. Waters that crash onto land are destructive, and waters that

Fig. 10.33 Landform that collects wind energy. The location in the center (marked by a small circle) receives wind energy from four diagonal directions (see dotted lines). Protected by dragon veins from four sides, it also absorbs energy from these veins. After a Ch'ing dynasty feng-shui manual.

approach land gently are nourishing.

Inlets and islands along a seacoast can contain water energy, but a coast that opens straight toward the ocean will dissipate energy very quickly.

Wind, Water, and Mountain. Wind is roving energy. Gentle breezes are benevolent, and strong winds (even seasonal ones) carry destructive energy. Wind in open spaces is generally destructive because there are no "cushions" to absorb and slow its ferocity. Wind tunnels in valleys and canyons are also places where wind is destructive. Wind along an exposed mountain ridge or a treeless slope is

also destructive, because there is nothing to soften its force.

Open land cannot gather wind energy. Land that is totally blocked from all wind flow is stagnant, for no wind energy can enter and be collected. Land that is sheltered from strong winds can prevent strong destructive forces from entering the area. Land that receives regulated wind flow can hold nourishing energy.

Wind can also animate water. Gentle winds in prevailing directions can create dragon formations in water, but water patterns can be destroyed by strong winds. Sheltered waters that receive gentle winds gather nourishing energy, but lakes and seas that are constantly whipped by winds have no beneficial energy.

Temporary Terrestrial Features. Some terrestrial features are temporary, for rivers and lakes can be seasonal, and sand dunes shift with wind strength and direction. Such temporary features do not contain inherent energy. However, they can act as barriers or conduits of energy while they are in existence.

Artificial versus Natural Landscapes. Artificially created landforms are called Later Heaven Formations, while natural landforms are Earlier Heaven Formations. Artificial landforms do not have inherent energy compared with natural landforms. This is because natural landforms are created over the millennia and have time to absorb the energy of the universe. However, artificial formations can direct the flow of energy or prevent the onslaught of destructive energy. Large-scale artificially created formations can include dams, dikes, and reservoirs. Small-scale artificial formations can include trees, hedges, walls, fountains, ponds, and gardens. (See chapter 18 for details of setting up artificial formations to counter the flow of destructive energy.) In fact, there is an interesting hypothesis that the Great Wall and some ancient Ch'in dynasty tombs were built as feng-shui devices, as conduits to direct and regulate earth energy.

Generally, there is no primordial energy embodied in artificial landforms to be absorbed, unless the artificial structures have been standing for a long time. It has been suggested that the Great Wall, the Pyramids,

megalithic stone monuments in Europe, and other ancient structures may have been around long enough to absorb some of the energy of the universe.

Natural Landforms That Emerge Abruptly. Volcanoes, landslides, and other formations that emerge abruptly in recent times do not have time to gather energy, and therefore do not have the same quality as formations that have been built up or weathered gradually. They can, however, conduct or block the passage of energy. On the other hand, volcanoes that were formed in geologic times do have enough time to absorb the essence of earth and sky energy and should have the same power as other nonvolcanic landforms.

Destruction of Natural Landforms. While it takes a long time for energy to be built up in landforms, it only takes a short time for energy in the land to be destroyed. When the formation that contains energy is destroyed, the power contained in that land is destroyed. Flooding a valley with the construction of dams, cutting a roadway or tunneling through a mountain, and reclaiming land from the sea are all examples where a natural landform can be destroyed in a short period of time, destroying the energy along with it.

The type of energy embodied in the land can also be modified by artificial structures that are built on it. Transmitters and antennas located on a mountaintop can turn benevolent and protective energy to destructive energy when a round-topped mountain has been changed to one having sharp points.

THE FIRST ENERGY

Being the first to absorb the energy of a location can be important in some places. Some landforms cannot regenerate energy once the energy is absorbed. The energy is therefore only good for the first house or burial site that is located there. Passive-type landforms have this characteristic. Passive animal formations are such sites. In dynamic-type landforms, where energy can be regenerated, being the first occupant is not so important. These include dynamic animal formations, human formations, and natural phenomena formations. In special regions where all the power of the land is used to create an extraordinary person or event, the energy will benefit only the first occupant. These are the magical animal formations and the immortal formations. Magical animal formations are likely to produce

kings and rulers if they are dragon formations. If they take the form of the other animals, they will produce persons of great talent who will affect the course of events. Immortal formations are likely to produce persons with high spiritual attainment.

As we come to the end of this chapter, we also come to the end of the theoretical part of feng-shui. You have entered the gateway into the universe of feng-shui. In the next section of the book you will learn how this theoretical knowledge is put into practice. If you decide to continue, your next step is to use the knowledge in these chapters with the tools outlined in the subsequent chapters to discover and experience the energetic nature of the land.

—

PART THREE

SWIRLING THE UNIVERSE

THE PRACTICE OF FENG-SHUI

—

Spirit reaches in the four directions, flows now this way, now that. It penetrates everywhere and everything. Above, it brushes the skies. Below, it surrounds the earth. It transforms and nourishes the ten thousand things.

—Chuang-tzu

11

Evaluating the External Environment

The first step in figuring out the feng-shui of a place is to evaluate its surrounding environment. I shall call it the external environment, in contrast to the internal environment, which is the architectural plan of the interior of a building (discussed in the next chapter). If the surrounding environment is not suitable, then there is no need to go further. This is true for the feng-shui of residences as well as the feng-shui of commercial buildings.

For purposes of convenience, I shall use the terms *house, site, location,* and *place* interchangeably since most readers will be concerned with the feng-shui of residences. The feng-shui of a business is intimately tied to the feng-shui of the residence of the owner of the business, but there are some unique considerations for the location of commercial buildings and retail shops. These will be discussed in a separate section at the end of this chapter.

The principles of residential feng-shui and the feng-shui of burial sites are quite similar. In general, a good place to live is also a good place to bury the dead. There may be some differences in the specific details, but energy that will benefit the occupants of a house is also energy that will benefit the descendants of a person buried at that same location. Where there are special considerations regarding the feng-shui of burial sites, I shall discuss them in the appropriate places.

The external environment consists of the immediate environment and the general environment. For any site, whether rural or urban, we evaluate first the features of its immediate environment and then the general layout of the land. What counts as the immediate environment and what constitutes the general environment is not defined by absolute measurement. Rather, it is dependent on the intuitive feel of the land. In rural areas the immediate and general environments will typically occupy a larger expanse of land, while in urban areas they will be more confined.

In rural areas, natural landforms make up both the immediate and the general environments. A location in a rural region has a closer relationship to the land and therefore a better chance to benefit from energy embodied in natural landforms. Therefore, if you have the choice, look for a house in a rural setting.

The previous chapter introduced some special landforms that have tremendous power. Those landforms are like works of art and are very rare. Most of the time your concerns will be finding a place that has nourishing energy but is also shielded from destructive energies. In other words, you don't want to be exposed to unnecessary problems, and at the same time it would be nice to benefit from any positive energies that are in the area.

In urban and suburban areas, the arrangement and shape of buildings make up the immediate surroundings, and the layout of the neighborhood will determine the general environment. In the city, you will not be able to absorb any energy that is intrinsic to natural landforms, but the artificial structures should function in the same way as natural landforms in collecting, dispersing, shielding, and rerouting energies.

THE IMMEDIATE SURROUNDINGS

1. Protection

In choosing a place to live, your first consideration should be protection. In feng-shui, protection means safety. You do not want harm to come to you and your family. Typically, safety means protection from dangers that will affect health, well-being, livelihood, and family relationships. In my feng-shui readings, I always counsel people that good health, well-being, and a contented livelihood are the most important things in life. If you don't have health or harmony, what is the use of having a lot of wealth?

A well-protected site is one in which the front, back, and sides are guarded by formations, whether natural or artificial. Recall that there are four protectors: Green Dragon, White Tiger, Red Raven, and Black Tortoise. The Green Dragon and White Tiger are land to the left and right of a site. This land should be higher than the site and should ideally be cradling it like arms.

RURAL AREAS

In a rural area, an effective Green Dragon should be high ground covered with trees or grass and should not be rocky or sandy or have gullies. An effective White Tiger should be a strong rock formation with no sharp features. Granite is best because the rock is hard and whitish in color. Red sandstone is not so ideal because it is soft and has the wrong color. If the dragon arm is long, then the tiger head needs to be high for both formations to be effective protectors. Likewise, a long tiger arm should be matched with a high dragon head.

The front of the site should be guarded by the Red Raven. An effective Red Raven should consist of several layers of mountain ranges in the distance. This is called the altar formation in traditional feng-shui, but you can also think of it as a coffee table. It cushions you from incoming forces, and yet your view is not blocked.

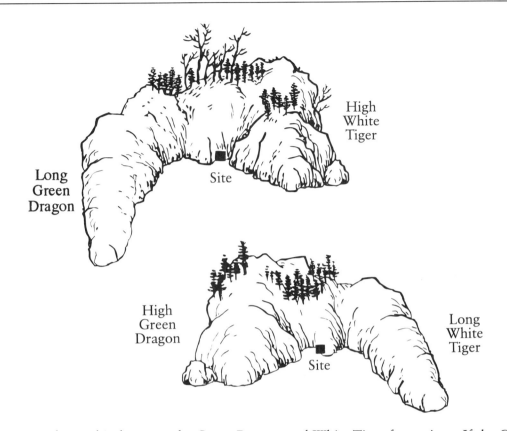

Fig. 11.1 Relationship between the Green Dragon and White Tiger formations. If the Green Dragon is long, then the White Tiger should be high. If the White Tiger is long, then the Green Dragon must be high.

The back of a site should also be well guarded. An ideal Black Tortoise formation should slope gradually toward the site. It should not be too high and should not be rocky. Ideally, it should resemble the back of a chair, and its top should be rounded, like a wood-type mountain. The next preferred shape is a flat top, like an earth-type mountain. In the immediate vicinity, there should be no sharp objects protruding from the Black Tortoise that point at the site. The Black Tortoise should also be the highest of the four formations. While your view in front should not be totally blocked by the Red Raven, the Black Tortoise should be the only thing that is seen from the back of the site.

If you are in a rural region where there is no natural high ground, then trees, hedges, and landscaped mounds can serve a similar purpose, but as protectors they are not as powerful as natural landforms.

URBAN AREAS

In an urban environment, the same principles of protection hold, except that you need to identify the appropriate equivalents in building structures.

An effective Green Dragon is ideally a

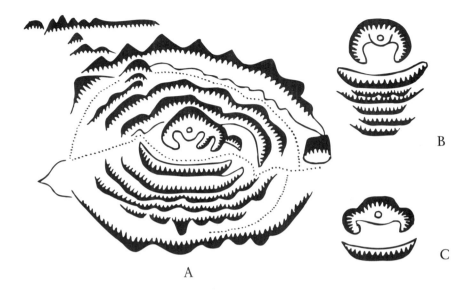

Fig. 11.2 (A) Black Tortoise and Red Raven formations, after a Ch'ing-dynasty illustration. Formations with hatch marks pointing downward depict Black Tortoise structures, and formations with hatch marks pointing upward depict Red Raven structures. (B) This illustration shows an ideal pair of Black Tortoise and Red Raven. Note that the Red Raven formation has many layers. (C) This is a passable pair of Black Tortoise and Red Raven. It is not so ideal because there is one tier of hills in the Red Raven.

building with a greenish or bluish tint. A building with a green stone facade or windows tinted the appropriate color will serve the purpose. Buildings with trees or hedges on their sides, or with ivy clinging to the walls, are also viable Green Dragons.

An effective White Tiger is a building that has a white stone facade. The next order of preference is a building simply painted white. The White Tiger should also be squat and strong. A building standing on pillars or positioned on top of a parking garage would therefore not qualify as an effective White Tiger. If the Green Dragon building is long, then the White Tiger building should be tall, and vice versa.

The Red Raven is the building in front. It should be lower than your building and should preferably be long, again like a coffee table. Ideally, the Red Raven building should not be too close to the front of your house. You should have a large front lawn, a wide street, or some open ground between it and your building.

The Black Tortoise is the building behind yours. It should be higher than your house, but again should not be too close. In a suburb, your backyard should provide enough distance between your house and the Black Tortoise. In the city, you would want to have a parking lot or even an alley between your building and the one behind you.

If the surrounding buildings are not effective protectors, you can build a fence, or plant hedges and trees around your house. I would advise you to have trees act as the Black Tor-

Fig. 11.3 Black Tortoise, Green Dragon, and White Tiger landforms. The White Tiger is the mound with exposed rock on the right hand side of the photograph. The Green Dragon is the mound with trees and bushes on the left side. The Black Tortoise is the ridge in the center of the picture. Notice that it slopes gently down into a valley.

toise and hedges or wooden fences as the Green Dragon and White Tiger. If the front of your house is too exposed, you may want to build a low brick wall to act as the Red Raven.

PROTECTION CHECKLIST

Here are some key points on what to look for when you consider protection.

- Choose a site that is protected on all sides.

- Land or buildings to the left and right of the site (the Green Dragon and White Tiger) should form cradling arms.
- Land or buildings to the back (the Black Tortoise) should be higher than your house. If the Black Tortoise is a natural landform, then it should not be ramrod-straight but should slope gently toward the site.
- Land to the front should be open in the immediate vicinity, but the horizon should not be empty. The house should

Fig. 11.4 A Red Raven formation. An opening in the branches reveals layers of ridges.

face a Red Raven formation and be "cushioned" by a layer of hills in rural environments, or buildings in urban environments. The more layers, the better the protection.

- Land should be sloping gently away from the front of the site. If you imagine the site as someone sitting on a chair, there should be room to stretch the legs.
- Land should not slope away from the back of the house. The site should have the feel of "security," as if there is something for it to lean against.
- The back of the house should not be too

close to the Black Tortoise formation, or the "guardian" will become an intimidator rather than a protector.

- The house should not be situated at the lowest point in the valley. In an urban environment, do not live in a building that is the lowest in the area. Positive energy will not reach it because the energy is absorbed by land that is higher. However, negative energy usually gathers at the lowest spot.
- Never live in a house built on a crag, a ridge, or the top of a mountain. These sites have no protection on any side.

Similarly, do not live on the upper floors of high-rise apartment buildings or in an apartment building that is the highest structure in the area. Exposed places get buffeted by untamed and destructive energy.

- Do not live in a house at the edge of a cliff or against a cliff. It is as if you are pushed to the brink of a fall or pushed up against a wall.
- Do not live in a house at the top of the Green Dragon (called the Horn of the Dragon) or the top of the White Tiger. These locations are too exposed and are buffeted by destructive energy that the Dragon and Tiger are meant to shield.
- Do not live in a house on a slope without vegetation as vegetation is a form of protection.

2. Influence of Objects in the Immediate Vicinity

Having considered protection, your next step is to examine objects in the immediate vicinity and see how they affect the building.

HARMFUL OBJECTS

Some objects, whether natural or artificial, are harmful because they can funnel or focus destructive energy toward your house. Below is a list of objects that are considered by feng-shui practitioners to be dangerous.

1. Sharp objects that point at a house are harmful because they contain destructive energy and focus it at you. (See fig. 11.5.) Look out for large tree branches that may be pointing at the house from the top and the sides. It is all right to have trees shade a house, but make sure that the branches do not point downward like a fork that is about to pene-

trate the roof. Jagged rocks that point at a site are also harmful. Other sharp objects to look out for include electrical transformers on power lines, transmitters, construction cranes, and antennas. The worst situation is when the sharp objects point at your front door or at your bedroom window.

Images of sharp objects are just as harmful as the real ones. Therefore, look out for advertisements on billboards, banners, and the like, that may have pictures of pointed objects (fig. 11.5F).

2. Large objects in the lot that dwarf the house are harmful. They compete with your house for energy and, being larger than your building, will absorb all the energy in the area, leaving you with none. For example, a large old tree with a lot of roots and branches, a big pile of rocks, or a deep pit can be competitors of energy.

3. Shiny objects directed at a house are also harmful. These objects collect malevolent energy and direct it toward you. They include reflections of sunlight from a glass door or window of another house, solar panels, reflective patterns off a distant lake, pond, or swimming pool, and light reflecting off metal objects (for example, parked vehicles). Even if they are far away, they can be harmful.

A word about satellite dishes. They have a bowl-like structure, which makes them reflecting surfaces even if they are not shiny. They also have an antenna, which is a pointed object. When a reflective object is combined with a pointed object, the danger is doubled because it collects destructive energy and focuses it. Therefore, get away from them at all costs. If you have no other choice, the next best strategy is to "neutralize" them with countermeasures (see chapter 18).

4. Long, thin objects that are oriented horizontally and are parallel to your building are

Fig. 11.5A Branches of a dead tree.

Fig. 11.5B Sculpture in the form of an upside-down dead tree with spreading roots.

Fig. 11.5 Examples of harmful objects. It is not desirable to have sharp objects pointing at your house.

Fig. 11.5C Power transmitter.

Fig. 11.5D Construction crane.

Fig. 11.5F A neon-lighted arrow (on top of the "liquor" sign)

Fig. 11.5E Sharp-edged rock.

Fig. 11.6A Objects that cut: power lines that appear to be slicing the house.

Fig. 11.6B Reflections of sunlight on a building making the building appear to be on fire.

Fig. 11.6C The "flames" are caused by sunlight reflected from the building with the shiny surface on the right hand side of the picture. The "burning" building is on the left.

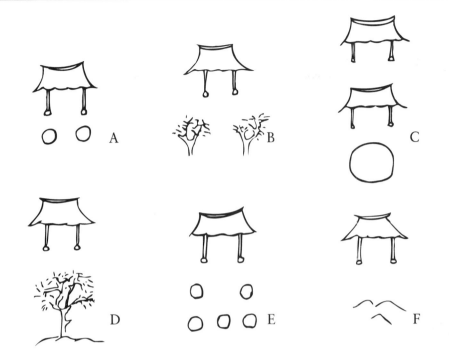

Fig. 11.7 Relationship of harmful objects to a house (from the notes of a feng-shui practitioner in Hong Kong). (A) Two large boulders blocking the front of the house. (B) Two large trees blocking the front of the house. (C) A large boulder blocking the front of the house. (D) A large tree blocking the front of the house. (E) A pile of rocks in front of the house. (F) Mounds of dirt in front of the house.

harmful. It is as if the blade of a knife is about to cut into your house. Obvious examples include power lines (fig. 11.6A), fences, and branches. Even clotheslines, if they are permanent fixtures, can be harmful.

5. Some patterns of light and shadows can be malevolent. Any pattern reflected onto the wall of your building that resembles flames, waves, and pointed objects, are all harmful. (See fig. 11.6B.)

6. Any large object located in front of your door blocks nourishing energy. It also obstructs your "way," so that you will meet with obstacles in all your undertakings. (See fig. 11.7.)

7. There are some special objects that you should pay attention to. It is impossible to provide an exhaustive list, but I shall give you a feel for what to avoid. Some sculptures have irregular shapes and sharp features. Others resemble objects of destruction or were once such objects. If you live in the city, you may need to watch out for these things. I once had a friend who complained that he had not felt well ever since he moved into his new apartment. When I paid him a visit, the first thing I noticed was a cannon from the naval memorial across the street pointing straight at his bedroom window! Any kind of object that resembles a weapon pointing at your home is

Fig. 11.8 More examples of harmful objects. It is not desirable to have such objects pointing at your house.

Fig. 11.8A Objects of destruction: sculpture that resembles pointing rifles.

Fig. 11.8B Objects of destruction: A "shooting" sculpture. Notice the gun and the arrows.

Fig. 11.8C Objects that reflect: satellite dishes.

harmful. Remember that pictures of such objects on billboards are just as destructive as the real ones. A picture of a jet fighter streaming toward you in an Air Force recruiting advertisement is just as harmful as living at the end of a runway. (See fig. 11.8.)

Ideally, you should try to avoid all the above objects. If you cannot avoid them, or if removing them is beyond your control, the next best alternative is to set up artifacts to counter them. These methods will be outlined in chapter 18.

BENEVOLENT OBJECTS

Some objects collect nourishing energy and are very beneficial if they are close to your house.

1. A small body of water right in front of a site is benevolent. Therefore, having a small pond or a fountain in front of your house is desirable.

2. Round objects near a house will bring nourishing energy. These include polished rocks and sculptures with smooth, round shapes, but *not* satellite dishes.

3. Structures in the Immediate Surroundings

These structures function the same way as objects in the immediate vicinity except that they are bigger, and therefore their effects are increased.

DESTRUCTIVE STRUCTURES

1. Structures that have a knifelike edge pointing at a house bring disaster. Look out for sections of rocky slopes that have sharp, thin edges oriented toward a house. The corners of other buildings can also "cut" sharply into a house. (See fig. 11.9A.)

2. Structures that have a shiny surface facing a house collect destructive energy and direct it toward the house (fig. 11.9B). These include glass or metal surfaces from skyscrapers that reflect sunlight onto your house.

3. Harsh-looking structures contain destructive energy (fig. 11.9C). It is harmful to have such objects "overlooking" your house. Outcrops of rocks, escarpments, and cliffs are all harsh structures. In fact, mountains are yin and contain malevolent energy. Buildings with strange shapes and uneven surfaces are also harsh structures.

4. Structures that are horizontally oriented and look like they are cutting into your house are destructive. These include bridges, viaducts, power lines (see fig. 11.6A), and elevated highways. Some examples of natural landforms are tops of mesas, buttes, and other flat-topped hills.

5. Structures that rise vertically in front or behind your house are destructuve (fig. 11.9F). They tower over you as if they are about to strike. These include cliffs, dams, and skyscrapers.

6. A rock formation that hangs over your house is destructive (fig. 11.9D). It gives the impression that the house is being crushed.

7. Buildings that have triangular shapes (fig. 11.9E) or have sections that protrude are also harmful, especially if the protruding sections point at your house like a lance.

8. Some structures can be harmful if they are close to your building. See figure 11.10 (page 118) for examples.

Fig. 11.9 Examples of destructive structures or large objects. It is undesirable to have these near your house.

Fig. 11.9A Escarpment with sharp and pointed rocks.

Fig. 11.9B Reflective side of building with images of transformers and power lines.

Fig. 11.9C Harsh-looking and knobby rock face.

Fig. 11.9D A large overhanging rock.

Fig. 11.9E A pyramid-shaped rocky ridge.

Fig. 11.9F A large rock that is very close to the building. In the picture, the rock on the left is up against the house. The house is partially hidden by trees.

A

B

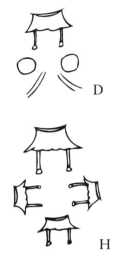

C

D

E

F

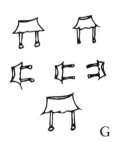

G

H

I

J

K

L

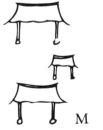

M

N

O

P

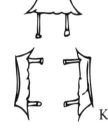

BENEVOLENT STRUCTURES

1. Gardens and parks with flowers and evergreen trees are benevolent. In Chinese culture, evergreens are the symbol of longevity and health because they do not shed their leaves and "die" in winter. Gardens and flowers are associated with growth and are symbols of prosperity. Preferably, the park should be located toward the front of your building.

2. Ponds and fountains are also benevolent structures. Water is associated with prosperity, so it is good to have a pond, a lazy stream, or a body of water near the front of your building.

3. Round structures are also beneficial. Roundness is the symbol of completeness and the contentment and satisfaction that come with it. Therefore it is good to live in an area where you can see domes or buildings with circular shapes. Having a rotunda or traffic circle in front of a building is good because its roundness smooths out intruding energy that may otherwise be directed toward the building. However, beware of structures that may appear round, but are actually not round. These are domes that have "spikes" on their roofs (see fig. 12.3D on page 155).

4. Roads and Rivers in the Immediate Vicinity

Rivers and roads are pathways of energy and can conduct, gather, and disperse energy depending on their pattern. In feng-shui, roads are evaluated the same way as river courses. The flow of traffic along a road becomes the equivalent of the flow of water in a river.

Road and river patterns may be benevolent or destructive, depending on their configuration and their relationship to a location. Beneficial patterns bring nourishing energy, and malevolent patterns bring destructive energy.

River patterns that have dragon formations bring nourishing energy (see page 87 in chapter 10). The same is true for roads that resemble river courses with water dragon formations.

Some patterns are unique to roads. If you live in an urban environment, you will encounter roads more often than rivers, and evaluating road and street patterns can be very important in choosing a location for your house.

Fig. 11.10 (opposite) Relationship of harmful structures to a house (from the notes of a feng-shui practitioner in Hong Kong). (A) Pits in front of and behind the house. (B) Edge of another building pointing at the house. (C) Large buildings in front and behind the house. (D) Two roads converging through a gap toward the house. (E) Large building immediately behind the house. (F) Three buildings forming a wedge that points at the back of the house. (G) Many buildings with edges of roofs pointing at the back of the house. (H) Many buildings with edges of roofs pointing at the front of the house. (I) Two buildings forming a triangular pattern that point at the back of the house. (J) Buildings that are close in front of and behind the house. (K) Two tall buildings with their sides pointing at the front of the house. (L) A bridge in front of the house. (M) Two tall buildings in the close vicinity. (N) Edge of another building pointing at the side of the house from the right. (O) Edge of another building pointing at the side of the house from the left. (P) Edges of sloping roofs from buildings pointing at the two sides of the house.

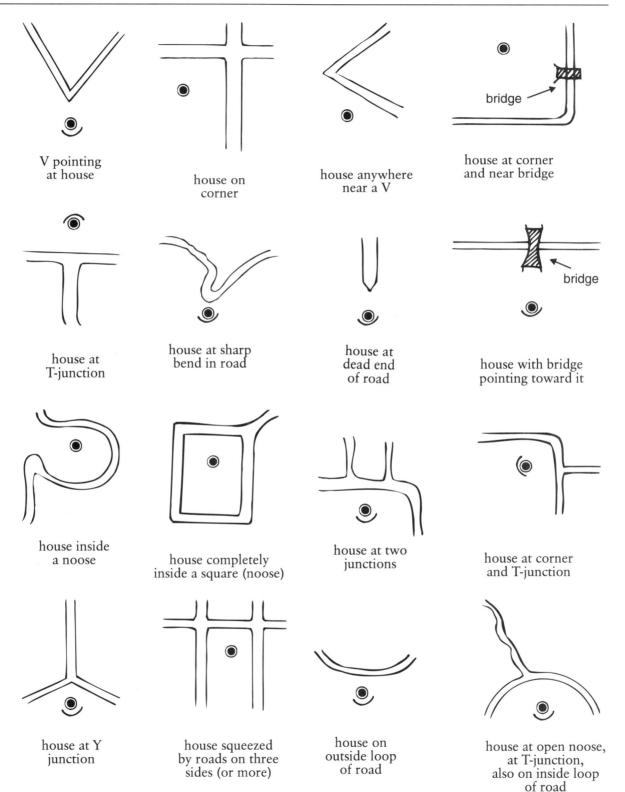

V pointing
at house

house on
corner

house anywhere
near a V

house at corner
and near bridge

bridge

house at
T-junction

house at sharp
bend in road

house at
dead end
of road

house with bridge
pointing toward it

bridge

house inside
a noose

house completely
inside a square (noose)

house at two
junctions

house at corner
and T-junction

house at Y
junction

house squeezed
by roads on three
sides (or more)

house on
outside loop
of road

house at open noose,
at T-junction,
also on inside loop
of road

DESTRUCTIVE ROAD PATTERNS

Destructive road paterns bring sha-ch'i, or malevolent energy. They are associated with ill-health, death, bankruptcy, failure in education, disharmony in the family, betrayal by friends and relatives, and other misfortunes. The following are some guidelines for recognizing destructive road patterns (see fig. 11.11). The conditions described are worsened where traffic flow is heavy and are minimized where traffic flow is light.

1. A road that terminates or intrudes into a site is destructive. Therefore, avoid a house that stands at a dead end, a T-junction, a Y-junction, or where a road makes a sharp turn.

2. A road that circles a house like a noose is harmful to the occupants. It is as if the road is "choking" the house.

3. A house situated between two parallel roads should be avoided. It is as if the roads are "squeezing" the house.

4. A house situated between two converging roads should be avoided. Here, it is as if the house is about to be cut by "scissors."

5. A road that veers sharply around a house is destructive. Energy along a path that changes course abruptly is malevolent.

6. Houses on the corners of intersections should be avoided.

7. Roads that curve into a site are destructive.

8. Houses near bridges, viaducts, elevated throughways, and highway interchanges are buffeted by destructive energy.

9. A road that runs downhill toward a house brings harm to the occupants.

10. Houses that are located along a steep road should be avoided. Energy rushing down will destabilize the house, making the fortunes and health of the occupants unstable.

11. Houses at a crest where steep roads run away from it on more than one side should be avoided. Anything gathered through hard work will roll away without warning.

12. Near airports, the orientation of runways to a house is important. Do not have a runway pointing straight toward your house.

13. You should not have a house in an area where the roads are like a maze. Mazelike pathways obstruct the flow of nourishing energy and trap destructive energy in the area.

BENEVOLENT ROAD PATTERNS

Benevolent road patterns bring nourishing energy, which is associated with health, well-being, good fortune in business, prosperity, harmony within the family, success in education, and good relationships with friends and relatives. (See fig. 11.12.)

1. A road that cradles a site, but does not wind around it like a tight noose, brings beneficial energy.

2. A house that is situated at the end of a series of loops in a winding road is also desirable.

3. Traffic circles are beneficial road patterns because they do not have the sharpness

Fig. 11.11 (opposite) Aversive road patterns. These are unfavorable positions for houses because the locations receive the greatest onslaught of destructive energy from the road. The curved line next to the dot designates the back of the building. The circle with a black dot in the center marks the location of the house in relationship to the road.

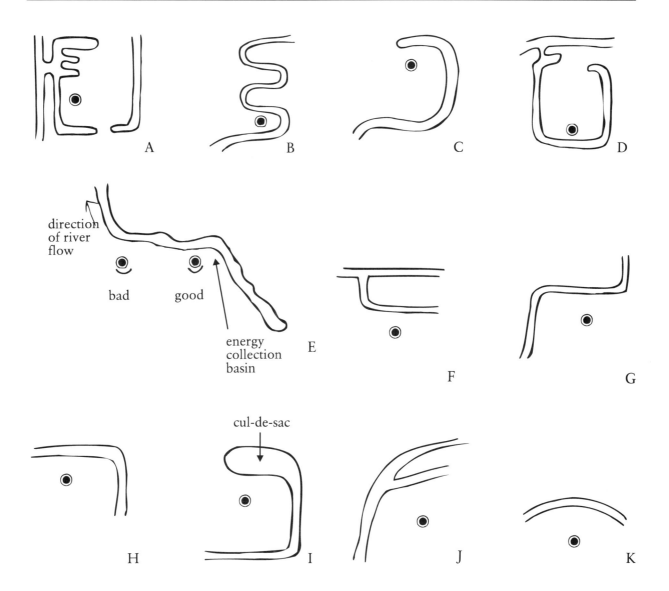

Fig. 11.12 Beneficial road patterns. The circled dot represents the location of a building; a curved line next to it indicates the back of the building. The first panel in the second row compares a good location with a bad one. The good location is situated where the road changes direction as it turns left. The road continues in the same direction for a while before it veers off in another direction. The house in the good location receives the flow of energy from the incoming road. This energy is collected where the road turns left (in the collection basin). The house in the bad location is situated where the energy flows away from the collection basin.

of an intersection, and traffic enters and exits with the flow of the circle.

4. Roads that resemble river courses with water dragon formations also bring nourishing energy (see figs. 10.30 and 10.31 on pages 93–95). Therefore, a house that overlooks such patterns is beneficial to the occupants.

5. In general, gentle, winding streets smooth out wild, rushing energy, and it is preferable to have a house in an area where the streets are curved rather than set in a square grid.

6. Dirt and gravel roads carry energy better than paved roads. Paved roads put a "lid" over the earth and therefore decrease the efficiency of energy travel.

TRAFFIC FLOW AND WATER FLOW

Recall from the previous chapter that water complements mountains and helps to spread energy. But also remember that yin waters are destructive and should be avoided. The nature of the flow will determine whether the water is yin or yang. Likewise, the flow of traffic on a road will determine whether yin or yang energy is carried by the road. Here are some guidelines for evaluating traffic flow and water flow near a house.

1. Yin water is water that drops from a great height. Energy that comes rushing toward, away from, and along a house is destructive. Therefore, do not live in a house that is near the bottom or the top of a waterfall. The same goes for a road that slopes steeply. Avoid a house that is at the top of a hill where roads slope steeply away from it. Also avoid a house at the bottom of a steep road or along a steep road. If the traffic on that steep road is heavy, then the power of the destructive energy is increased.

2. Fast-flowing waters are yin in nature. Therefore, do not live in a house right next to whitewater or a fast-flowing stream. Likewise, you do not want to live in a house along a road with fast-moving traffic. These include busy streets and highways.

3. Water that rises is also yin. Therefore, avoid a house where waves crash up against a shore. The urban equivalent is a location where a house stands at the dead end of a busy street.

GENERAL ENVIRONMENT

After you have looked at the immediate environment, you should try to get a feel for the general surroundings. Sometimes you may have to walk away from the site to get a clear perspective of the land. In a hilly region, you will want to get to a high point in the region. In an area where land is flat, you may have to drive or walk several miles around the region to get the feel of the layout of the land. In an urban area, you can get a good panoramic view from the higher floors of a skyscraper.

Effects of General versus Local Environments

In considering general versus local environment, the following points should be noted.

1. If both local and global environments are beneficial, the power of the nourishing energy is enhanced.

2. If both local and global environments are harmful, the power of the destructive energy is multiplied.

3. Local features tend to affect only those who are currently living in that location.

4. General environmental features tend to affect several generations, even if the second or third generations do not live in that location.

5. Effects brought by local features are generally Later Heaven effects: that is, effects caused by human activity. Effects brought about by global environments are generally Earlier Heaven effects: that is, effects that are not associated with human actions. For example, a fire started by a child playing with matches is a Later Heaven calamity, and a fire caused by a lightning strike is Earlier Heaven calamity.

1. Mountain Environments
EFFECT OF DRAGON VEINS

In the previous chapter you were introduced to dragon veins, which are pathways of concentrated energy in mountains. Recall that dragon veins can bring energizing or destructive energy, depending on their pattern. We shall now evaluate various types of dragon veins and see how they affect people who live in the path of their energy.

Dragon veins can be strong or weak, energizing or destructive, alive or dead. (See fig. 11.13.) A strong vein is organized, follows a straight path, and has many branches. A weak vein twists around and has sparse and disconnected branches. An energizing vein has thick branches that connect to a larger trunk. A destructive vein has disconnected branches ending in cliffs or has a branch that cuts into the main trunk of the vein. A dead vein is one that has no branches. A vein in which energy runs backward instead of forward also carries destructive energy.

Figure 11.13 shows thirteen different kinds of dragon veins, described below. Sites that

are most affected by the energy of these veins are marked by small circles. These locations are called the "head" of the dragon.

The Emerging Dragon. Also called Birth of the Dragon, this vein resembles a dragon emerging from its egg. Movement or development, whether waxing or waning, starts from the part of the vein nearest you, which is the head of the dragon. The tail is the part farthest from you. The energy of the Emerging Dragon is youthful and strong. This energy is most beneficial for enterprising activities.

The Prosperity Dragon. This vein has many branches cradling and protecting the site. Its energy is more mature than that of the Emerging Dragon, and it is most beneficial to enterprises that are building on an existing foundation, be it prosperity or sphere of influence.

The Receding Dragon. This is a weak vein. Notice how the spine of the dragon gets smaller and smaller until it disappears. This is not to be confused with the gradual termination of a vein (see "Dragon Veins," page 65, and figs. 10.4 and 10.5). A strong vein that ends gradually retains the majesty of its spine and branches, and their slopes do not end in cliffs. Energy in the Receding Dragon is associated wtih weakness of personality. Occupants born in a house located in the head of the Receding Dragon will be dominated by others in business or in social status.

The Growing Dragon. This is a vein that gains in strength and power. Compare it with the Receding Dragon and you will see that its branches and "arms" get thicker and bigger toward the top of the picture. Energy in this dragon vein brings prosperity and wealth to many generations. Occupants born in a house at the head of this dragon will have many achievements.

The Dragon on Its Back. This is a destructive vein. It resembles a dragon rolled over on

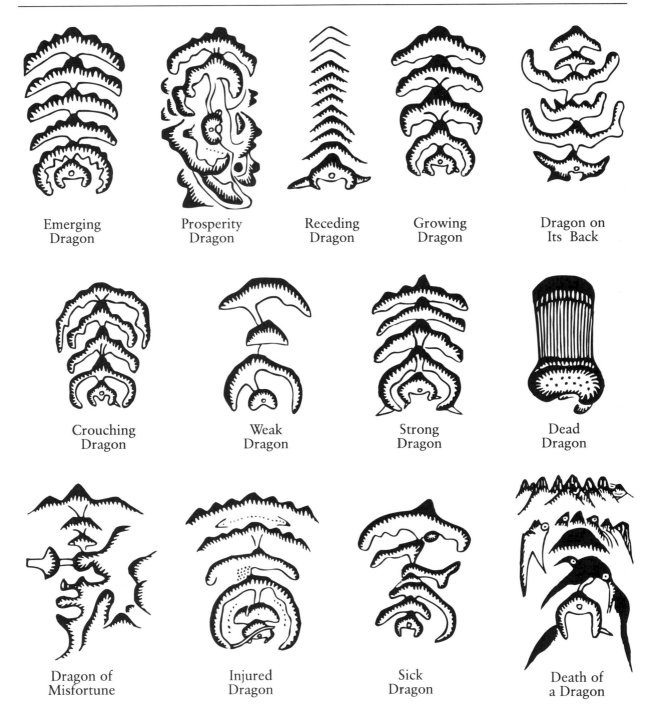

Emerging
Dragon

Prosperity
Dragon

Receding
Dragon

Growing
Dragon

Dragon on
Its Back

Crouching
Dragon

Weak
Dragon

Strong
Dragon

Dead
Dragon

Dragon of
Misfortune

Injured
Dragon

Sick
Dragon

Death of
a Dragon

Fig. 11.13 Types of dragon veins. See the text for a discussion of each of these veins and their effects. The small dots in the Dead Dragon and Injured Dragon indicate unevenness in the terrain.

its back with its feet in the air. Notice that the "legs" of the dragon are pointing away from its head. Only dead animals assume this posture. Therefore, this is a dying or dead dragon. This dragon vein brings loss of fortune associated with bankruptcy. Moreover, the family living here will be entangled with legal problems involving young children.

The Crouching Dragon. This is a nourishing vein and is the opposite of the Dragon on Its Back. The "feet" of the dragon point toward its head as if protecting it. The occupants of a house at the head of this dragon will be surrounded by many descendants who will be filial and caring. The energy of this vein is associated with wealth, prosperity, and harmony within the family.

The Weak Dragon. The spine of this dragon is weak because it is not aligned. There is no central trunk and the branches are sparse. It is as if the spine of the dragon, or the vein, is broken. The occupants of a house at the head of the dragon will meet with accidents associated with wind and water. Children will be orphaned young, and the family will become poor as the result of the early death of the head of the family.

The Strong Dragon. This vein is mature and strong, as indicated by the coherent and thick branches. Moreover, the first two pairs of "legs" of the dragon cradling the head have extra "claws." The claws are associated with power and energy. The occupants of a house located in the head of this dragon will have wealth, fame, and strength of character. The head of the family or a descendant of the family living here will achieve renown and success.

The Dead Dragon. This vein is dead because it has no branches. Its shape resembles the inert body of a dead animal. Its energy is extremely destructive and should be avoided

at all costs. Occupants of a house built at the head of this dragon will meet with poverty and death.

The Dragon of Misfortune. This vein carries destructive energy because it does not have a strong central spine. In fact, there are two formations that cut into the middle of its spine, severing it into segments. Moreover, there is no coherent "head," as indicated by the disorganized branches at the bottom of the picture. In this dragon, the primordial vapor has gone sour. It forebodes illness and death to children in the family in addition to loss of possessions in robbery and theft.

The Injured Dragon. The vein of the dragon along the central spine is broken. There are no connections between the last three pairs of legs. Furthermore, cliff edges mark the slopes of the legs of the dragon, and the branches are separated by parallel intermontane valleys. Finally, the head of the dragon is cut in half by a road or a river. This vein forebodes the death or disability of young children in the family.

The Sick Dragon. This vein is characterized by imbalance in its branches (the feet of the dragon). As shown in the illustration, the branches are lopsided, some long, some short, making the dragon vein look very unbalanced. Imbalance is an indication of instability, and this vein forebodes fluctuations of fortune in the family whose house is located in the area of the head of this dragon.

The Death of a Dragon. This is the most destructive of dragon veins. It is called the Death of the Dragon because the mountain ranges are jagged and descend as cliff faces. The general shape of the mountains in this vein is harsh and sharp, and there is no central spine at all. This vein brings death to the entire family whose house is located in the area of the head of this dragon.

EFFECT OF GENERAL MOUNTAIN ENVIRONMENTS

Recall from the previous chapter that yin-type mountains are associated with destructive energy. The following are some guidelines on what to avoid and what is desirable in evaluating general mountain environments.

Harmful Mountain Environments

1. Do not live in a house close to mountains with jagged peaks and rocky slopes (fig. 11.14A). It is all right for them to be in the distance, but you do not want them to be towering above you.

2. Do not live in an area with a lot of cliffs (figs. 11.14B, C). These include valleys and canyons with steep, rocky walls.

3. Do not live in an area where there are a lot of gullies or loose rocks on the slopes (fig. 11.14D)

4. Slopes that are permanently in shadow are very destructive, for they do not receive the yang energy of the sun. Therefore, do not live in a house in a valley that is always in the shade.

5. Slopes that are covered by cloud or fog for many days of the year are not beneficial because too much sky energy will smother the earth.

6. Do not live on a bare slope because there will be too much energy from the sun and not enough earth energy from vegetation.

7. Road cuttings generally expose rocky or sandy formations (fig. 11.14E). Do not live in a house that overlooks a road cutting.

Beneficial Mountain Environments

All yang-type mountains are associated with nourishing energy.

1. An area with green mountains is a desirable place to live.

2. Areas where mountains have gentle slopes and rounded tops are also places of nourishing energy.

3. Shifting shadow patterns on mountain slopes are also signs of good energy. When moving clouds create areas of light and shade on mountain slopes, it is said that earth and sky energy are copulating. Out of this interaction comes nourishing energy. Therefore, if your house has a view of these patterns, it is very beneficial.

4. The same can be said for mist or cloud on mountain slopes (fig. 11.15). When parts of a mountain range are temporarily hidden by cloud or mist forming an image of partially hidden mountains (as seen in many Chinese landscape paintings), this is a sign of the movement of energy. Mist and clouds are energy of the sky, and when they hug mountains, nourishing energy is created and circulated.

2. Water Environments

Evaluation of a water environment includes the land around it, since we do not live in environments where there is only water. The place where water meets land is where yang and yin energies interact. When water and land are both yin, no constructive interaction is possible. They end up fighting each other for dominance and create destructive energy. Waves crashing against a cliff is an example of yin waters competing against yin mountains.

Destructive waters bring harm and calamity. Benevolent waters bring nourishing energy. However, regardless of whether the water is destructive or beneficial, you do not want a house right against the water. You should have a buffer of land between the house and the water.

Fig. 11.14 Examples of destructive mountain environments.

Fig. 11.14A Jagged peaks and rocky slopes.

Fig. 11.14B Rocky escarpment with cliff face.

Fig. 11.14C Cliffs at the sudden termination of a dragon vein.

Fig. 11.14D Scree: slope with loose rocks.

Fig. 11.14E Road cutting exposing a rocky outcrop.

Fig. 11.14F Bare slope. Houses built on a bare slope have poor protection. Bare slopes are also a poor source of nourishing energy.

Fig. 11.14G A house should not overlook a road cutting that reveals a harsh layer of rocks. Harsh-looking rocks carry destructive energy.

Fig. 11.14H Canyons surrounded by steep cliffs are unfavorable locations for houses because they tend to be wind tunnels, which carry destructive energy.

Fig. 11.15A Wispy layers of mist that partially covers a mountainside are an indication of the copulation of sky and earth energies. Creative energy is born of this interaction and such locations are filled with power. *Watching the Waterfall among the Clouds* (1975), from the author's collection.

Fig. 11.15B Mist on a mountainside as sometimes seen from the author's house. This is very auspicious. It is a meeting of earth (mountain) and sky (vapor) energies.

DESTRUCTIVE WATERS

1. Water that crashes onto land brings destructive energy. Therefore, do not live in a house on top of a sea cliff or on a rocky platform along the coast.

2. Water that funnels into land like a long finger brings destructive energy. Do not live in a house that stands at the end of an inlet surrounded by two headlands.

3. Fast-flowing rivers, especially whitewater that runs over rocks, are destructive. Do not live in a house on the banks of a fast-flowing river.

4. Tidal flow can be destructive if the onset of high tide is fast.

5. Fluctuating water patterns are associated with erratic energy flow. Although they can sometimes be beneficial (if they form a water dragon), they can turn malevolent without any warning. Drainage areas and flood plains in delta regions have that characteristic. So do swamps. Therefore, avoid these kinds of water environments.

6. Stagnant water environments are destructive because they are "dead." No energy exists in them. Some swamps or inland lakes

Fig. 11.16 Fast-flowing water carries destructive energy.

have that characteristic. Again, avoid this kind of water environment.

BENEVOLENT WATERS

1. Water that laps gently as it meets land is beneficial. Therefore, a house with a view of sandy beaches and trees is a good place to live.

2. Water that has surface patterns, such as dragon formations (described in fig. 10.31 on pages 94–95), brings nourishing energy. Therefore, a house with a view of the sea where you can see differences in surface colorations resembling water dragon patterns

is very desirable (fig. 11.17A).

Sometimes, water dragon formations are seen in the difference between colorations of grass in a pasture. These are extremely rare and are very auspicious. In feng-shui, they are called Green Dragons Frolicking in Water (fig. 11.18).

3. Water that is "connected" to earth is beneficial. Therefore, springs and water that run into underground drainage in limestone areas have life energy in them, and a house in the area will benefit from that energy.

4. In an urban setting, the equivalent of water surface patterns can be found in the layout of a parking lot in a shopping plaza. Surface pattern is defined by the relationship of roadways, shape of parking lots, dividers, and flow of traffic. A shopping plaza with circular roadways brings benevolent energy. An ideal plaza is one that has buildings, some high, some low, circling the parking lot, with exits and entrance partially hidden or off to the corners. A building overlooking such a structure will have good feng-shui.

5. A parking lot enclosed by a wall with entrances oriented to the corner of the lot is the urban equivalent of a sheltered lake. You tend to find this type of arrangement in older buildings with courtyards that have been converted into parking lots. European cities and in sections of Hong Kong and Singapore with colonial-era architecture have many of these structures.

WIND, WATER, AND LAND

One general principle in feng-shui is to maximize yang environments and minimize yin ones. Here, yin and yang are regarded not as complementaries but as opposites. In this context, yin is associated with decay, illness, and death, and yang is associated with birth, nourishment, and life. Most Westerners are

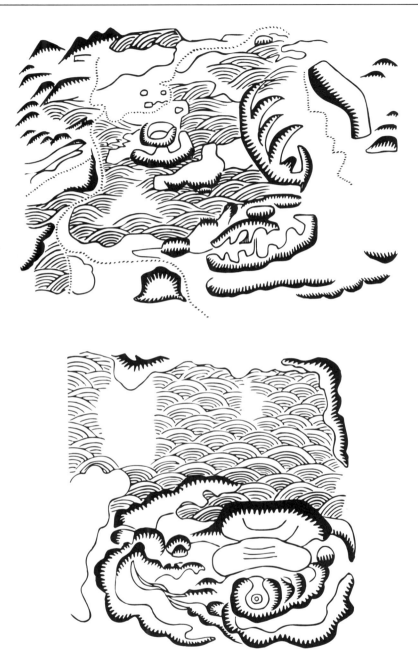

Fig. 11.17 (A) Water patterns along a coast (after a Ch'ing-dynasty feng-shui book on landforms). The drawing shows an inlet where the water is surrounded by land on three sides. In the middle of the inlet are some islands. The presence of the islands create different patterns in the water, depicted by the shadings of curved lines and white areas. (B) Water patterns along a coast that has no protection from islands—a destructive water environment.

Fig. 11.18 Green Dragons Frolicking in Water. Some water patterns are not necessarily associated with different colorations in water. This photograph shows a Green Water Dragon—the dark, snake-like pattern in the center. The Green Water Dragon is vegetation, typically long grass, that is greener than the surrounding vegetation. Most Green Water Dragons are associated with a stream or subsurface runoff that makes some plants more lush than the ones farther away from this water source.

only familiar with the idea of yin and yang as complements describing two equal parts necessary to achieve a state of balance. The other meaning of yin and yang, that of opposites, is seldom discussed in the popular literature. However, in Chinese thinking and in Taoist philosophy, the notion of yin and yang as opposites is just as common as conceiving them as complements. In fact, the usage of yang and yin as opposites is older.

Before the *I-ching* was compiled by Confu-cius in the sixth century BCE, the meaning of yin and yang was tied to their concrete qualities, yin meaning shade and yang meaning light. One of the earliest usages of yin and yang was the description of mountain slopes. South-facing slopes are sunny (in the Northern Hemisphere) and therefore are yang. North-facing slopes are shady and therefore are yin. The symbolic meanings attached to yin and yang came several hundred years later, when yin became associated with receptivity, softness, and inward-looking, and yang became associated with strength, expansion, and outward-looking. I remember that in my studies in Hong Kong, these two dimensions of meaning of yin and yang were common knowledge and always discussed together.

In order to understand the feng-shui of yin and yang environments, you need to recognize that there are two usages of yin and yang. In this context, yin and yang symbolize opposites, and the goal is to maximize yang (life-giving) qualities and minimize yin (death-inducing) qualities.

Recall from chapter 10 that sharp, rocky formations are yin and tempestuous waters are yin. Whitewater and breakers form a sharp transition between water and land. Similarly, rocky outcrops form a sharp transition between land and land. In both cases, there is a feeling of discontinuity in the boundaries between the two environments. Therefore, the worst conditions for feng-shui occur when an environment contains both yin mountains and yin waters.

Also recall from chapter 10 that gentle green slopes are yang and calm waters are yang. The gradual termination of a dragon vein is the smooth transition between land and land. Similarly, there is a sense of smoothness in the transition between surface colorations in water dragon patterns, which are found in calm waters. Therefore, the best conditions for feng-shui occur when an environment contains both yang mountains and yang waters.

Given this understanding, the following are some guidelines in evaluating the combined presence of water and land.

1. Do not live in a house on a seacliff, as this is where yin waters (breakers) meet yin mountains (cliff).

2. Avoid a house by a fast-flowing stream with steep banks.

3. Do not live near cliffs and rocky outcrops even if whitewater is absent, because there are still destructive effects from the yin mountains.

4. Frozen lakes are considered dead and therefore yin. Do not live in a house where there are rocky slopes on one side and a lake that freezes on the other.

Wind is also an important consideration in feng-shui. Wind is modified by land, and wind affects water. Because wind is transitory, it is a carrier of roaming energy. Winds that are strong and gusty are yin. They are carriers of destructive energy. In contrast, gentle winds carry nourishing energy.

Here are some guidelines in evaluating the effect of wind on the feng-shui of a place.

1. Do not live in areas where it is windy all the time. These include open coastline, lakefront, wide stretches of flatland, and exposed ridges and slopes. Wind tunnels are also undesirable, and these are generally found in narrow valleys and canyons.

2. Winds that swirl or create funnels are destructive, for they uproot energy and carry it away, leaving the earth "barren."

3. Even if the top of a ridge is covered with trees, a house located there is still buffeted by wind. In fact, when wind lashes at the trees, the trees will sway as if they too are "beating" the house.

Vegetation and Animals

Vegetation is associated with life force. An area that does not support vegetation lacks life energy.

1. Do not live in an area that is too dry

A

B

Fig. 11.19 Harmful interactions of yin waters with mountains. (A) Fast-flowing water next to cliffs. (B) Frozen lake (stagnant water) next to cliffs.

to support greenery. Such places do not have enough life energy.

2. Do not live in an area where plant life is too thick. This area has excessive earth energy and not enough sky energy.

3. High altitude and cold climates also rob vegetation. Therefore, tundralike conditions and places above the tree line are also low in earth energy.

4. Even if you live in a city, try to find an area where there are trees. These areas are generally found in older neighborhoods, where trees have had enough time to grow. Newly developed housing areas tend to be barren.

5. An area with wildlife usually has nourishing energy. Animals are generally more sensitive to the energy of the land than humans and can give valuable guidance as to where there are concentrations of energy. Among animals, the deer, fox, monkey, and wolf are most sensitive to energy in the land. Therefore, it is good to have a house in a region where these animals are frequently seen.

6. Where farming or other human activity has cut a swath through the land, finger-like sections of earth may be stripped of vegetation (fig. 11.20A). These strips are harmful, although they may be seasonal.

7. There is one special case about vegetation. Vegetation on a slope that looks like boils on a head brings harm. Hills with stubby bushes and brush have that appearance (fig. 11.20B).

Types of Land Use around Your Building

Land use affects the flow of energy in an area. Usage transforms the feel of a space, and the feng-shui of a place can become suddenly good or bad because of land use.

In general, land use that is associated with illness, death, decay, and violence brings destructive energy to the area. Land that is used for growth, healing, spiritual development, learning, and harmonious interactions among people brings nourishing energy to the area. Given this understanding, the following are some guidelines for evaluating the effects of land use on the feng-shui of your house.

These are undesirable conditions:

1. You should not choose a house where there is a graveyard in the vicinity. Graveyards create and enhance yin (death) energy.

2. Your house should not be situated next to a mortuary, funeral home, or crematorium, or any kind of business associated with death. This includes manufacturers of caskets and engravers of headstones.

3. You should not build your home on ancient burial grounds. The spirits of the dead will be disturbed and will turn against the occupants of the house.

4. A house next to a hospital or hospice brings misfortune to the occupants.

5. A house near a power station should be avoided (fig. 11.21). Generators produce a lot of electrical power, and this powerful concentration of energy will distort the natural flow of energy in the area and create a vortex of destructive energy in that place.

6. Do not live in a house near prisons, police stations, or other government facilities that deal with crime and violence. Violent actions carry destructive energy, and in an area where there is a concentration of incidents associated with crime and violence, there will be a lot of destructive energy lurking around.

7. You should not live in a home that is close to a garbage dump. Waste products have a lot of death energy in them, which will be absorbed by the house.

8. Do not live in a house next to a meat-

Fig. 11.20 Unfavorable vegetation. (A) A section of earth with topsoil removed (the light, T-shaped area), appearing like a scar on the land. (B) A stubby slope that look like sores on a head.

Fig. 11.21 Power stations disturb the natural flow of energy and may create destructive vortices of malevolent forces.

packing plant, slaughterhouse, or butchery. Activity associated with killing brings violent energy.

These are desirable conditions:

1. The best kind of land use is natural land use. Forests, woods, or grasslands with plenty of wildlife are the best environments. Energy inherent in the land is most likely undisturbed here, and if other landform factors are conducive, houses built in these natural environments normally have the best feng-shui.

2. An agricultural region is the next most beneficial land use in feng-shui because the activities are associated with growth. These include farmland, orchards, and ranches where livestock are not raised for slaughter.

3. If you live in an urban area, choose a house close to a park or garden, for plants and water bring nourishing energy.

4. A house with a playground in its vicinity is good. The presence of children brings life energy to an area. The effect of the playground is enhanced if it doubles as a park and is not simply a concrete enclosure.

5. A house near a spiritual training center is also desirable. Activities that help spiritual development generate nourishing energy and can tame wild energy that roams the area.

6. Places of healing also give nourishing energy to the area. These include services dedicated to improving health in a wholesome way. The typical hospital does not fit this category because in our society, hospitals are too much associated with injury, illness, and death. The "feel" of a hospital is very different from the "feel" of, say, an acupuncture clinic, an herbal clinic, or even a chiropractor's office. In my experience of practicing feng-shui, I would class hospitals as negative, chiropractor offices as neutral, and t'ai-chi centers, yoga centers, meditation centers, and acupuncture and herbal medicine clinics as places with positive energy.

7. Places where there is harmonious interaction among people also produce nourishing energy. Community centers, friendly shopping plazas, neighborhood stores and restaurants, churches, public town squares, and spiritual training centers all generate beneficial energy. Therefore, it is good to live in areas with these establishments around.

8. Nurseries, preschools, and day-care centers are areas where there are children. Since children bring life energy, these institutions are also good to have in your neighborhood.

9. Schools where the activities of the students and teachers are dedicated to learning and self-improvement generate nourishing energy.

Special Considerations

BUSINESSES

Although the feng-shui of a business is closely tied to the feng-shui of the home of the owner, there are some special considerations in choosing a good feng-shui environment for a business.

1. If the feng-shui of the business location is bad, then the owner's residential feng-shui must be extraordinarily good to tip the balance. If the feng-shui of the business location is neutral, then the owner's residential feng-shui will determine the fortunes of the business. If the feng-shui of the business is good but the owner's residential feng-shui is problematic, then the business will follow the fortunes of the owner.

2. Generally, any environment that is harmful for a home will be harmful for a business, and any environmental factors that are

beneficial for home will be beneficial for a business.

3. However, there are some environments that will help the prosperity of a business but are harmful to the employees. These are situations in which certain configurations of the geomantic chart are matched with an environmental condition where untamed and strong energy funnels into the business site. Under these conditions, the business will prosper, but the owner and/or the employees may meet with accidents or illness. In my feng-shui readings, I never counsel anyone to enhance the prosperity of a business at the expense of the welfare of the employees. Therefore, I shall not discuss these conditions in the book. Should you come across them in your other readings, remember that the spirit of feng-shui is to help everyone to live a good life and that no one should suffer harm so that another may benefit.

4. A good location for a retail business is in a shopping plaza or on streets with a good flow pattern (see paragraph 4 of the section "Benevolent Waters." page 133). It should preferably be situated along the rim of a circular traffic way but should not be at the entrance to the plaza.

5. No business should have its door facing a four-way intersection. Destructive energy is carried by the sharp corners of the intersection, and it is increased by the traffic crisscrossing the area.

6. A retail business should preferably be located on a street where there is moderate traffic, and not on a large boulevard where traffic is dense and sometimes fast. Fast traffic is aversive to prosperity. It may bring in profit, but the profits will not hold. On the other hand, a street with low traffic does not give a business enough exposure.

7. If there is a large parking lot between the shops and the busy street, the above effects are cushioned.

8. A retail business is best located where there are terraces, balconies, awnings, and verandas in the buildings around it. Anything that breaks up a smooth surface that reflects on your business is good.

9. Do not locate a retail business in an arcade with roofs held up by long posts. Thinness of support means thinness of profits.

TEMPLES AND MONASTERIES

There are some special considerations for the feng-shui of a temple or a monastery. Temples, monasteries, and shrines are places where the human and the sacred meet. Being a human-made edifice, the temple or monastery should be located in a place worthy of meeting the sacred powers in the area. Moreover, spiritual sanctuaries are places that help people cultivate body and mind to attain enlightenment. Therefore, they should be built in an area that has absorbed the timeless energy of heaven and earth. As discussed in chapter 10, landforms that resemble immortals, magical animals, or natural phenomena are places where there is a concentration of the primordial energy of the Tao, so these are therefore ideal spots for temples and monasteries.

In traditional feng-shui, we recognize two kinds of sacred or spiritual places. The first kind is designed to affect the flow of energy. Placed at the appropriate location, it can tame, conduct, and regulate energy. This kind of structure is typically built in areas where there are powerful concentrations of wild energy that, if directed properly, can be extremely beneficial. The second kind is designed to gather energy so that the spiritual development of persons living in these places can be enhanced.

A lone shrine, a pagoda perched on top of a rounded rock with sheer cliffs dropping down the edges, and a temple on a ledge over-looking a steep slope are structures designed and placed to affect the flow of energy. They work like valves in regulating the powerful flow of energy and are best situated on soli-tary peaks or crags, where there is maximum exposure to the energy swirling around the re-gion, or where the concentration of earth en-ergy is tremendous. Sometimes these places are inappropriate for human habitation be-cause only enlightened individuals or immor-tals have enough foundation to withstand the onslaught of power. Examples are isolated pa-godas or stupas in deserted areas. In mainland China and Taiwan I have seen ten-story pago-das with no stairs!

Monastic complexes with multiple struc-tures built on dragon veins that run along ridges are designed as conduits, to conduct and direct powerful energy flow. They are best located in the "dip" of the spine of the dragon vein, where the dragon is "inhaling." The Taoist monasteries of Hua-shan were built as regulators and conductors of energy. So are Buddhist retreats in the Himalayas. Be-cause these temples or shrines are built to tame wild energy, they are not places suitable for the casual person to live in. Only people with already strong spiritual foundations should live and train in such monasteries or temples.

The second kind of spiritual sanctuary rec-ognized by traditional feng-shui is designed to help spiritual training and is typically built on gentle slopes in rolling hills, preferably over-looking a lake or a river with water dragon formations (see chapter 10). The monastery complex is in an area where energy from the surrounding area is gathered and contained. Thus, these locations are generally sheltered.

The Lo-kuan Tai Taoist monastery of the Complete Reality sect in the Chung-nan Mountains is an example (fig. 11.22A). In the Sun Moon Lake district of Taiwan there are many Buddhist temples built on the slopes of a hill surrounding a lake fed by an underwater spring. Water from the spring bubbles up to produce surface patterns on the lake that re-semble interlocking swirls. Such an environ-ment is ideal for spiritual training and a good place for the casual visitor who stays for a weekend retreat.

The most important thing in selecting a site for a spiritual training center is to remember that places of power should not be toyed with casually. The nature and strength of the power of the land should be matched with the foundation of the inhabitants. If the power in the place is too strong and wild, it will over-whelm the inhabitants and cause harm.

Some temples are not recognized as spiri-tual sanctuaries in traditional feng-shui, be-cause they resemble businesses more than spiritual training centers, and their success is based on income. One such temple in Hong Kong is Huang Ta-hsien, which is named after its patron immortal (fig. 11.23). Huang Ta-hsien was a Taoist monk who attained en-lightenment in southern China and used his powers to heal and foretell the future. The temple named after him is in an urban envi-ronment. Located close to a large under-ground rail station and the terminus of several bus routes, it is easily reachable from any-where in Hong Kong. It is surrounded by low-cost housing apartment buildings, therefore giving it good protection and a steady clien-tele. A circular covered walkway leads to the main temple complex, and the various shrines are linked by courtyards and gardens. The main shrine is located in the center of the complex and overlooks a large courtyard.

Fig. 11.22A (left) The Taoist monastery Lo-kuan Tai in the Chung-nan mountains of central China. Situated on gentle slopes with good protection on all sides, it is an ideal place for spiritual training.

Fig. 11.22B (right) Taoist monastery on Wu-tung Mountain. Notice the protective mountain behind it. This monastery is also located among gentle mountains, making it a place conducive to spiritual training.

The temple grounds are crowded all the time, and the income of the temple—from donations (called incense and oil money), sale of merchandise such as incense and talismans, and commissions from concessions that sell food and services (such as fortunetelling)—is tremendous. Such a temple may not be a conducive environment for spiritual training, but it is successful in its own way. Temples whose chief function is business follow the same principles of feng-shui as any other business establishment.

Interestingly, environments that are appropriate for temples oriented toward spiritual development are not suitable for "commercial" temples, and vice versa. Maybe this reflects the differences between these two paths

Fig. 11.23 Huang Ta-hsien Temple in Hong Kong. Note that the temple grounds are surrounded by high-rise apartment buildings that offer protection but are not in the immediately vicinity.

of life: the secular life of business and commerce versus the spiritual life of inner development.

Another category is the neighborhood temple or church that functions as a community center. These are places where people can share common interests, do something together, and help each other, whether through devotion, study, or community service. Although the neighborhood church or temple provides a link between spiritual and the mundane life, it is not a monastery or retreat.

It maintains close ties with the social and business worlds and serves the needs of those who choose a balance between their social and professional life and their spiritual life.

Where, then, would you want to locate a neighborhood temple? In the same kind of location that would make a successful local restaurant or general store. While a commercial temple like Huang Ta-hsien in Hong Kong should have the feng-shui of a department store, the neighborhood church or temple should have the feng-shui that draws the members of the community together. Therefore, all the factors that are beneficial to residences and retail businesses hold for the neighborhood temple and church.

In North America and Europe, it may be hard to imagine using feng-shui to help select a site for a church. However, this practice is not uncommon in Hong Kong. I have helped several Christian congregations (both Protestant and Roman Catholic) choose locations for their church or retreat. The philosophy and practice of feng-shui should not conflict with whatever religious beliefs you hold, if you have a sense of respect for all things in creation, animate and inanimate. Once you understand that feng-shui is the art of living in harmony with the environment, then you will realize that its philosophy and practice transcend all sectarian beliefs.

Burial Sites

The feng-shui of burial sites is intimately tied to landforms. In ancient times people had more freedom to choose where to bury their dead, so the feng-shui of burial sites developed to a high level of sophistication. However, in our times, we have created cemeteries, and the burial of our dead is regulated by local ordinances regarding land use.

Although the focus of this book is on the feng-shui of the yang domain, I shall also provide a brief discussion of the feng-shui of the yin domain in case you have a chance to use it. Even if a burial site is located in a cemetery, there is still some freedom in choosing the location of the lot, and some cemetery grounds are large enough so that the choice of the lot may place the site in a different geographical surrounding.

Consider the following things when you evaluate the landform surrounding a burial site.

1. The burial site should have the same protection as a residential site. See the discussion titled "Protection" (beginning on page 104).

2. The burial ground should not overlook or be near destructive mountain formations or river formations. It should overlook benevolent environments. Refer to the sections "Harmful Mountain Environments" and "Beneficial Mountain Environments" (page 127), "Destructive Waters" (page 132), and "Benevolent Waters" (page 133). The most ideal condition is to have mountains to the back and water to the front.

3. There should be no harmful objects pointing at the burial site. Refer to the section "Influence of Objects in the Immediate Vicinity" (page 109).

4. Examine the road patterns around the cemetery. There should be no destructive road patterns in the immediate surrounding. Do not use a cemetery that is next to a highway. The fast transient energy carried by the traffic disturbs the peace of those buried in the cemetery.

5. Ideally, the burial site should not be very windy. This may be a problem in cemeteries in North America since most of them are lo-

cated in open land. The next preference is a cemetery that is windy only seasonally.

6. In the feng-shui of burial sites, "guardian rocks" are very important. These are rocks that resemble shapes of animals or special objects. They are sometimes called "spirit rocks" because it is said that these rocks have the spirit of an animal or plant in them. The feng-shui of a burial site is enhanced tremendously if there are such objects in the immediate vicinity. They are markers of places where the primordial energy of the universe once gathered. A grave in the area will absorb this energy and bring fortune to the descendants of one who is buried there. However, some rock spirits are malevolent, and a grave or human dwelling should not be situated near these types of rocks.

7. Among the Chinese, it is quite common to purchase a cemetery plot well before it is needed, if one finds an ideal location. My granduncle and his friends chose their own burial sites while they could. In this way, there is time and leisure to pick the best spot, instead of choosing one under pressure after someone has died.

8. In general, when you look at a burial site, you should follow the same feel as you would for a house. Walk around the site. Sit down on the ground. Get a feel for the surrounding area. If you get a good feel for the place, then the one buried there will rest peacefully.

Cremation is a common practice today. Some cemeteries have a memorial hall where the ashes are kept. Although the ashes are concealed in cubicles, it is advisable that the building be situated in a sheltered spot on the cemetery grounds. Some people choose to keep the ashes of their family members at home. In this case, the ashes should be put in the most sheltered part of the house. In Chi-

Fig. 11.24A A cemetery in the United States. The area of the cemetery shown in the photograph has two layers of protection from the Black Tortoise, is sheltered by trees, and overlooks a reservoir.

Fig. 11.24B The same cemetery showing a sharp pointed structure on the grounds. The burial site should not be directly behind this structure because the sharp point carries destructive energy and will have aversive effects on the descendants of the person buried there.

nese tradition, typically it is not advised to have ashes scattered, but if this is the wish of the deceased person, then the best place to scatter the ashes is a valley or lake.

There are more complex factors in the feng-shui of burial sites that are beyond the scope of this book. Anyhow, most of these factors involve walking the dragon veins to determine where the energy of the land is gathered. This may be possible in another time or culture, but may be unfeasible in ours. However, if your local ordinances allow it and if you have the time and inclination, why not walk the dragon veins and look for a good burial site for yourself?

Fig. 11.25 Spirit rocks. Some rocks have absorbed the energy of the sky and earth, and have taken on shapes resembling animals, humans, or special objects. Spirit rocks can be guardians if they have a benevolent appearance. They can be destructive spirits if they have a mean appearance. Areas with spirit rocks are sites of power and can benefit persons who live there or are buried there if the spirits are benevolent. Rock spirits can harm both the living and the dead if they are malevolent.

Fig. 11.25A Benevolent spirit rock in the form a frog.

Fig. 11.25B Extremely rare and benevolent rock spirit in the form of an "immortal peach." It is said that a rock attains this form by absorbing the energy of the Tao.

Fig. 11.25C Benevolent spirit rock in the form a bird.

Fig. 11.25D Benevolent and very powerful spirit rock in the form of a wolf.

Fig. 11.25E Extremely rare formation of spirit rock called "Buddha's fingers."

Fig. 11.25F Two benevolent spirits rocks: Immortal's face (*right*) and guardian animal (*left*).

Fig. 11.25G Malevolent spirit rock in the form of an angry head.

Fig. 11.25H Malevolent spirit rock in the form of a sinister head.

CONCLUSIONS

Having a beneficial environment is the first step in choosing a good place to live. The points discussed in this chapter are guidelines for living in harmony with the ways of the earth, and the examples are hardly exhaustive. Your first goal is to use these guidelines to evaluate the environment around you; then develop your intuition to get a natural feel for the land. Much of the practice of feng-shui depends on intuition and common sense. For example, it does not feel good to wake up and see a large branch pointing at you. Likewise, it is spooky to have a cliff towering over you, or have cars driving straight toward your house at a T-junction. Most important of all, if you do not feel good about a place, don't stay there. As you cultivate intuition and dissolve the barrier between yourself and the universe, you will begin to sense the energies around you. Follow your intuition and trust your commonsense rationality. You will find that most of the time you are right.

12

Evaluating the Internal Environment

After looking at the feng-shui of the external environment, the next step is to examine the feng-shui of the internal environment. The internal environment is the building itself and the frontage. It includes the shape of the house, the floor plan, the interior structures, the front and back yards, the driveway, and the building materials. In commercial or apartment buildings, the internal environment includes the layout of the hallways, the floor plan of the entire building, and the position of your unit in relationship to the building.

I shall start with a discussion of the internal environment of houses. Again, for convenience, I shall use the words *house* and *building* interchangeably when discussing the internal environment. Typically, what is good for a house is also good for an apartment or a business, and what is bad for a house is also bad for an apartment or business. However, there are some special considerations for apartments and commercial buildings. These will be covered in a separate section.

STEPS IN EVALUATING THE INTERNAL ENVIRONMENT OF A HOUSE

1. Shape of the House

The shape of the house is the most important consideration in the internal environment. If the shape is not right, you don't need to look at other factors.

Your choice of shape for a house should be guided by three principles. They are stability, balance, and smoothness.

A stable shape gives stability to health and livelihood. Generally, the shape of a house is balanced if parts of the building are "stacked" up in a solid way and none of the levels is significantly larger than the others. Also, a building is stable if the upper levels are resting on a firm, solid foundation.

A balanced shape is associated with harmony within the household and cooperation among the occupants of the house. Generally, a house is balanced if it does not have an irregular shape.

Smoothness is the absence of harsh, protruding structures and is the best protection against unexpected problems and accidents. A house is smooth if there are no sections or blocks jutting from it vertically or horizontally. A house with a uniform surface gives better protection of the internal environment from destructive energy.

Here are some key points in evaluating the shape of a building and its feng-shui. Since shape is three-dimensional, you need to consider the shape of the area outlined by the floor plan as well as the general appearance of the house.

GENERAL SHAPE OF HOUSE

1. A house with an irregular shape is considered unbalanced, unstable, and harsh (figs. 12.1, 12.2). These are examples of elements that cause a house to be classed as irregular:

- Some parts of the house form a triangular shape.
- The building is shaped like a pyramid (fig. 12.1)
- Parts of the house are cut off from the rest (fig. 12.2).
- The house is L-shaped.
- The house is shaped like an H.
- The house has rooms that form irregular shapes jutting out of the main part of the building.
- Parts of the house are physically sepa-

rated from the rest, even though they may be connected by a covered walkway.

Triangular shapes are especially undesirable (fig. 12.3A). Destructive energy is carried in the sharpness of the triangle. Moreover, malevolent energy gets collected in the apexes of the triangle where they cannot escape. Triangular shapes also squeeze and constrict the occupants of the house.

Houses with sections that jut out, creating an irregular or knobby shape, are also untenable. Examples of these are buttress-type structures on the surface of a building, and houses with bedrooms or sunrooms that protrude from the side of the building. In feng-shui, these kinds of houses are also considered imbalanced and harsh, especially if the structures on the upper level are large (figs. 12.3A, B, C). Alcoves, window seats, bay windows, and enclosed flower boxes are excluded because the volume of space occupied by these structures is insufficient to unbalance the general shape of the house.

2. Round or rectangular shapes are preferred for buildings because they are balanced and stable. Roundness smooths out harsh energy, and the rectangular and symmetrical shapes do not allow destructive energy to build up in restricted corner sections. However, make sure that the round structures are not punctured by spikes (fig. 12.3D).

3. Long, thin structures that extend upward from the building makes the building look irregular and harsh. Moreover, the towers act like beacons to attract destructive energy. Also, because they are higher than the rest of the house, they are targets for destructive energy that flows that way.

4. Chimneys should not protrude like thin towers for the same reasons described above.

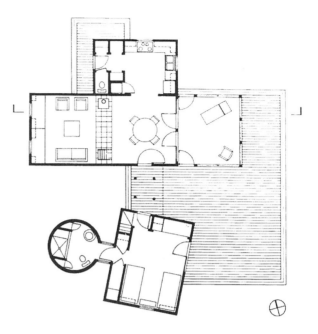

Fig. 12.2 A house with an irregular floor plan.

Fig. 12.1 A house with an irregular shape.

Moreover, this design creates the feeling that parts of the house are "fighting" the sky, a most disharmonious relationship with nature.

5. Do not live in a house with walls that lean (fig. 12.4). It creates a visual impression of instability or a feeling that the house is about to collapse. Occupants in this house will also be in danger of bankruptcy or loss of job.

ROOFS

1. A house with a domelike roof or skylight is desirable since roundness gathers en-

ergy and is the best protector against destructive energy. All parts of a sphere have the same resistance and there are no weak points. (An exception is shown in fig. 12.3D.)

2. Do not live in a house with many small rooms protruding from the top. Dormer windows are an example. This design makes the roof very irregular. It also makes the house appear dominating and harsh. A flat roof or one with a small angle of slope is the best choice.

3. If the house is an A-frame, the roof should not be too steep. A steep roof creates a harsh triangular structure, which is associated with destructive energy. Moreover, the smaller the angle at the apex, the more pointed will be the appearance. Again, this creates the impression that the house is fighting the sky.

Fig. 12.3 Undesirable structures for both residential and commercial use.

Fig. 12.3A A house that is top-heavy and balanced precariously.

Fig. 12.3B A building with a very pointed top. It is also sitting on "small" legs.

4. Do not live in a house with cascaded roofs. These buildings create the feel of falling and sliding. Occupants in the house will lose money in investments, as wealth within the family will "fall" off the house.

5. Do not live in a house where the roof slopes all the way to the ground. This kind of design makes the roof look very heavy and gives the impression that the house is capped by a lid that prevents benevolent energy from entering the building.

FOUNDATION

1. A house should be "balanced" between its different levels. One in which the higher levels are larger than the lower levels is unstable and imbalanced. Although it may be sound from the mechanical point of view,

Fig. 12.3C Cars seeming to drive into an apartment complex make for bad feng-shui. Also notice that the building appears to be sitting on stilts, making it top-heavy and unstable.

Fig. 12.3D A building with a deceptive "round" top. The geodesic top is highlighted with points. Such "spiky" roofs do not have good feng-shui.

these structures are unstable as far as feng-shui is concerned. This is because it gives the feel that the lower level is straining to support the upper level or that the house is topheavy. (See fig. 12.3B.)

Some houses have very small upper levels compared with the lower levels. Although these houses are "stable" because they are not topheavy, they are unbalanced because the areas of the levels are not equal.

Ideally, if a house has several levels, the size (area) of the levels should be about the same. This makes the house balanced. If there is any discrepancy in area between levels, the upper levels should be smaller, but not too much. If the upper floors are too small, then although the house is not topheavy, it is not balanced.

2. Houses sitting on top of posts or a large

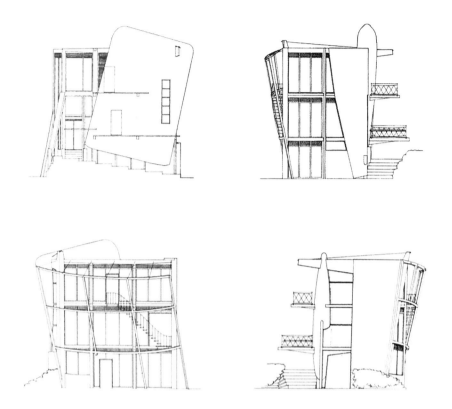

Fig. 12.4 A house with leaning walls. This creates the impression that the house is about to fall down.

pillar, or houses with large sections supported by thin posts, are unstable. An example is a house that has a section of the upper floor "resting" on posts with a courtyard underneath.

3. A house built on a slope is unstable if parts of the house are resting on posts. It is stable if the lower levels are built in so that they are in contact with the ground. The difference between these two structures is that the latter has a type of walk-in basement.

GENERAL APPEARANCE AND STYLE

1. Do not live in a house that looks like a military installation. Its occupants will meet with problems associated with armed violence, or members of the family will be injured or meet with death in a war. I knew some people who lived in a house that resembled a castle. One of their sons, who was a journalist, was killed in Vietnam.

2. Do not live in a house with structures that resemble equipment or machinery associ-

Fig. 12.6 An unstable house. Notice that the house is standing on stilts and does not have a solid feel.

Fig. 12.5 A stable house built on a slope. Notice that the basement is built into the slope. The brick facade also gives a stable feel. Compare this house with the one shown in fig. 12.6.

ated with death. I have seen houses that look like missiles. In figure 12.8 the framelike structure in front of the house looks like a gallows.

3. Do not live in a house that resembles a crag (fig. 12.9). Craggy landforms are yin and carry destructive energy. Similarly, a building with an irregular shape that resembles a crag embodies some of those qualities.

4. Do not live in a house that appears like cards stacked on their edges (fig. 12.10). This

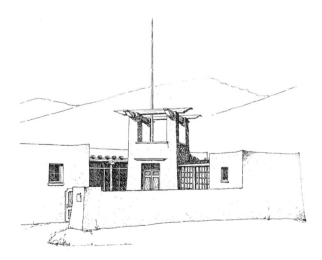

Fig. 12.7 A house that looks like a fort or garrison has bad feng-shui.

Fig. 12.8 A house with a structure that appears like gallows. Underneath the "gallows" is the garage. The location of the garage also creates bad feng-shui because the cars seem to be colliding with the house.

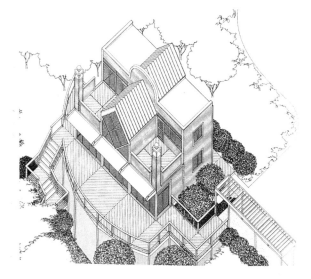

Fig. 12.9 A house with a craggy appearance does not make good feng-shui.

Fig. 12.10 This house creates the impression that it is a stack of cards held together precariously by wires. Moreover, it is sitting on thin legs.

is a very unstable structure and forebodes the imminent collapse of the fortunes of the occupants.

5. Do not live in a house that looks like it is being crushed by a large object (fig. 12.11).

Fig. 12.11 A house with a "plunger" on top, ready to crush the building.

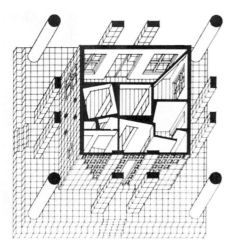

Fig. 12.12 A building surrounded by pillars, giving the impression that the structure is confined by iron bars. Also notice the irregularity in the partition of the rooms.

Fig. 12.13 Another example of a house "jailed" by pillars.

Occupants will be dominated by others, and business ventures will never get started.

6. Do not live in a house that is surrounded by pillars (figs. 12.12, 12.13). Pillars are like rods that are prepared to strike the building. However, the presence of pillars is

good for government buildings because they convey the image of strength and power.

2. Floor Plan

The floor plan is the arrangement of rooms, hallways, doors, windows, and stairs. It is the next most important consideration in evaluating the internal environment. To some extent, the general shape of the house affects the floor plan. However, a house with a balanced and stable shape can have a floor plan that is not conducive to harmonious living. For example, a square or rectangular area can be divided into two triangles, depending on the floor plan.

When evaluating the floor plan, remember two things. First, you need to have an idea of the frequency of usage of particular parts of the house. Rooms that are used a lot are important and should be placed in such a way to maximize benefits. Areas that are used less often are less important and, if necessary can occupy less desirable positions. Second, you need to figure out the type of usage for each room. For example, a room that is not suitable for a bedroom may be all right for a study. Of course, frequency of usage and type of usage may interact to some extent. For example, the kitchen and family room tend toward high usage because of their functions.

The following are some guidelines for evaluating the floor plan of a house.

THE ENTRANCE

The entranceway is very important in determining the feng-shui of a building. Energy, positive or negative, enters the house through the front entrance. The entrance also affects the general fortunes of the occupants. A "good" entrance enhances the well-being of the occupants, while a "bad entrance" brings obstacles and problems. There is an old feng-shui saying: "Outside the entrance, the occupants are not part of the house; inside the entrance, they become a part of the house and the house becomes a part of them."

The following are guidelines for evaluating the entrance to a house.

1. The entrance should not open into a narrow corridor. Circulation of nourishing energy to the rest of the house is constricted, and negative energy gets trapped in the entranceway.

2. The entrance should not funnel from the outside into the front door of the house (fig. 12.14). A funneling type of entrance gathers negative energy and focuses it at the house.

3. The path leading up to the front entrance should not funnel into it. Not only does this form a "pointing" structure toward the house, but funnels collect destructive energy, directing it into the building. Therefore, do not line the pathway leading to the front door with trees.

4. Do not live in a house where the entrance room is walled on all sides with only one doorway into the rest of the house. In this condition, positive energy will be constricted and negative energy will get trapped.

5. The entrance should open into a foyer or entrance room that buffers the rest of the house from the outside. This allows nourishing energy to gather and be distributed evenly to the rest of the building. Moreover, if any malevolent energy makes its way in, the foyer is there to absorb or thin out the destructive energy, thus lessening the impact on the rest of the house.

6. The entrance room or foyer should open to several rooms. This allows benevolent incoming energy to circulate easily to the other parts of the house.

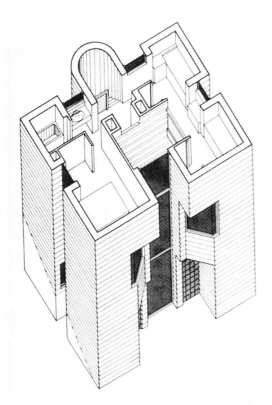

Fig. 12.14 A building with a "funneling" entrance. These types of entrances do not make good feng-shui.

CORRIDORS

Corridors connect different parts of the building to each other and therefore are conduits of energy in feng-shui. Whether a house has a good circulation of nourishing energy or traps destructive energy will depend on the arrangement of corridors.

1. There should not be too many corridors in a house. Long, winding corridors are especially problematic. Winding corridors can transform positive energy into a twisting and unmanageable form of energy that is destructive.

2. Do not live in a house where the doors of rooms open into a long corridor (fig. 12.15). Long, narrow corridors "squeeze" energy, turning positive energy into malevolent forces. Doors opening into the long corridors also let malevolent forces get into the rooms without any buffer.

3. Corridors should not be too narrow, even if they are not long, for the reasons listed above.

4. Corridors tend to give a dark gloomy feel. Any area that is not lighted well gathers yin or death energy. Give these areas as much light as possible. Doorways opening onto corridors should reveal windows looking outside. This allows yang energy from the sun to filter into the corridor.

STAIRWAYS

Stairways connect various levels of a building to each other. Therefore, they are conduits of energy between the upper and lower levels. Effective staircases can distribute nourishing energy and ensure that it gets to every part of the building. Harmful staircases will restrict energy flow and even transform positive energy into destructive energy.

Here are some guidelines for looking at the feng-shui of stairways.

1. Spiral staircases are undesirable because they enhance malevolent energy. Ascending vapor or energy should rise evenly as a cylindrical column. Energy that is forced to twist or funnel up as it rises becomes destructive. A curved stairway is not a spiral staircase. To qualify as a spiral, the stairs must curl around themselves at least once.

2. Narrow stairs that lead straight to the upper levels with only a small landing at each floor are undesirable. The gradient of the ascending and descending energy is too steep,

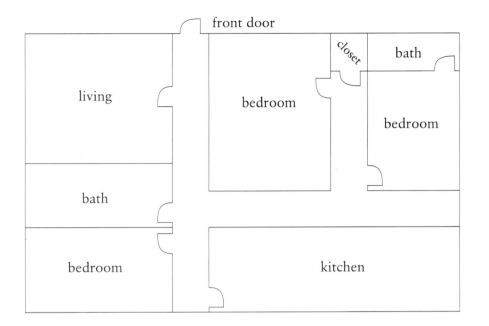

Fig. 12.15 A house with corridors that are bad feng-shui. Notice the corridors are long and narrow. Moreover, there is a large section of corridor that has no openings into rooms.

and the rush of energy can be overwhelming. Moreover, energy flowing through a long, narrow stairway is like wind through a wind tunnel. It is wild and unpredictable, and its onset is too sudden to allow sufficient preparation to avoid its destructive influences.

3. Stairs should be wide and shallow. This facilitates the gentle rise and fall of energy. Do not have stairs with steep steps.

4. Typically, the stairs should not face the front door except in special circumstances. (See chap. 15 for a discussion of how the stars of the Nine Palaces affect different areas of the house. If auspicious stars occupy the front door and the stairs, then it is all right for the stairs to face the front door.)

5. A ladder is not a stairway, because it does not occupy a sufficient volume of space to be considered as a stairwell. Therefore, it is

all right to have ladder-type steps leading up to attics and lofts.

GARAGE

The relationship of the garage to the rest of the house affects the health and safety of the occupants. Being associated with travel and transport, the garage is especially pertinent to the safety of the occupants while they are in transit.

1. The garage should ideally be separate from the house. The movement of cars disturbs energy flow that is native to the area and creates complications in the flow of energy in the house. If the garage is separate from the house, then the disturbance is both isolated and buffered. Moreover, vehicle movement carries destructive energy. If the garage is iso-

lated from the rest of the house, this destructive energy will not spread into the living areas.

2. The next order of preference is a garage that is attached to the side of the house but does not have any residential part of the house behind it. In this way, the vehicles do not enter the garage as if they are driving into the residential part of the home.

3. If the above arrangements are not possible, then the next preference is to have a seldom-used room buffering the garage from areas of the house that are frequently used. For example, a laundry room or a storeroom is a good buffer.

4. The worst case is when the back of the garage is flush against a bedroom so that the incoming vehicles drive toward the room. Next worse is when the back of the garage is against a room that is frequently used by the whole family, like the kitchen or family room. Such situations create a feeling that the cars are about to run down the occupants of the house. The family living in such a house will often be ill or will be involved in road accidents.

5. A residential part of the house should not be situated above the garage. Again, it creates the feel that the vehicles are driving toward the occupants. Moreover, the vehicles entering the garage bring destructive and foreign energy right into the living quarters.

POSITION OF KITCHEN

In feng-shui, the kitchen is associated with the health and livelihood of the family. It is said that illness enters through the mouth and prosperity is associated with having enough to eat. Having the kitchen located in an untenable position in the house can lead to illness and loss of livelihood. Moreover, the kitchen is where cooking and eating take place, and

areas of the house that get used a lot should be in an area that is best for them. In North American households, where many families use the kitchen for activities other than meals, having the kitchen in the proper place is especially important.

When I moved to the United States, I was astonished by how central the kitchen is to the North American household. People plan the household finances, read the Sunday papers, do homework, and chat with family and friends in the kitchen. This makes the kitchen more important than any other room in the house. In Hong Kong, where I grew up, the situation is different. The kitchen is not a gathering place. It is the place where food is prepared, not where you have meals. Food is served in the dining room, and if a cook prepares your meals (and many households in Hong Kong have houseworkers who double as cooks), chances are that you will rarely be in the kitchen yourself. However, even in these circumstances, the kitchen still symbolizes health and livelihood, and many people in Hong Kong take care in choosing an apartment where the kitchen is in the "correct" relationship to the rest of the house. In the North American household, because of the important place of the kitchen in family life, the location of the kitchen relative to the rest of the house is of the utmost importance.

1. The kitchen should be shielded from the front entrance. When you enter, you should not get an unobstructed view of the entire kitchen. In this way, any malevolent force that enters through the front entrance does not make its way to the part of the house most important to the occupants.

2. Ideally, the kitchen should be located centrally in the house. It should be sheltered by the rest of the house and preferably not

be exposed on more than two sides. In many North American homes there is an informal eating area attached to the kitchen that resembles a large alcove, with windows on all sides. This arrangement is fine as long as the cooking section of the kitchen is not exposed on more than two sides.

3. The entrance to the kitchen should not be a narrow doorway, as this creates a funnel for negative energy to collect and enter. Preferably, it should have more than one doorway to ensure good circulation of energy.

4. The shape of the cooking area of the kitchen should be symmetrical and regular. An irregular shape creates pockets where negative energy can be trapped.

5. The kitchen should preferably be aligned with the central axis of the house and not diagonal to it, so that nourishing energy entering the house makes its way to the kitchen in the least convoluted way.

BEDROOM

Considering that most people sleep at least six hours a day, the bedroom is used quite a lot. Sleeping is a passive activity, however, so its requirements differ from those of a room where there is a lot of movement, like the kitchen or family room. In many ways, the bedroom should be the most protected part of the house because we are most vulnerable while we are asleep. We do not have control over our thoughts and actions, and are oblivious to things that happen around us.

1. The bedroom should not have more than one doorway. Sleeping is a way of gathering energy for the body. If the bedroom has more than one entrance, then benevolent energy can flow out of the room, and the sleeping body will not have a chance to absorb it.

2. The bedroom door should not face a stairway. Destructive energy rushing up the stairs will enter the bedroom right away.

3. There should be no exposed beams in the bedroom. You do not want to get the feeling that a log or steel girder is about to land on you while you are sleeping.

4. The bedroom should not have a ceiling shaped like an inverted V. This kind of ceiling traps negative energy, and its danger is enhanced because you are most vulnerable while sleeping.

5. The bedroom should be a regular, symmetrical room. This kind of shape invites smooth, beneficial energy.

GENERAL ARRANGEMENT OF FLOOR PLAN

Below are some guidelines for choosing a beneficial arrangement for the general layout of rooms in a building.

1. The front and back doors should not be lined up (fig. 12.16). You should not be able to see the back door from the front entrance. Otherwise, beneficial energy entering through one entrance will go straight out the other.

2. One portion of the house should not be higher than another. If the front half is higher than the back, the younger members of the family will have difficulty achieving independence. If the rear portion of the house is higher than the front, the family wealth will flow outside. In other words, split-level houses are not very desirable.

3. The levels within the building should be defined well. Some houses have uneven levels, lofts, or interior balconies. If the levels of a building appear to be confused, energy flow will be confused.

4. The arrangement of rooms should not be too irregular (fig. 12.12). Irregularity transforms smooth, circulating energy into harsh, destructive energy.

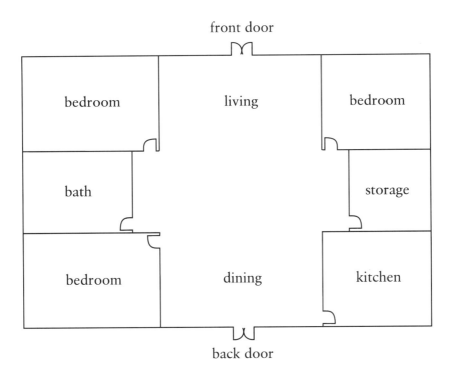

Fig. 12.16 In this floor plan, the front and back entrances are lined up with each other. This creates unfavorable feng-shui, for fortunes coming in from the front will exit immediately at the back.

5. A well-lighted house receives yang (life) energy, and a dark house traps yin (death) energy. Therefore, rooms should receive adequate natural lighting, and no part of the house should need artificial lighting if it is sunny outside. It follows that you do not want a house with windows like slits.

6. However, the windows should not be huge. Some houses have a "picture" window overlooking a scenic landscape. A house with large windows or glass walls has very poor protection against destructive energy. Moreover, an exposed room leaks nourishing energy.

7. The passage between rooms should not feel constricted. Therefore, long winding corridors are undesirable. Energy circulation is like ventilation. If ventilation is not good, then positive energy cannot circulate well and negative energy will collect.

8. A flat or dome-shaped ceiling is desirable. Ceilings that are shaped like an inverted V and ceilings that continue to slope all the way to the ground are not desirable. They constrict the flow of nourishing energy and gather destructive energy. (See fig. 12.1, page 153, for examples of very uneven ceilings.)

9. Ceilings with uneven height are also undesirable. The irregularity of the ceiling will affect the circulation of energy in the house. Most houses with uneven levels tend to have ceilings with irregular height.

10. Ceilings should not be too high. Nourishing energy rises and will be trapped on top.

Moreover, nourishing energy will be thinned out in a room with a high ceiling.

11. Arches, rounded vaultlike ceilings, and flat ceilings are preferred. Energy circulation will be even if the ceiling is flat. Energy circulation will be enhanced in certain areas if the ceiling is vaulted.

12. In general, rooms that are frequently used by all the occupants should receive good natural lighting, should not have an irregular shape, and should not have doorways aligned directly with any door that exits the house. These include the kitchen and the family room.

13. The bedrooms should not have doors facing the stairway or any door that exits the house.

14. The study or office should not have a door that is lined up directly with a door that exits the house. The office and study are associated with work and enterprise. If the door is aligned to a door that exits the house, prosperity and success will be easily lost.

3. The Frontage and the Driveway

The frontage and driveway are part of a property, and because they surround the house, they act as buffers between the outside and inside. Depending on its arrangement, a frontage can enhance or ruin the feng-shui of a house. Here are some guidelines for considering the frontage of a property.

1. The backyard should be larger than the front lawn.

2. Do not have your driveway run straight toward the living quarters of your house. Circular driveways are always preferable.

3. The driveway of the house across the street should not point at your front door.

4. Do not have a long, narrow path leading up to the front door.

5. Do not have fences with sharp points.

6. Do not have trees in the front yard blocking your front door.

7. Round structures like fountains, ponds, and gazebos are desirable to have in the front or back yard. However, these structures should not dwarf the house or dominate the space in the yard.

8. It is desirable to have a buffer between the house and the street. Buffers protect the house from wild and destructive energy and enhance the effects of nourishing energy. Gardens, trellised walks, a terrace, or even a front porch are all very viable buffers.

4. Other Features: Bridges, Landings, Verandas, and Decks

1. Do not have a bridge or covered walkway connecting two houses or two sections of a house. In Chinese tradition, bridges and paths are associated with parting. Couples will get divorced or separated. Children will leave home early and have strained relations with the parents. (See fig. 12.2 for an example of a house with two sections connected by a walkway.)

2. Verandas on the upper levels should be supported by strong, thick pillars.

3. Decks should be supported by strong legs. Circular-shaped decks are best.

4. Structures on decks, such as hot tubs or gazebos, should preferably be round.

5. Interior Structures

1. Do not have exposed beams in the house. They are destructive because it feels like you are being crushed under a log or a concrete girder.

2. It is all right to have fireplaces and

woodstoves, but they should not dwarf the room. These structures enhance the presence of the fire element in the house. If the fireplace is too big, then the house will be dominated by the fire element and will have a fire hazard. (See also chapter 15 for the placement of fireplaces.)

3. Wooden doors should not have excessive knotty patterns that are harsh-looking. The same goes for wooden paneling. Harsh-looking knotty patterns will disrupt the circulation of energy.

4. Do not use vertical blinds, because when opened, they look like knives cutting into your room.

5. A "hanging" light that suspends low from the ceiling is extremely harmful. It suggests that the occupants are being hanged at the end of a rope.

6. Crystal lights and lamps that cast spotty and discontinuous shadows on the walls are also harmful. The purpose of lamps is to illuminate a room, and lights that cast shadows give the impression that yin (shade and decay) is dominating yang (light and growth).

6. Building Materials

1. Do not use bright red bricks. They belong to the element of fire and will attract problems associated with fire.

2. Do not use materials that reflect. They send nourishing energy away. Aluminum siding is all right if it does not create reflections.

3. Rock facades are acceptable if the rocks do not protrude sharply (fig. 12.17). Sometimes an uneven surface may appear even if the rocks are arranged properly.

4. Do not use large glass windows to form a wall. They dissipate nourishing energy and are poor protection against destructive energy.

Fig. 12.17 A rock facade that does not consist of protruding rocks. This kind of wall does not harm the occupants or the neighbors.

5. It is best to have a dirt or gravel driveway, which gives the same advantages as dirt roads. The unpaved driveway can enhance nourishing energy from the earth and cushion negative energy more effectively.

APARTMENTS

1. Do not live in an apartment building where there are long hallways.

2. Do not live in a unit that is at the end of the hallway with the corridor running straight to it.

3. Do not live in a unit with a door facing the stairs.

4. Do not live in an apartment building where the landings on each floor are narrow.

5. Do not live in a building where the stairs to the upper floors are not buffered by a landing.

6. Do not live in a unit that is next to the elevator or the stairway.

BUSINESSES AND COMMERCIAL BUILDINGS

See figure 12.18 for examples of commercial buildings.

1. An office building with a fountain inside or outside its entrance is good.

2. An office building with a large foyer is good. The foyer serves as a gatherer of positive energy and a buffer against negative energy.

3. Do not have an office in a building whose elevators face the front entrance. The onslaught of energy will enter the elevator and be carried swiftly through the building.

4. Do not have the suite right next to the elevator or stairway. Prosperity flows out easily.

5. Your unit should not face the elevator doors. Any onrush of negative energy will enter your suite first.

6. Your business should not be in a unit that is at the end of the hallway.

7. Do not have an office in a building with windows that reflect. Wealth and prosperity cannot enter a reflective building.

8. Do not have an office in a pyramid-shaped commercial building. Its triangular shape traps malevolent energy and constricts the flow of benevolent energy. This is especially so in the upper floors, where the area decreases and the walls close in.

9. Do not have an office in a building that is situated on top of a parking garage. Too much movement of vehicles below will destabilize the business.

10. Do not have an office in a building where the upper levels are larger than the lower levels. It forebodes the collapse of the business or the domination of the upper executives over the middle- and lower-level employees.

11. Awnings are good, especially for retail businesses, because they provide just enough shelter against negative energy and collect positive energy.

12. A retail business is best situated in a building with balconies and verandas, which break up smooth surfaces that may reflect.

13. A retail business should not have glass windows that go all the way down to the floor. When the business is too exposed, profits leak out. Large glass windows should be covered by blinds so that the exposure can be regulated.

Fig. 12.18A Business with a "funneling" entrance.

Fig. 12.18B Building that is top-heavy and is buffeted by the onslaught of destructive energy from cars. Notice that the front of the building is sitting on two pillars. The location of the parking area forces vehicles to drive right into the building.

Fig. 12.18C Building with triangular roofs.

Fig. 12.18D Building with a "cascading" roof. Fortunes will roll off this building.

Fig. 12.18E Building with a "reverse cascading," another instance of a topheavy and unstable structure.

Fig. 12.18F Building complex with uneven and slanting roofs. Fortunes will roll off this type of roof.

CONCLUSIONS

The interior of a building affects the health and prosperity of the occupants, whether it is a residential or a commercial building. The more time you spend in it, the more important is the internal environment.

The materials covered in chapters 11 and 12 are from the Landscape School of Feng-shui. They are concerned with the feel of the environment, and involve more intuition than calculation. How would you go about cultivating an intuitive feel for the environment? First, you should stop your internal thought processes and try to look at things without any preconceptions. How does a building feel? Forget about what's popular in aesthetics, the current design fads and prevailing architectural theories, or what other people say. Cultivate your own feel for the natural and human environments. It is amazing how many feng-shui practitioners come to the same conclusions without comparing notes. If you dissolve the barrier between yourself and the universe, you will have direct contact with the energies swirling in it. You will experience the smoothness, the harshness, the disturbance, the playfulness, the youthful vigor, the mature stability, the wicked, the volatile, and the many nuances of energy that are present at all places and in all times.

Knowing the environment is only half of the practice of feng-shui. The second half involves calculation and logical deduction of principles. This is the more analytic aspect of feng-shui, from the Compass School or Computation School, and this is what we will turn to in the next six chapters.

13

Taking Readings
with the Geomantic Compass

After you have evaluated the external and internal environments and found them to be satisfactory, your next step is to take the geomantic compass reading for the building. This will give you the orientation, or facing direction.

The geomantic compass is probably the most important piece of equipment you will need in practicing feng-shui. It gives you the information necessary to generate the geomantic chart, which describes the flow of energy in a particular place. Although there are many rings in the geomantic compass, the information they provide is used primarily for the feng-shui of burial sites. In yang-domain feng-shui, you will only need the Twenty-four Directions Circle. It is this ring that is used to determine the orientation of a building, the information that is used to generate the geomantic chart.

Again, for the sake of convenience I shall use the words *building* and *house* inter-

changeably when we discuss how to take readings with the geomantic compass. In the latter part of the chapter, we shall look at conditions where you may need multiple readings. For example, in apartments or business suites, where the front door of your unit may face a different direction than the main entrance of the building, you will need multiple compass readings.

Every geomantic compass reading consists of a pair of directions, called the Facing Direction (the front orientation), and the Mountain Direction (the back orientation). Typically, what is designated as the front facing is based on the characteristics of landform. (See fig. 13.1.) The side of the house overlooking lower ground is normally designated as the front, regardless of the position of the entrances. If there are no visible landforms determining the facing orientation, then the front of the house is identified by the orientation of the front door. In most houses, the

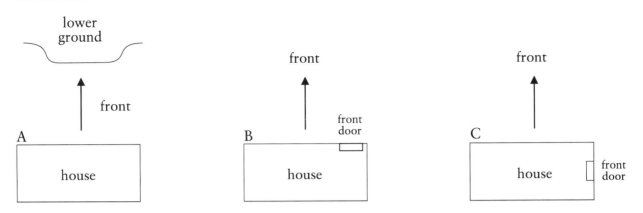

Fig. 13.1 How to determine the front of a house. Typically, the front of a house faces the lower ground in the area. If there are no elevation differences in the region, then the "long" side of a house designates its front.

front door faces the same direction as the general orientation of the building. However, for houses with front doors that face a different direction than the orientation of the building, two readings are required: one for the front door, and one for the general orientation of the building.

USING A CHINESE GEOMANTIC COMPASS

If you read Chinese and can get hold of a geomantic compass, then follow the instructions described in this section. If you do not read Chinese but would like some challenge, you can match the Chinese characters of the Twenty-four Directions from the compass with the English romanization given in fig. 13.2, and follow the procedures described in this section. If you cannot obtain a geomantic compass, or don't want to bother with recognizing the Chinese characters, go to the next section, where you will be shown how to determine the Twenty-four Directions with a regular compass.

Before you begin to take a reading, you need to learn to handle your equipment.

First, identify the features on the geomantic compass that you will be working with when

Jen	壬		Ping	丙
Tzu	子		Wu	午
Kuei	癸		Ting	丁
Ch'ou	丑		Wei	未
Ken	艮		K'un	坤
Yin	寅		Shen	申
Chia	甲		Keng	庚
Mao	卯		Yu	酉
I	乙		Hsin	辛
Ch'en	辰		Hsü	戌
Shun	巽		Ch'ien	乾
Ssu	巳		Hai	亥

Fig. 13.2 The Twenty-four Directions in Chinese characters and romanized.

you are taking a reading. They are: the needle, which is the magnetic sensor; the red line with two red dots on one end; the cross-hairs on top of the compass, made of nylon or string; and the Twenty-four Directions ring, which is located toward the center of the compass.

Second, you need to get used to handling the equipment. Rotate the black disk of the compass. You will find that by moving the disk, you can get the needle to line up on top of the red line. You will also notice that the black disk can be rotated beneath the cross-hairs.

If you look at the needle closely, you will find that at one end of it is a small ring. This end of the needle points north. See if you can move the disk until the needle is perfectly on top of the red line and so that the ring on the needle is on the same side as the two dots. This is very crucial in manipulating the compass. The more accurate you are in lining up the needle with the red line, the more accurate you will be in figuring out the Facing Direction and the Mountain Direction of the building.

When you are ready to try a reading, follow the steps described below. For simplicity, we shall assume that the front door faces the same direction as the general orientation of the building.

1. Line one side of the geomantic compass parallel to the front door. Do not put the compass flush against the door, as metal fittings may distort the magnetic sensor.

2. Rotate the black disk until the needle is perfectly on top of the red line. Remember that the small circle on the needle must be on the same side as the two red dots.

3. Now locate the Twenty-four Directions ring and see where the cross-hairs lie. The part of the compass pointing toward the front is the "facing" portion of the compass. The part of the compass pointing toward the back of the house is the back portion of the compass. (See fig. 13.3.)

4. You are now ready to identify the pair of directions designating the front and back orientation of the building. The segment of the twenty-four partitions where the cross-hair goes through the facing portion of the compass is the Facing Direction of the building. The segment of the twenty-four partitions where the cross-hair goes through the back portion of the compass is the Mountain Direction of the building. Remember from chapter 7 that in feng-shui terminology, the pair of directions are designated such that the first of the pair is the Mountain Direction and the second is the Facing Direction.

This is how you take a reading from a geomantic compass to obtain the front and back orientations of a building. Once you are familiar with this procedure and have memorized the Twenty-four Directions in pairs of twelve, you will only need to get the reading of the front facing, for the Mountain Direction is determined by the Facing Direction.

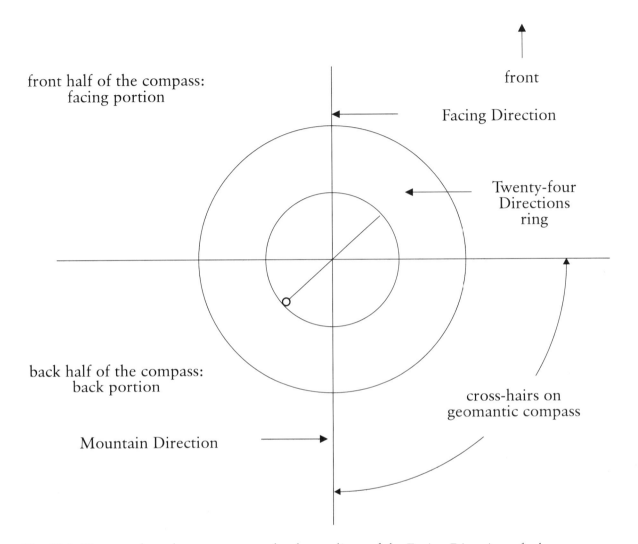

front half of the compass: facing portion

front

Facing Direction

Twenty-four Directions ring

back half of the compass: back portion

cross-hairs on geomantic compass

Mountain Direction

Fig. 13.3 How to place the compass to take the readings of the Facing Direction of a house.

MAKING YOUR OWN GEOMANTIC COMPASS

If you don't want to deal with the Chinese characters on the geomantic compass or you can't get hold of a geomantic compass, this section will show you how to use a regular compass as a substitute.

First, you need to get a fairly good compass with clear markings. You can purchase a good compass from any hiking and camping equipment store. I would suggest that you get a compass that is used for orienteering. At

Fig. 13.4 Two models of an orienteering-type compass. The line of sight in the top one is marked by a notch in the dark knob. In the bottom one it is indicated by an arrow. Both models are made by Silva and can be easily obtained from camping and hiking equipment stores.

the time of writing this book (1994), I found suitable compasses costing between ten and fifteen dollars.

Here are some guidelines for finding a compass suitable for geomantic purposes. You should get a basic protractor compass that is graduated in two-degree steps. North is 0 degrees, and going clockwise, east is 90 degrees, south is 180 degrees, west is 270 degrees, and north is also 360 degrees. You would also want a compass with a rotating capsule or dial. This allows you to align the magnetic needle with the bar underneath it simply by turning the capsule. In compasses used for orienteering, the needle is color-coded, and to find north, you simply line up the colored por-

tion of the needle with the arrow underneath. Some models even label the arrowhead with an N, so there is absolutely no confusion as to which end points north. If you have a hard time figuring out which end of the pointer is north, don't get that model. Your compass should be easy to read and easy to use. You should also get a compass with a rectangular base plate. This helps in aligning the compass with the front door of a building. Finally, one very useful feature on the base plate is the "line of sight." On some models, it is indicated by an arrow; on others it may simply be a marker.

The geomantic compass is divided into twenty-four segments, called the Twenty-four

Directions, each segment measuring fifteen degrees. Three segments make up each point of the eight-point compass. (See chapter 7 if you need a review of the geomantic compass.) For example, north consists of the three segments jen, tzu, kuei. Due north lies in the segment tzu. Jen is north with a westerly inclination, and kuei is north with an easterly inclination. Translating this to the 360-degree circle of the Western compass, tzu occupies + and − 7.5 degrees from 0 degrees, where the 0 line bisects the tzu segment. Another way of putting it is that tzu extends from 352.5 degrees to 7.5 degrees. Jen occupies the next fifteen degrees from tzu in the counterclockwise direction, from 337 degrees to 352.5 degrees. Kuei occupies the next fifteen degrees from tzu in the clockwise direction, from 7.5 degrees to 22.5 degrees.

To convert the 360-degree regular compass to the geomantic compass, make a cardboard ring with the twenty-four partitions. When it is attached to your compass, you can read off the Twenty-four Directions for any given compass bearing.

To prepare the ring, trace or photocopy the template shown in figure 13.6, cut it out, and paste it onto a piece of cardboard. Or you can cut out the template in Appendix D (page 264) and paste it onto a piece of cardboard. This is the Twenty-four Directions ring of the geomantic compass. The marker that bisects the segment tzu indicates due north. Next, cut a circular hole in the center of the cardboard so that it fits the capsule of your compass. The inner circle in the template provided in this book should be large enough to fit the largest models of a common orienteering compass. If the capsule of the compass is smaller than the inner circle of the template, you can draw a smaller circle that matches the diameter of your compass. This will allow you to cut the

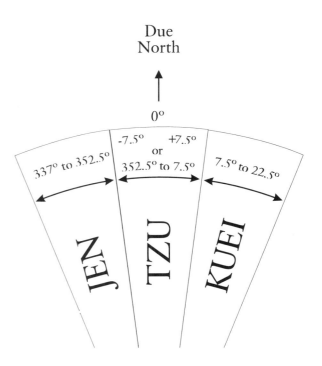

Fig. 13.5 Comparing the geomantic compass with the regular compass. Due north, or 0 degrees on the regular compass bisects the segment tzu onf the geomantic compass. Each of the Twenty-four Directions of the geomantic compass covers 15 degrees on the regular compass.

appropriate opening to fit your compass. I shall show you how to use this tool to transfer degrees into the Twenty-four Directions when we get to that step in taking a reading.

Here are the steps in finding the orientation of a building using a regular compass. We shall assume that the front door faces the same direction as the general orientation of the building.

1. Set the base plate of the compass on the ground so that one of its four sides is parallel to the front door. Do not line the base plate flush against the door, as

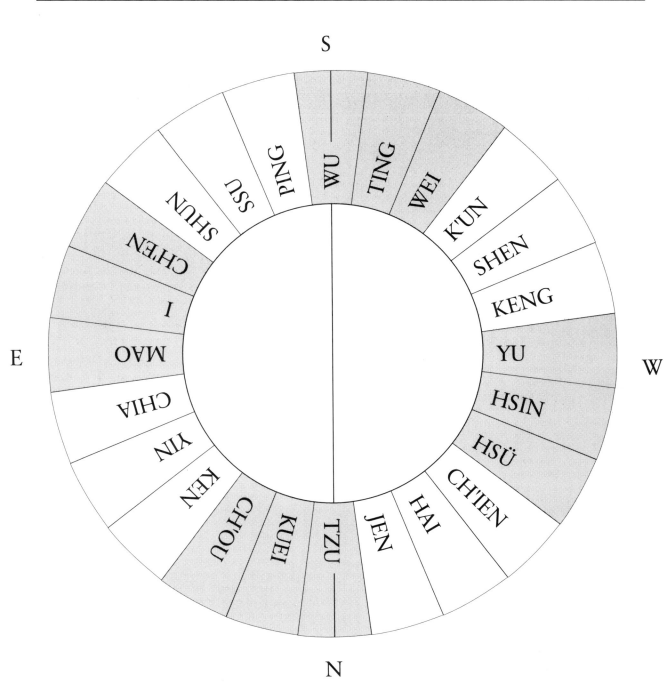

Fig. 13.6 Template of the Twenty-four Directions of the geomantic compass. When it is fitted to the regular compass, you can easily convert the reading in degrees to the Twenty-four Directions. (See text for instructions.)

metal fittings can distort the magnetic sensor.

2. Rotate the capsule so that the needle lies on top of the bar underneath. Make sure the correct end of the needle is lined up with the arrowhead pointing north.

3. Do not move the compass. Now read off the degrees at the line of sight. This is the orientation, or Facing Direction, of the building.

4. To convert degrees into the Twenty-four Directions, you can use the cardboard ring described above. Put the ring on the capsule of the compass so that due north on the compass (0 degrees) is lined up with the mark that bisects the tzu segment. Take care not to move the compass. Check the needle to see that it is still aligned with the bar underneath after you attach the ring.

5. To obtain the Facing Direction, simply look at where the line of sight lies in the Twenty-four Directions. This is the Facing Direction of the building. To obtain the back orientation or Mountain Direction, simply find the segment directly opposite the front-facing segment.

Let us go through some examples. You have lined up the magnetic needle with the bar underneath, and you have obtained a reading from the line of sight, say at 320 degrees. Now put the ring around the capsule of the compass so that 0 degrees on the compass lines up with the marker in the middle of the tzu segment on the ring. The line of sight lies in the segment ch'ien. This is the Facing Direction of the house. Correspondingly, the Mountain Direction (opposite ch'ien) is shun. For another example, say you take a reading with the line of sight at 230 degrees. With the ring in place, the 230 degree line lies in the segment k'un. This is the Facing Direction. The corresponding Mountain Direction is ken.

You've learned how to obtain the most important piece of information required in a feng-shui reading, using a regular compass as a substitute. Of course there is much more information contained in the other rings of the geomantic compass, but for the purposes of learning the basics of feng-shui, this is all you need.

MULTIPLE ORIENTATIONS AND READINGS

There are some circumstances in which you would need to take multiple readings:

1. If the front door of the house faces a different direction than the front of the house, you will need to take one reading for the front door and one for the general orientation of the house (see panel C in fig. 13.1, page 173).

The front of the house is typically on the long side of the building. However, in figure 13.1 (panel C), the front door opens on the short side of the house. In this condition, you need to take two readings. The first reading is based on the orientation of the front door. Use the procedure outlined above to obtain this reading. The second reading is based on the front of the building. To obtain this reading, set the geomantic compass, or the base plate of the regular compass, parallel to the wall. The rest of the procedures are the same.

If the shape of the house is very irregular, you will not be able to figure out the Facing Direction for the house, and all you have is information based on the front door. This is another reason why you do not want a house with an irregular shape.

2. If the entrance to an apartment faces a different direction than the apartment building, you will need to get two readings. I would suggest that you take readings for both the apartment entrance and the building entrance anyway. Even a small difference in matter of degrees can give two different readings and therefore generate two different geomantic charts (covered in the next chapter).

3. If the entrance to a business suite faces a different direction than the commer-cial building it is in, again you will need two readings.

If you are building a house on a plot of land, how would you go about figuring out what is the best direction for the house (and front door) to face? First, you need to gener-ate all the possible geomantic charts of the Twenty-four Directions for houses built within the current cycle of the Nine Cycles. Find the chart that describes the best feng-shui conditions, and find out what direction the house and front door must face. Since this requires knowledge of materials covered in the next chapter, I shall discuss this matter there.

14

Setting Up the Geomantic Chart

We are now ready to set up the geomantic chart. The chart tells you how energy flows in a building and the way it affects the occupants. Recall from chapter 8 that the geomantic chart is essentially the Nine Palaces arranged in a particular order, and that order is dependent on the year the house is built.

After you have obtained the Facing and Mountain Directions of a house, the next step is to find out in which of the Nine Cycles the house was built. The table in figure 6.2 on page 49 below shows the starting years of each cycle. To go back before 1864, subtract twenty years for each cycle. To go beyond 2024, add twenty years to each cycle.

You can find out when a house was built by looking at the deed. If you are renting an apartment, consult the owner of the building. In many North American cities you can generally get this information from the buildings department in the city or county offices. If, for some reason, you can only get an approxi-

mate date of when the house was built, you may need to work out two geomantic charts. Also, you will need to work out two geomantic charts if you are not sure whether the house was built in one cycle or another. This is sometimes the case for old houses that were built around the turn of a cycle. Also, if the house was built in January or February in the year when the change of cycle occurs, you will need to compute two geomantic charts if you do not know when the Chinese year changes. Anytime you have uncertainty about when a house was built, it is safer to compute two charts. Of course, having two charts will make the use of space more complex, but my advice is not to sacrifice safety to avoid some extra work.

The information contained in the diagrams in figure 14.1 is the key to setting up the geomantic chart. These charts are collectively called the Nine Cycles chart.

Before we go on, a clarification of terminol-

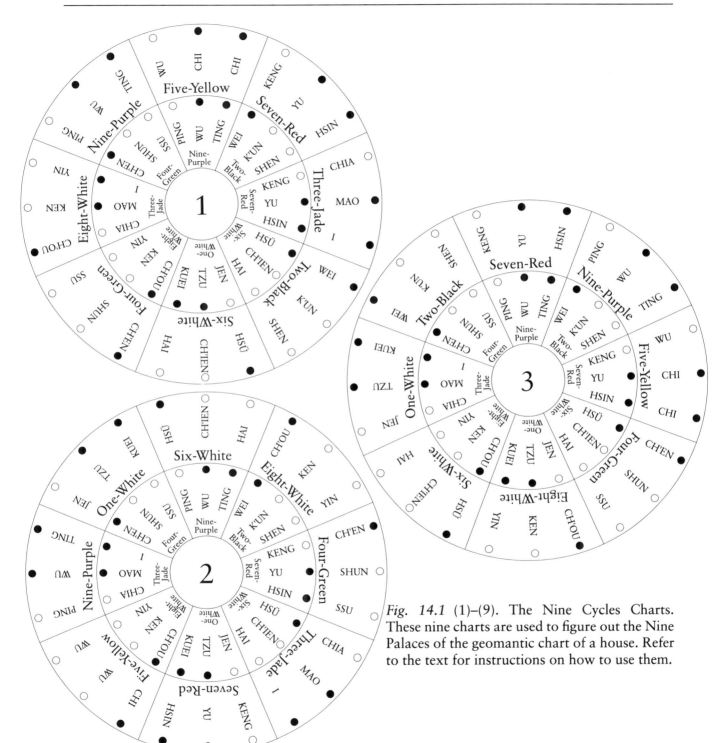

Fig. 14.1 (1)–(9). The Nine Cycles Charts. These nine charts are used to figure out the Nine Palaces of the geomantic chart of a house. Refer to the text for instructions on how to use them.

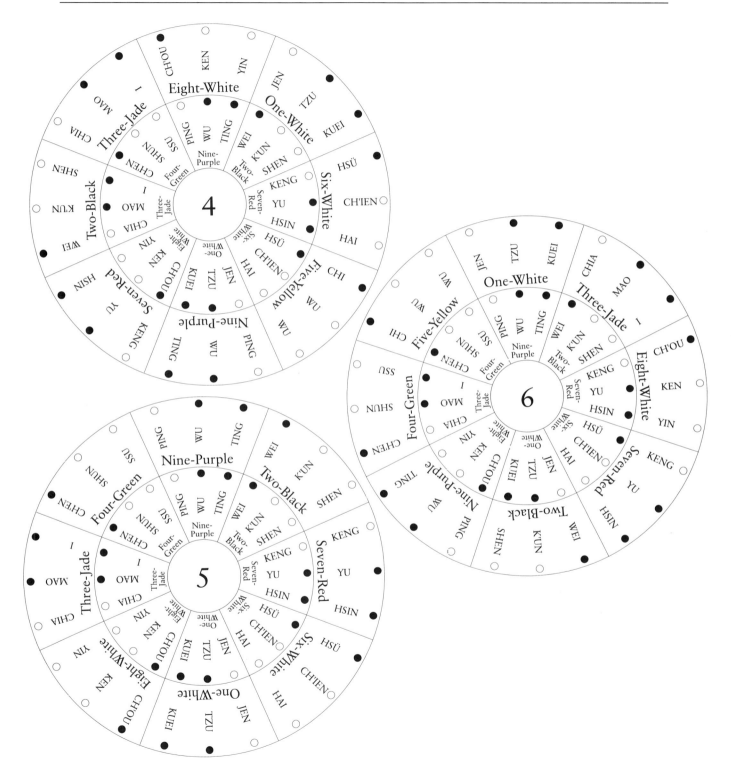

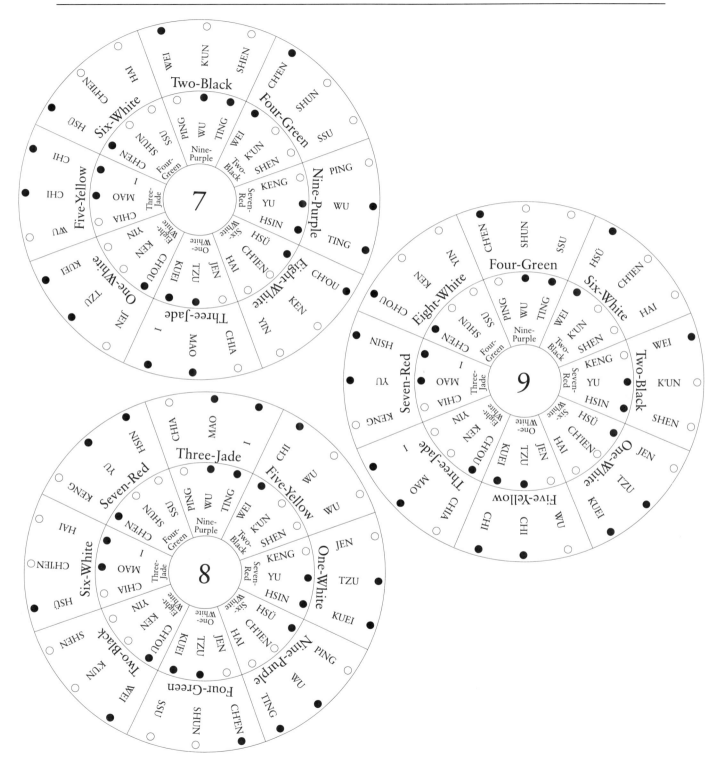

ogy is needed. The terms *Mountain Direction* and *Facing Direction* refer to the Twenty-four Directions, and the terms *Mountain Star* and *Facing Star* refer to the Nine Palaces. Thus, tzu and wu are Directions, and one-white and nine-purple are Stars.

The following is the procedure for setting up the geomantic chart. It is illustrated by an example.

EXAMPLE 1

1. Find out the year in which the house was built. For example, for a house built in 1972, we find by consulting the table on page 49 that 1972 is in the sixth cycle.
2. Now look through figure 14.1(1)–(9) and locate the chart with the number 6 in the middle (page 183). This is the cycles chart used for setting up the geomantic chart for houses built in the sixth cycle.
3. Three items make up the geomantic chart: the Earth Base, the Facing Star, and the Mountain Star. The construction of the geomantic chart begins with setting up the numbers of the Earth Base. Recall from chapter 9 that the Earth Base is based on the structure of the Nine Palaces. From the Nine Cycles chart, we obtain the numbers of the Earth Base from the large number in the center and the eight numbers in the outer ring of the chart. Lay out a grid of nine squares. Continuing with our example, put the number 6 in the center and fill in the rest of the positions with the numbers from the outer ring of the chart. (See fig. 14.2.) These are the large numbers of your nine squares. (If you need a review of the Nine Palaces and the basic information concerning the geomantic chart, refer to chapters 8 and 9.)
4. The next step is to fill in the numbers of the Facing Star and the Mountain Star.

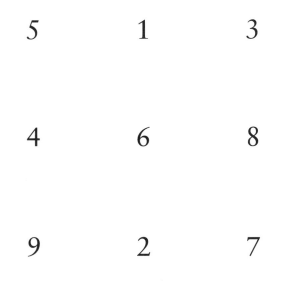

Fig. 14.2 The Earth Base numbers of the Nine Palaces of the geomantic chart from example 1 in the text.

These are determined by the Facing Direction and the Mountain Direction.

a. Take the readings for the Facing Direction and Mountain Direction for the house. In this example, let us say that they are tzu for Mountain and wu for Facing. Now look at the sixth-cycle chart again. Locate the inner ring of numbers and find the position tzu. You will notice that it lies in the segment of one-white. Next, if you work your way outward from this position, you will find the segment two-black in the outer ring. Two-black is therefore the number of the Mountain Star that will go into the center square of the Nine Palaces in the Mountain Star position, typically as the smaller number in the upper left.

b. Now you are ready to fill in the other Mountain Stars in the rest of the Nine Pal-

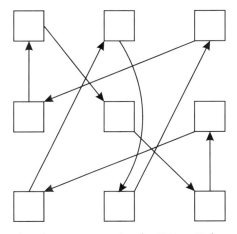

path of movement in the Nine Palaces

4	9	2
3	5	7
8	1	6

clockwise
sequence

6	1	8
7	5	3
2	9	4

counter-
clockwise
sequence

Fig. 14.3 The numbers of the Nine Palaces in clockwise and counterclockwise sequence. When yin conditions dominate, energy flow in the Nine Palaces is counterclockwise. When yang conditions dominate, energy flow is clockwise.

aces. Directly lined up with tzu's position (two-black) is k'un. Next to k'un is an open circle. Open circles indicate yang, and yang movement follows a clockwise direction. Therefore, the numbers counting from 2 through 9 and back to 1 go in a forward sequence. Here you need to use your knowledge of the movement of numbers in the Nine Palaces. For a quick review, look at figure 14.3.

Counting forward (in the clockwise sequence), we fill in the numbers 2 through 9 and back to 1, and complete the Mountain Star component of the geomantic chart (fig. 14.5).

c. Next we put the Facing Star numbers in the Nine Palaces. The Facing Direction in our example is wu. Locate wu in the inner circle of the sixth cycle chart. You will find it in the segment nine-purple. Work your

```
  1           6            8
  5           1            3

              M F

  9           2            4
  4           6            8


  5           7            3
  9           2            7
```

Fig. 14.4 The Earth Base numbers and Mountain Star numbers of the Nine Palaces of the geomantic chart from example 1 in the text.

way outward and find the segment one-white in the outer circle. One-white is the Facing Star number that will go into the center of the Nine Palaces as the smaller number in the upper right.

d. Now put the rest of the Facing Star numbers in the Nine Palaces. Directly lined up with wu is tzu in the segment one-white. Beside tzu is a filled circle. Filled circles indicate yin movement, which is counterclockwise. Therefore, the numbers counting from 1 will go in a reverse order. Use your knowledge of the movement of numbers through the Nine Palaces to place the numbers. From 1 in the center, count backward to place 9 in the lower right-hand corner, then 8, and so on until all nine positions of the Facing Star are filled. You should get a chart like the one shown in figure 14.5.

5. One last item. We need to orient the geo-

mantic chart and identify the Facing Palace in the Earth Base. In figure 14.5 you will see an arrow. The arrow indicates the orientation of the geomantic chart, that is, the Facing Direction of the chart. The sixth-cycle chart tells you how to orient the geomantic chart. Look at the inner ring of the sixth cycle chart, and find tzu and wu. The arrowhead should point in the direction of wu, the Facing Direction. Draw the arrow above the Facing Palace, which is one-white, and point it in the Facing Direction, wu.

The geomantic chart for the house in our example is complete. Let us run through another example so that you can be more comfortable with the procedure.

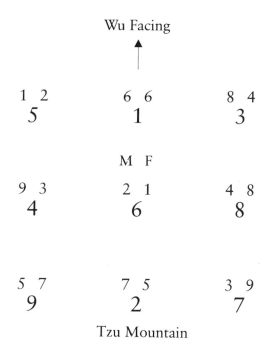

Fig. 14.5 The Earth Base, Mountain Star, and Facing Star numbers of the Nine Palaces of the geomantic chart from example 1 in the text.

EXAMPLE 2

1. The house was built in 1990. This places it in the seventh cycle.
2. Therefore, the chart for the seventh cycle (page 184) will be used.
3. The Mountain Direction is chia, and the Facing Direction is keng.
4. Now set up the Earth Base. This is done simply by copying the numbers of the outer ring of the seventh-cycle chart into their appropriate positions in the Nine Palaces. You should get panel A in figure 14.6.
5. Next, put the Mountain Star numbers in the Nine Palaces. The Mountain Direction is chia. Locate it in the inner circle. It is aligned with wu in the five-yellow segment in the outer circle. Five-yellow is therefore the number of the Mountain Star in the center of the Nine Palaces. Wu is next to an open circle and therefore yang. Thus, the numbers for the Mountain Stars in the Nine Palaces will follow a forward sequence. The next number, 6, will occupy the lower right-hand corner of the Nine Palaces, and so on, until all the numbers of the Mountain Star are placed. This gives you panel B in figure 14.6.
6. Next, put the Facing Star numbers in the Nine Palaces. The Facing Direction is keng. Locate it in the inner circle. It is aligned with ping in the segment nine-purple. Nine-purple is therefore the Facing Star number in the center of the Nine Palaces. Ping is next to an open square and therefore yang. The placement of the Facing Star numbers in the Nine Palaces will thus follow a forward sequence. The next number, 1, will occupy the lower right corner of the Nine Palaces, and so on, until all the numbers of the Facing Star are placed.

This gives you panel C in fig. 14.6.

7. The last step is to put in the orientation indicator and identify the Facing Palace. Locate keng, the Facing Direction, in the inner circle. The head of the arrow will point in that direction from the Facing Palace, which is nine-purple. This completes the geomantic chart.

To familiarize yourself with the above procedures, try several examples on your own. First, set up a geomantic chart for a house built in 1954. You will find that for the fifth cycle, the inner and outer rings of the Nine Cycles chart are identical. Don't let this confuse you. In fact, geomantic charts of the fifth cycle are the easiest ones to generate.

Now try these four scenarios:

• You want to look at the feng-shui of a historical building that was built in 1868. The Mountain and Facing Directions are ch'ien and sun respectively.
• You want to examine the feng-shui of a house that you are considering buying. The house has just been completed and is ready for immediate occupancy. The Mountain and Facing Directions are ken and k'un respectively.
• You have just inherited a house from your grandparents, and you want to find out about its feng-shui. The house was built in 1924, and the Mountain and Facing Directions are wei and ch'ou respectively.
• You are looking at the architectural plans of a house that will be completed in the year 2005, and you want to know its feng-shui. From the drawings, you find the Mountain and Facing Directions to be hai and ssu respectively.

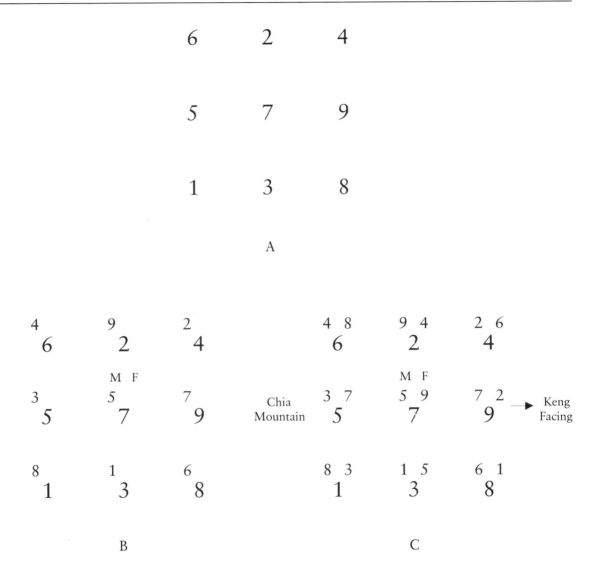

Fig. 14.6 Steps in setting up the geomantic chart in example 2 in the text: (A) Putting in the Earth Base numbers. (B) Filling in the Mountain Star numbers. (C) Filling in the Facing Star numbers and designating the Facing and Mountain Directions.

After you have set up these four charts, you will discover that there are four combinations of the sequencing of the Mountain and Facing Stars in the Nine Palaces. They are:

• Forward-Mountain / Backward-Facing
• Backward-Mountain / Forward-Facing
• Forward-Mountain / Forward-Facing
• Backward-Mountain / Backward-Facing

There are a few things to note concerning these combinations of number sequences:

- The Forward-Mountain / Backward-Facing combination is called the Descending Water condition. A house with this combination will have its fortunes enhanced if it has water in front.
- The Backward-Mountain / Forward-Facing combination is called the Ascending Mountain condition. A house with this combination will have its fortunes enhanced if it has a mountain at the back.
- The Forward-Mountain / Forward-Facing combination is called the Ascending Mountain and Descending Water condition. A house with this combination will have its fortunes enhanced if it has water in front and a mountain at the back.
- The Backward-Mountain / Backward-Facing combination is called the Reverse Mountain and Reverse Water condition. A house with this combination will have its fortunes enhanced regardless of its position relative to mountains and water. It is the most powerful combination. There are no Reverse Mountain and Reverse Water conditions in the first and ninth cycles.

EXPLANATION OF THE STRUCTURE OF THE GEOMANTIC CHART

When I was learning feng-shui, I always asked the how and why of things. Some of you may be curious about how the Nine Cycles charts in figure 14.1 were generated and whether there is a general pattern to them. The charts, or look-up tables, in figure 14.1 provide the easiest way to learn how to set up the geomantic chart, but are by no means the only way. In fact, you can easily generate these charts yourself. The pieces of information required to generate the Nine Cycles charts are knowledge of the Twenty-four Directions ring of the geomantic compass, the principles of the movement of the numbers in the Nine Palaces, and how to put them together.

In this section, I shall show you how to generate the Nine Cycles charts. It is actually quite straightforward, but you need to be very familiar with the Nine Palaces and the Twenty-four Directions. If you are not interested in these details, you can skip this section and go on to the next part on the interpretation of the numbers in the geomantic chart.

Looking at the Nine Cycles charts, you will notice several features. First, the inner rings for all the nine charts are the same. Only the outer rings change with the cycle. Second, the circular charts are made up of the Nine Palaces: one-white, two-black, three-jade, four-green, five-yellow, six-white, seven-red, eight-white, and nine-purple. Third, the small segments in the inner ring are made up of the Twenty-four Directions of the geomantic compass. The segments in the outer ring are made up of segments of the Twenty-four Directions plus two new items, wu and chi, which appear in all the charts except the fifth cycle. Last, the yin or yang designation associated with each of the Twenty-four Directions, and with wu and chi, is constant. Moreover, the designation of yin and yang follows a pattern. It starts out with jen, tzu, kuei being yin/

yang/yang. The next segments, ch'ou, ken, yin, are yang/yin/yin. Then it is back to yin/yang/yang in chia, mao, i, and so on, alternating until the Twenty-four Directions are completed. Therefore, you only have to know the beginning configuration of yang/yin/yin for the first three segments (jen, tzu, kuei) to figure out the rest.

The positions of the numbers of the Nine Palaces in the outer ring in each of the Nine Cycles chart are determined in the following way. The number for the particular cycle occupies the center of the chart. The next number will occupy the next position in the sequence of the Nine Palaces (fig. 14.3), and so on, until all nine numbers are in position. Thus, for example, in the first cycle, the number 1 is in the center, and 2 is in the lower right-hand position. In the ninth cycle, the number 9 is in the center, and 1 is in the lower right-hand position. To generate the chart for each cycle, simply draw the concentric circles and fill in the numbers of the Nine Palaces in the two rings.

In the fifth cycle, the positions of the numbers of the Nine Palaces are identical in the inner and outer rings, but in the other cycles, five-yellow is positioned on the periphery. Just like the other positions, five-yellow is subdivided into three segments, but two of them are the same. From the Nine Cycles charts you will notice that sometimes the segments in five-yellow are wu/chi/chi, and sometimes chi/wu/wu. These are not segments from the Twenty-four Directions of the geomantic compass. They are the "hidden stems," so called because wu and chi are from the Ten Celestial Stems, and they only reveal themselves when five-yellow does not occupy the center position. In feng-shui terminology, we call this condition "five-yellow flying to the periphery."

Why is the five-yellow segment sometimes wu/chi/chi and other times chi/wu/wu? First, notice that wu/chi/chi is yang/yin/yin and that chi/wu/wu is yin/yang/yang. The way you determine which of these two compositions goes into the five-yellow segment is by looking at the configuration of yin and yang in the number that five-yellow is replacing. For example, in the fourth cycle, five-yellow replaces four-green on the periphery because four-green occupies the center. The components in four-green are ch'en, sun, ssu, which are yin/yang/yang. Therefore, five-yellow should be composed of a similar configuration, making it chi/wu/wu, which is yin/yang/yang. In the ninth cycle, five-yellow replaces nine-purple in the periphery because nine occupies the center. The components in nine-purple are ping/wu/ting, which are yang/yin/yin. Therefore, to match the yin and yang configuration that is being replaced, five-yellow should be composed of wu/chi/chi, which is yang/yin/yin. You can go through all the cycles and work this out.

Given these principles that determine the structure of the Nine Cycles chart, you can easily generate them from scratch. As you become more proficient in taking directions with the geomantic compass and setting up the geomantic chart, you will not need to rely on the look-up tables as much, and you can generate the chart when you need it.

INTERPRETING THE NUMBERS IN THE
GEOMANTIC CHART

The Earth Base

When a site is marked for a house or a grave, the flow of energy at that time is captured and contained in the microcosm of the place. This microcosm is called the Earth Base because it describes the life span of the energy of a site. The cycle in which a house is built is its "birth" cycle. Thus, houses built in 1996 have the seventh cycle as their birth cycle. Each cycle has a Ruling Star. The Ruling Star is one-white for the first cycle, two-black for the second cycle, three-jade for the third cycle, four-green for the fourth cycle, five-yellow for the fifth cycle, six-white for the sixth cycle, seven-red for the seventh cycle, eight-white for the eighth cycle, and nine-purple for the ninth cycle.

Earth Base energy does not last forever. Its rise and fall follow changes in the Nine Cycles. Typically, a site is at the highest level of Earth Base energy in its birth cycle. Energy starts to wane in the next cycle. However, as the years go by, it will return to its birth cycle once more. Its Earth Base energy will be renewed, and the process starts over again. The table in figure 14.7 shows the rise and fall of the Earth Base energy for each birth cycle.

Looking at the table, you will see that a house built in the first cycle is at the height of its Earth Base energy in its birth cycle. In the second cycle, the energy begins to decay. At the third cycle, it is at its lowest, and by the fourth cycle it starts to rise again. A house built in the fifth cycle is at the height of its Earth Base energy in the fifth cycle. Energy wanes in the sixth cycle and is dead for the rest of the cycles until the fourth cycle, when the Earth Base energy begins to rise again. If you look through the entire table, you will realize that some cycles are better than others, in that the Earth Base energy lasts longer, or their periods of "fall" or "death" are shorter. Thus, the first, sixth, and eighth cycles are the best, followed in order by the fourth, third, seventh, ninth, and second, with the fifth cycle as the worst. Houses built in the fifth cycle have the shortest life span of Earth Base energy, while those built in the first cycle have the greatest life span.

The life span of Earth Base energy for any house can therefore be figured out by the table in figure 14.7 if you know when a house was built. Look at the table again, and you will see that all houses built between 1984 and 2004 are in the height of their Earth Base energy. This is because we are currently in the seventh cycle. Houses built between 1964 and 1984 are in the process of waning, but by 2004 the Earth Base energy will be on the upward swing again.

The Facing Palace

The square in the Nine Palaces of the Earth Base that contains the Facing Direction is called the Facing Palace. This was introduced earlier when we identified the Facing Direction and Facing Palace in the geomantic chart. We shall now examine the meaning of the Facing Palace in more detail.

Figure 14.8 shows a geomantic chart for a house built in the first cycle, with tzu as the Mountain Direction and wu as the Facing Direction. The arrow shows the facing orientation of the geomantic chart. It points in the direction of wu from five-yellow (the large

Birth cycle of house (year built)	THE NINE CYCLES								
	1	2	3	4	5	6	7	8	9
1	H	F	R	G	G	G	G	G	G
2	R	H	F	D	D	D	N	R	D
3	N	R	H	F	DES	D	F	R	D
4	G	G	R	H	F	R	N	G	G
5	D	D	D	R	H	F	D	D	D
6	G	G	G	G	R	H	F	G	G
7	D	N	R	D	D	R	H	F	D
8	G	G	G	G	G	G	R	H	F
9	F	D	D	N	D	D	N	R	H

Fig. 14.7 The rise and fall of Earth Base energy in the Nine Cycles.

H = highest level of energy
R = energy is rising
N = energy is passive or neutral
D = energy is dead

G = energy is good
F = energy failing
DES = energy is destructive

number 5). Thus, the Earth Base, five-yellow, is in the Facing Palace.

Some stars of the Nine Palaces are undesirable to have in the Facing Palace. In the example, the Earth Base, five-yellow, is in the Facing Palace. Recall from chapter 8 that five-yellow is a star associated with destructive energy. The extent of its malevolent influence will be affected by the Facing and Mountain Stars that appear with it in that square. (See the sections below for a discussion of the interaction of the Earth Base with the Facing and Mountain Stars.)

The following stars of the Nine Palaces are desirable to have as the Earth Base in the Facing Palace because they carry nourishing energy: one-white, four-green, six-white, and eight-white. Five-yellow, nine-purple, and two-black are the worst stars to have in the Facing Palace. Three-jade and seven-red are negative, but not so severe as five-yellow and two-black.

The overall auspiciousness of a site does not depend on Earth Base energy alone. So you need not worry if you find out that your house was built in the fifth cycle or is currently in a downward swing of energy. There are other factors that are equally important as, if not more important than, the Earth Base energy. These are the Facing Star and the interaction between the Facing Star and the Earth Base.

The Facing Star

The Facing Star determines how energy enters a site. Energy coming from the front is expansive and is stronger than energy that enters from the back. Therefore, if the Facing Star is destructive, its harmful influence will spread very fast. However, if the Facing Star is nourishing, its beneficial influence will be increased. To understand the influence of the Facing Star, we shall use an example. Look again at the geomantic chart in figure 14.8. The Facing Star in the Facing Palace is one-white. In that example, the house was built in the first cycle. One-white is the Ruling Star of the first cycle. When the Ruling Star is the Facing Star, and it is in the Facing Palace, conditions are extremely auspicious. However, the benefits are canceled if the star is two-black, five-yellow, or nine-purple. In the example in figure 14.8, the destructive effect of five-yellow can almost be neutralized by one-white alone. With the help of some countermeasures and enhancers (these techniques will be covered in chapter 18), all the bad influence of the five-yellow can be erased.

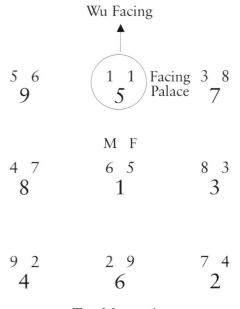

Fig. 14.8 Geomantic chart for a house built in the first cycle. (See page 192.)

The Mountain Star

The Mountain Star exerts less influence than the Facing Star. As long as five-yellow, two-black, and nine-purple are not the numbers of the Mountain Star in the palace, you need not worry about it. Chapter 18 discusses how to deal with aversive Mountain Stars.

INTERACTION OF THE EARTH BASE AND FACING STAR

The interaction of the Earth Base and Facing Star in each of the Nine Palaces is not cumulative. Each combination has a unique meaning.

There are two kinds of interactions—conditional and unconditional. Conditional interactions have alternate results depending on circumstances, and unconditional interactions have only one result regardless of other factors. Conditional interactions apply only in the Facing Palace, and unconditional interactions apply to all Nine Palaces.

Conditional Interactions

The results of conditional interactions depend on whether the combination of the Earth Base and Facing Star is waxing, strong, or malevolent. And these conditions themselves are dependent on which direction of the compass (technically, the positions of the Later Heaven pa-k'ua) they are located in.

The following list describes the nature of the numerical combinations (waxing, strong, and malevolent) and the positions of the pa-k'ua that they occur in. These combinations are in effect as long as the pairs of the numbers are present. It does not matter which number is the Earth Base and which is the Facing Star.

- The one-six combination is in its waxing cycle in the pa-k'ua positions chen (east) and sun (southeast). It is at its height in k'an (north) and is malevolent in li (south).
- The two-seven combination is waxing in the positions k'un (southwest) and ken (northeast). It is at its height in li (south) and is malevolent in ch'ien (northwest) and tui (west).
- The three-eight combination waxes in li (south). It is at its height in chen (east) and sun (southeast) and is malevolent in k'un (southwest).
- The four-nine combination waxes in k'an (north). It is at its height in tui (west) and ch'ien (southwest) and is malevolent in chen (east).

Each numerical combination has a unique interpretation. The following is a list of the results of conditional interactions between the Earth Base number and the Facing Star number. Remember, conditional interactions occur only in the Facing Palace.

When the combination of the Earth Base or the Facing Star is in its waxing or strong phase:

- A one-six combination yields successful scholarly pursuits. Children in the house will be intelligent and talented.
- A two-seven combination yields financial success, but seedy connections may be involved.

- A three-eight combination means that you will be successful in politics or will have filial descendants.
- A four-nine combination yields tremendous success in business through ethical means.

When the combination of the Earth Base and Facing Star is in its malevolent phase:

- A one-six combination means that the head of the family will be injured in accidents. Children may be unfilial, and descendants may become thieves and bring harm to family members.
- A two-seven combination leads to infant death, illness, and accidents.
- A three-eight combination leads to suicidal death. Children may die young.
- A four-nine combination leads to injury or death in war. Children will become orphans.

Here is the procedure for determining conditional interactions between the Earth Base and the Facing Star. It is illustrated with an example.

EXAMPLE 1

1. First, examine the Facing Palace of the geomantic chart, and see if there are any of the above combinations of numbers. For example, say you find the combination one-six in the Facing Palace.
2. Now find out whether one-six is in its waxing, strong, or malevolent phase. To do this, you need to find the Facing Direction of the building. Suppose the Facing Direction is mao (due east). Mao is in the pa-k'ua position chen.
3. Next, look at the list that determines which phase (waxing, strong, or malevo-

lent) one-six is in for mao (due east). You will find that it is in the waxing cycle.

4. Finally, look up the interpretation of one-six in its waxing cycle. You will find that in its waxing cycle, one-six indicates success in scholarly pursuits and intelligent and talented children.

Let us go through another example.

EXAMPLE 2

1. Looking at the Facing Palace you find the combination three-eight.
2. Next you find out that the Facing Direction for the building is wei. Wei is in the k'un position of the Later Heaven pa-k'ua.
3. From the list determining which phase three-eight is in for the k'un position, you find that three-eight is malevolent.
4. The interpretation for three-eight in the malevolent phase is suicidal deaths and early deaths of children.

Unconditional Interactions

Unconditional interactions do not depend on any other factors and will occur whenever the specific numerical combinations of the Earth Base and Facing Star appear. Interactions in the Central Palace affect everyone in the household. Interactions in specific rooms affect activities in those rooms and the individuals using them (see chapter 15).

In unconditional interactions, we need to identify the Earth Base number and the Facing Star number because the numerical combinations are not reciprocal. In the interpretations of unconditional interactions listed below, the first number refers to the Earth Base and the second number refers to the Facing Star.

AUSPICIOUS COMBINATIONS

A one-four or four-one combination means success in scholarly pursuits.

A six-eight combination means success in the military arts or business.

An eight-six combination means success in scholarly or artistic endeavors.

A four-six combination means talent and fame.

An eight-nine combination means the family will have many happy occasions and celebrations.

A nine-eight combination means fame.

A two-eight combination in the northwest position means great wealth.

A three-one combination in the western position means many descendants.

Combinations of one-one, one-six, one-eight, six-four, six-six, and eight-eight all forebode good fortune and good health.

DESTRUCTIVE COMBINATIONS

A seven-nine combination forebodes problems associated with political intrigues.

A two-five or five-two combination means severe illness.

A three-seven combination means loss of fortunes through robbery or legal hassles.

A nine-seven combination means Later Heaven fire—that is, fire caused by human activity.

A two-seven combination means Earlier Heaven fire—that is, fire caused by natural occurrences.

A five-five combination means severe illness or death.

A five-nine combination means accidents that lead to injury or death.

Anytime a five is present in the Earth Base or Facing Star, it means illness.

A combination of seven-red and six-white or six-white and seven-red forebodes armed robbery that may lead to injuries.

A three-two or a two-three combination means quarrels and disharmony.

A seven-three combination means unexpected gains in business, but these gains will invite robbery and trickery.

A three-seven combination means illness associated with worries and anxieties. There is also the possibility of being victimized by politics.

A six-nine combination means illness involving failure of internal organs. The eldest member of the family has the highest risk.

A seven-nine-five combination means terminal illness.

An eight-four or a three-eight combination means that children will be unhealthy.

A two-nine combination means obstacles in business ventures.

A two-three combination means having too many mouths to feed.

Any combination not specified above has no special effects. When evaluating interactions in the Facing Palace, conditional interactions take priority over unconditional interactions.

SPECIAL CHARTS

There are two geomantic charts that warrant special attention. They are called the Three Combinations and the Combination of Ten.

The Three Combinations

The Three Combinations refer to combinations of these three sets of numbers: one, four, seven; two, five, eight; and three, six, nine. If these combinations are present in all of the Nine Palaces of the geomantic chart, then a special interpretation overrides all the other combinations discussed earlier. It does not matter which number is in the Earth Base and which is in the Facing or Mountain Stars. As long as these numbers are present, then the geomantic chart fits the condition of Three Combinations. Figure 14.9 is an example of such a chart.

The Three Combination chart is very auspicious and is associated with good health, great fortune, fame, respect from society, familial harmony, and filial descendants. The three sets of numerical combinations describe the ideal conditions for the copulation of yin and yang energies in Upper, Middle, and Lower Eras. One, four, and seven are numbers of the "head" of the Three Eras. Two, five, and eight are numbers of the "shoulders" of the Three Eras. Three, six, and nine are numbers of the "feet" of the Three Eras. When all the numbers are present, it means completeness, and completeness comes from primordial energy. Therefore, a house having

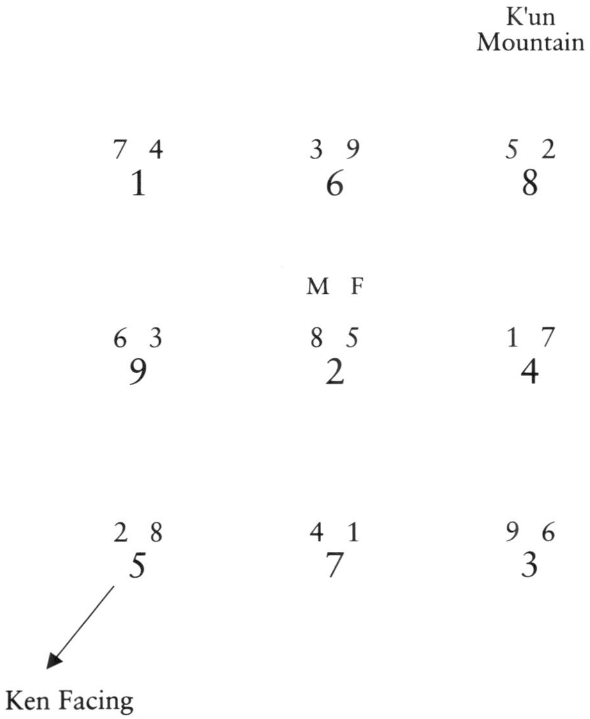

K'un
Mountain

7 4	3 9	5 2
1	6	8

M F

6 3	8 5	1 7
9	2	4

2 8	4 1	9 6
5	7	3

Ken Facing

Fig. 14.9 Example of a "Three Combinations" geomantic chart.

a chart of the Three Combinations means that it will receive energy in all of the Eras. The life span of this site is eternal.

The Three Combinations chart does not occur in all of the Nine Cycles. It does not occur in the first, third, seventh, and ninth cycles. There are three occurrences each in the second, fifth, and eighth cycles, and they occur in the following Mountain/Facing configurations: ken Mountain/k'un Facing, yin Mountain/shen Facing, k'un Mountain/ken Facing, shen Mountain/yin Facing. In the fourth and sixth cycles, there are two oc-

currences each, and they occur in the following Mountain/Facing configurations: ch'ou Mountain/wei Facing, and wei Mountain/ch'ou Facing. Thus, there are a total of sixteen occurrences of the Three Combinations throughout the one hundred and eighty years of the Nine Cycles.

The Combination of Ten

This combination refers to the condition in which the sum of the numbers of the Earth Base and Facing Star or Mountain Star in all the Nine Palaces adds up to ten. Ten symbolizes completeness, and when all Nine Palaces exhibit this condition, the benefits are similar to those of the Three Combinations. (See fig. 14.10 for examples.)

Recall that in the first, third, seventh, and ninth cycles there are no geomantic charts with the Three Combinations. It would appear that houses built in those cycles are at a severe disadvantage. However, the Combination of Ten appears in the first, third, seventh, and ninth cycles, and so these occurrences make up for the absence of the Three Combinations in those cycles.

There are a total of twenty occurrences of the Combination of Ten throughout the one hundred and eighty years of the Nine Cycles. In the first and ninth cycles it occurs when ch'ien, sun, ssu, and hai are either the Facing Direction or Mountain Direction. In the second and eighth cycles it occurs when ch'ou or wei is either the Facing Direction or the Mountain Direction. In the third and seventh cycles it occurs when tzu, wu, kuei, ting are either the Facing Direction or the Mountain Direction. In the fourth and sixth cycles, it occurs when keng and chia are either the Facing Direction or Mountain Direction.

Sun Facing

Sun Facing

| 1 1 | 6 5 | 8 3 | | 2 8 | 6 3 | 4 5 |
| 9 | 5 | 7 | | 8 | 4 | 6 |

M F

M F

| 9 2 | 2 9 | 4 7 | | 3 6 | 1 8 | 8 1 |
| 8 | 1 | 3 | | 7 | 9 | 2 |

| 5 6 | 7 4 | 3 8 | | 7 2 | 5 4 | 9 9 |
| 4 | 6 | 2 | | 3 | 5 | 1 |

Ch'ien
Mountain

Ch'ien
Mountain

Fig. 14.10 Examples of a "Combination of Ten" geomantic chart.

CHOOSING AN ORIENTATION IN A GIVEN CYCLE

We can now examine the matter of choosing an orientation for a newly built house. This was mentioned at the end of the previous chapter, but we needed information covered in this chapter to discuss it properly.

Suppose you are planning to build a house within the next three years and would like to know what is the best geomantic condition. Here's how it is done.

First, determine the current cycle. Here, it is the seventh cycle. If you plan to build the house in 2004, it will be the eighth cycle. I would suggest that you buy the land and build the house in the same cycle. It reduces the complication of having to work out two geomantic charts, one based on the cycle when the land is purchased, and one based on the cycle when the house is built.

Second, work out all the geomantic charts for all the twenty-four possible Facing Directions of the cycle that the house is to be built.

Next, use the guidelines set up above to select the best chart. Remember, the most important squares in the Nine Palaces are the Central Palace and the Facing Palace. The most important components in the palaces are the numbers of the Earth Base and the Facing Star. Make sure that five-yellow and two-black are not in the Central Palace and the Facing Palace. This serves as an initial guideline for ruling out certain Facing Directions.

Once you have selected the chart, and

therefore the Facing Direction, your next step is to translate this information onto the land. To do this, you need the geomantic compass, a long string, and nonmetal spikes. (Plastic tent pegs are excellent for this purpose.) Now follow the instructions below.

1. Line up the needle of the compass with the north-pointing arrow on the face of the compass. Now find out where the Facing Direction is, using the technique described in the previous chapter. The line extending through the Facing Direction is called the Facing Direction Line.
2. Hammer a peg into the ground and tie the string around it, leaving enough length on both ends. This spike will locate the center of the front door of the house.
3. Unroll the string and walk away from the first spike toward the Facing Direction. Approximately ten feet away, with the string tied around the second peg,

hammer the peg into the ground so that the two pegs are perfectly lined up.
4. Do the same thing for the third peg, which is to be placed behind the first one.
5. You may need to adjust the positions of the second and third pegs to get the three of them aligned perfectly. You may also want to place your compass at each of the pegs to check the alignment. This is why nonmetal pegs are preferred. You now have the Facing Direction Line, which specifies the Facing Direction of the house. When the foundations are poured, this line will determine the front orientation of the house.
6. If you want more accurate measurements, you can set up more than three anchor positions. This is helpful especially if you plan to have a very large house. Normally, I find three anchor points to be enough for the typical house in North America.

MULTIPLE CHARTS

Sometimes you will need to set up more than one geomantic chart for a building. Some of these conditions were discussed in the previous chapter. Here are other conditions for which multiple charts are required.

First, as I have mentioned, when the land is purchased in a cycle different from when the house is built, two charts are required. The chart from the cycle in which the house is built is given a more important consideration than the chart for when the land is purchased.

Second, when a house has undergone a major renovation and the renovation occurs in a different cycle than when the house was

built, multiple charts are required. Here you need to set up one chart based on the cycle when the house was built and one based on the cycle when the major renovations occurred. In evaluating the feng-shui of the house, the cycle when the major renovations occurred is given more weight—so much so, in fact, that many feng-shui practitioners recommend that when the geomantic conditions turn disastrous in a new cycle, one way to improve the conditions is to renovate the house. This gives the house a new Earth Base and, depending on the nature of the renovations in the floor plan, possibly a new Facing Direction and, subsequently, a new Facing Star.

Third, when a house undergoes major renovations within the same cycle it was built, the Facing Star may change. This is especially so if the floor plan changes in such a way that the front door or the front orientation of the building is changed. The Earth Base, however, remains the same in this case.

What kinds of renovation warrant a new geomantic chart? Here are a few guidelines:

- if there are structural changes to the building
- if there are changes in the room partitions
- if you add or remove a level
- if you add some rooms, thus changing the general layout of the house. This includes changing an attached garage into living quarters.

The following conditions do not warrant a change in the geomantic chart even though these changes are made in a different cycle than the one the house was built.

- putting in a new porch
- any repairs, including changes in window panes and ceilings
- building a deck or a separate garage
- repaving the driveway or putting up a fence
- painting or putting in new wallpaper or carpeting
- installing new lighting

The conditions listed are hardly exhaustive. Common sense can usually tell you whether the renovations are great enough to change the Facing Star or the Earth Base.

Now that you have learned to set up the geomantic chart, the next step is to superimpose the chart onto the floor plan of a house and interpret the meaning of the numbers in the Nine Palaces on each room. This is what we shall do in the next chapter.

15

Superimposing the Geomantic Chart
onto a Building's Floor Plan

The geomantic chart describes the flow of energy in the universe. In Taoist cosmology, the structure of the universe is reflected in both the macrocosm and the microcosm. This philosophy is expressed in the *Chuang-tzu* as the principle of the "unity of things." To the Taoist sage Chuang-tzu, the stars in the skies, the tides in the sea, and each grain of sand on the earth are all governed by the same laws of existence, for they are all reflections of the Tao. The parallel structure of the microcosm and macrocosm is the most important principle in understanding the flow of energy in the Nine Palaces and seeing how it affects the life and health of a building and its occupants.

When the geomantic chart is superimposed onto the floor plan of a building, it describes the flow of energy, benevolent and malevolent, in that place. The chart is first superimposed on the entire building, which is the macrocosm, and then onto each room, which is the microcosm. The interaction of the numbers in each of the Nine Palaces is then interpreted for each level of superimposition.

These are the steps in fitting the geomantic chart onto a building and interpreting its meaning for the inhabitants.

1. orienting the geomantic chart
2. superimposing the geomantic chart onto the floor plan
3. interpreting the meaning of the numbers of the Nine Palaces in their positions in the floor plan

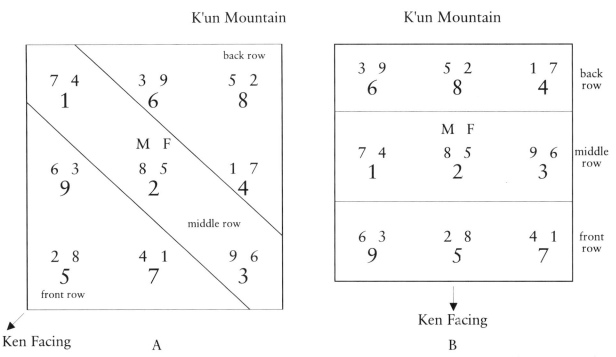

Fig. 15.1 How to adjust a geomantic chart when the Facing Palace is in a corner. The Facing Palace in panel A is in the lower left-hand corner. Panel B shows the adjusted grid. In the adjustment, the lower triangle becomes the bottom row, the diagonal in the middle becomes the middle row, and the upper triangle becomes the upper row. Note that the Facing Palace is now in the center of the bottom row.

ORIENTING THE GEOMANTIC CHART

First, we need to make sure that the geomantic chart is oriented properly. You have learned to identify the Facing Palace and the Facing Direction of the geomantic chart in the previous chapter. If the Facing Palace is located in a corner square, we need to rearrange the chart before we can fit it onto the floor plan. If the Facing Palace is not located in a corner square in the Nine Palaces, no adjustment is needed.

Figure 15.1 shows a geomantic chart with the Facing Palace in the lower left-hand corner (panel A) and its adjusted version. When rearranged (panel B), the Facing Palace now occupies the middle square in the bottom row of the chart. It is easier now to see how it fits into the floor plan.

FITTING THE GEOMANTIC CHART ONTO A FLOOR PLAN

The next step is to learn to superimpose the geomantic chart onto different designs of floor plans. Floor plans that have regular shapes are easiest to work with. Floor plans

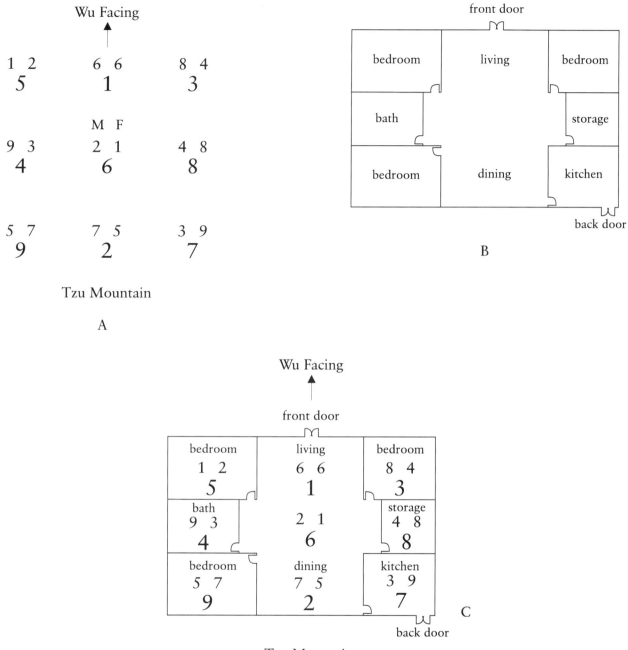

Fig. 15.2 Superimposing a geomantic chart onto a floor plan. (A) The geomantic chart. (B) The floor plan. (C) The geomantic chart is superimposed onto the floor plan.

that are irregular require more care to ensure that the geomantic chart is fitted properly.

When the Floor Plan Has a Regular Shape

Panels A and B in figure 15.2 shows a geomantic chart next to the floor plan of a bungalow. To fit the geomantic chart onto the floor plan, first divide the house into roughly nine squares. This should be simple for a floor plan with a regular shape. Thus, superimposing the two panels A and B in Figure 15.2, we get what is shown in panel C. Make sure that the geomantic chart is oriented in the same direction as the house it is associated with. Usually,

the Facing Palace and the Facing Direction should be pointing in the same direction as the front door, or toward the front of the house.

Most houses are rectangular, so that the square shape of the Nine Palaces would have to be "stretched" when fitted into the floor plan. A general rule that I use is that if a room occupies more than one-half of a square, I assign it the entire square. Similarly, if a room occupies more than one and a half squares, I assign it two squares. (See Fig. 15.3.) If the Facing Palace in a geomantic chart occupies a corner square, simply rearrange it as shown in Figure 15.3, and fit it onto the floor plan accordingly.

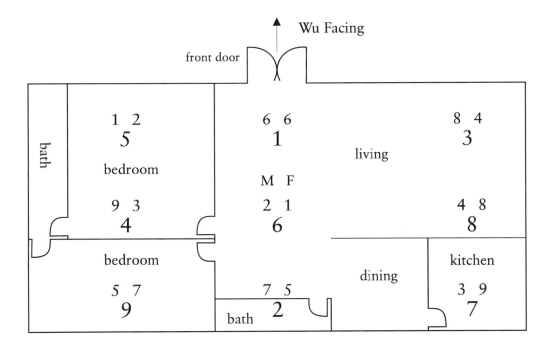

Tzu Mountain

Fig. 15.3 Stretching a geomantic chart to fit onto a rectangular floor plan. Notice that the bedroom occupies two squares in the Nine Palaces, and the living room occupies four squares.

When the Floor Plan Has an Irregular Shape

Superimposing the geomantic chart onto a floor plan with an irregular shape is a bit more challenging. Figure 15.4 shows a condition where some parts of the chart have to be "stretched" and other parts fall on areas outside the house.

When the floor plan is too irregular, it will be extremely difficult to fit the geomantic chart into its floor plan. In fact, you probably won't get to this stage of evaluating the feng-shui of the building, because you would have ruled out such a house based on the factors of Internal Environment (see chapter 12).

When the Building Has Multiple Levels

If a building has multiple levels, the geomantic chart is simply superimposed onto each level separately. If the dimensions of the levels are different, the chart will have to be stretched differently on each level, as described above.

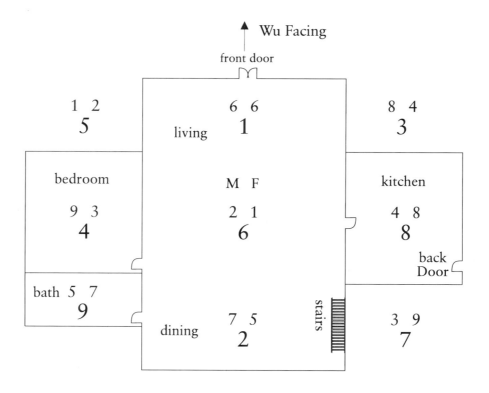

Fig. 15.4 Fitting a geomantic chart onto a irregular floor plan. Notice that some squares of the Nine Palaces fall outside the building.

THE MEANING OF THE NUMBERS OF THE EARTH BASE, FACING STAR, AND MOUNTAIN STAR FOR EACH AREA OF A BUILDING

Now that you know how to fit a geomantic chart onto the floor plan of a building, the next task is to learn to interpret the meaning of the numbers in the Nine Palaces for the area they occupy. As you already know from the previous chapter, some numbers are associated with beneficial influences and others with malevolent effects. In this section we shall go through each area of a house and discuss which numbers are worst and which numbers are best for it.

The influence of the Facing Star is greatest. If the number of the Facing Star is malevolent, it takes auspicious numbers in both the Earth Base and the Mountain Star to neutralize it. If the number in the Earth Base is bad, an auspicious Facing Star will neutralize it. If the Mountain Star is bad, either an auspicious Facing Star or Earth Base number, or an artifact acting as a countermeasure (see chapter 17), can neutralize it.

In the following discussion, all references to numerical interactions in the Nine Palaces involve the Earth Base and the Facing Star, and no specific designation of ordering is implied.

Front Door

The front door plays a very important part in determining the feng-shui of the house. Energies, benevolent and destructive, enter through the front door and spread to the rest of the house. If the Earth Base and Facing Star at the front door are destructive, then energies entering the house will be colored by their malevolent influence. On the contrary, if the stars in the Palace where the front door is situated are beneficial ones, then energies entering the house will take on the benevolent characteristic of the stars of the Palace.

Auspicious Earth Base and Facing Star numbers for the front door are one-white, four-green, six-white, and eight-white. The worst numbers for the front door are two-black, five-yellow, and nine-purple. Three-jade and seven-red are neutral, and their effects will depend on the presence of the other numbers in the Palace. Combinations of one-one, one-six, one-eight, one-four, four-six, four-eight, six-six, and six-eight are also very auspicious for the front door and entrance area. They bring health, prosperity, and success. The combinations two-two, two-five, two-nine, five-five, and five-nine bring illness and death to the occupants of the house. A combination of two and seven brings fire from natural causes. A combination of seven and nine brings fire due to human negligence. A combination of three and two brings disharmony and problems with neighbors. A combination of seven and six means break-ins through the front door.

In general, the numbers two-black, five-yellow, and nine-purple are not good for the entrance, whether they are the Earth Star or Facing Star, or even the Mountain Base. If these numbers are accompanied by one-white, six-white, or eight-white, their destructive influence is lessened.

Back Door

The back door is generally not as important as the front door, but nonetheless it should not have stars like five-yellow and two-black in its Palace. Its importance, though, is increased if that door is used a lot. In North American households, it is quite common for the family and close friends to enter the house through the back (or side) door, especially if the parking area is closer to the back door. If this is the case, your back door becomes as important as the front door.

Hallways and Stairs

Hallways and staircases are passageways where there is a lot of traffic. Moreover, because hallways and stairways connect different parts of the house, they are conduits of energy (see chapter 12). Therefore, when a malevolent star is in these places, there will be unfortunate events associated with travel and movement. Moreover, a destructive force present in a passage can block the flow of beneficial energy from one part of the house to the other. On the contrary, if a beneficial star is located in the hallway or stairway, positive energy associated with the star will be distributed effectively throughout the house. In addition, an auspicious star in these locations can facilitate prosperity associated with travel and movement.

Again, one-white, four-green, six-white, and eight-white are auspicious stars for hallways and stairways. The worst conditions are when twos and fives and nines make up all three numbers of the Palace where the stairs and hallways are located. The next worse condition is when twos, fives, and nines constitute two of the three numbers in the Palace, especially when they are the Earth Base and the Facing Star.

Specifically, a combination of five-yellow in the Earth Base, five-yellow in the Facing Star, and five-yellow or two-black or nine-purple in

the Mountain Star forebodes injury and death occurring at the location of the stairs or hallway. I once did a feng-shui reading for a house with this condition and, after explaining this situation to the occupants, was told that a year before, a miscarriage had occurred when a pregnant woman slipped and fell down the stairs. A combination of nine-purple in the Earth Base, nine-purple in the Facing Star, and either two-black or seven-red in the Mountain Star forebodes injury and death occurring at that location. I know of several houses with this condition. In one incident, an elderly man slipped and fell down the stairs and became paralyzed. Another incident involved a child who slid down a banister, fell, and injured his head.

The best combination for the stairs is one-white in the Earth Base, six-white in the Facing Star, and either one-white or six-white in the Mountain Star. This condition predicts great wealth and prosperity associated with multinational enterprises. One of the owners of a large textile manufacturing plant in Hong Kong has this combination for the stairway in his house.

Bedrooms

The stars of the Nine Palaces in the bedrooms affect the health of the individuals sleeping there. Therefore, bedrooms with two or more stars that are five-yellow, two-black, and nine-purple forebode illness. A bedroom with five-yellow as the Earth Base, five-yellow as the Facing Star, and five-yellow or two-black or nine-purple as the Mountain Star will bring severe illness leading to death. A combination of five-yellow as the Earth Base and two-black as the Facing Star forebodes chronic illness for those who sleep in that bedroom. A bedroom with two-black as the Earth

Base and five-yellow as Facing Star means frequent health problems that are not life-threatening. The threat of illness is lessened when one-white and six-white are present in that square.

The best stars for bedrooms are one-white, six-white, and eight-white. They are all stars of health and longevity. When all three stars are one-white, six-white, and eight-white (in any position), the individuals sleeping in that room will have excellent health and a long life. These three stars are so strong that even if the Mountain Star is five-yellow, two-black, or nine-purple, the malevolent influence is totally neutralized.

Living Room

The living room is the place where guests are welcomed and entertained. Therefore, the stars of the Nine Palaces in this room affect business matters and relationships with friends and relatives.

The best Earth Base and Facing Stars for the living room are one-white, four-green, six-white, and eight-white. Whenever one or more of these stars are present, good business connections will be made, and friends and relatives will be harmonious and helpful. The worst stars are two-black, five-yellow, nine-purple, and three-jade. Whenever one or more of these stars are present, there will be bad luck in business ventures and quarrels with friends and relatives.

Specifically, the presence of two-black and three-jade in the Earth Base and Facing Star forebodes constant quarreling among business partners that may lead to litigations. A combination of seven-red and six-white predicts loss of fortunes through deceit in business dealings.

Family Room

The stars of the Nine Palaces in the family room affect all members of the family because this is a place where they do most of their activities together. The best Earth Base and Facing Stars for the family room are one-white, four-green, six-white, and eight-white. These are stars of health, longevity, harmony, and well-being. Having one of them in the Palace(s) where the family room is situated is enough, provided that the other two stars are not a combination of two-black and five-yellow, or a combination of two-black and three-jade, or of seven-red and nine-purple. The worst conditions are combinations of two-black and five-yellow in all three stars of the Palace.

Specifically, a combination of two-black and three-jade means disharmony, quarrels, and competition between family members. A combination of five-yellow and two-black means illness and accidents occurring in vacation or leisurely activities, whether at home or abroad. A combination of seven-red and nine-purple predicts fire caused by activities in the room.

Kitchen

The kitchen is a very important area in the house. As mentioned in the discussion on internal environment in chapter 12, the kitchen is associated with livelihood, health, and harmony. Therefore, the part of the geomantic chart occupying the kitchen area is examined in detail in feng-shui readings.

First, we look at the stars affecting livelihood, for the kitchen is associated with "having enough to eat." A combination of three-jade and seven-red, or of seven-red and six-white, forebodes instability of employment and hardships in livelihood. A combination of one-white and six-white, or of four-green and six-white, means that the family will always have enough to eat.

Second, we examine the occurrences of events in the kitchen. A combination of seven-red and nine-purple, or of seven-red and two-black, predicts fire started by activities in the kitchen. A combination of eight-white and nine-purple means many family reunions and happy events. In general, if the Palace where the kitchen is situated has nine-purple as the Earth Base, there will be a constant threat of accidents associated with fires and burns.

Third, we look at the stars that govern health. Combinations of two-black and five-yellow, of five-yellow and five-yellow, and of five-yellow and nine-purple all forebode illness associated with food. A combination of five-yellow and five-yellow means frequent food poisoning, whether the food is consumed at home or in a restaurant. A combination of two-black and five-yellow means chronic problems with food, such as food allergies. A combination of five-yellow and nine-purple means illness associated with the internal organs related to the digestive system. Anytime a five-yellow or two-black is present in the kitchen as the Earth Base or Facing Star, there will be minor but frequent illness.

Finally, the harmony of the family is affected by the stars two-black and three-jade. A combination of two-black and three-jade predicts quarrels occurring in the kitchen. When seven-red is also present, the quarrels may lead to fights and injuries.

Dining Room

The most auspicious stars for the dining area are the stars of health and longevity: one-

white, six-white, and eight-white. The worst stars are the stars of illness: five-yellow, two-black, and nine-purple. In general, the combinations of stars that govern health for the kitchen also apply to the dining room.

Study

When a study is used by students, the best combination for the Earth Base and Facing Star is eight-white and six-white or four-green and six-white. The combination one-white and four-green means that the student will become an expert in his or her field. The combination eight-white and six-white predicts excellence in academics, especially in the arts and humanities. When the Earth Base or Facing is one-white or eight-white, and the Mountain Star is six-white, the student will excel in all subjects—humanities, sciences, and practical skills. The worst stars to have for a student's study room are the combination seven-red and six-white in the Earth Base and Facing Star. It means that the student's academic career will be a constant struggle. When five-yellow is present, the combination forebodes misdemeanor and behavioral problems in school. A combination of two-black and three-jade means stiff competition and peer pressure in school.

When the study is used as a home office, the best Earth Base–Facing Star combination is one-white and four-green. It means that ingenious business ideas will be generated, leading to promotion and increase in wealth. A combination of three-jade and seven-red means that good ideas are generated, but you do not get the merit for them. A combination of seven-red and six-white means that business ideas will be failures, leading to loss of job and income. A combination of two-black and three-jade means that competition in the work environment will be stiff and chances for promotion are slim.

Bathroom

The best star to have for the bathroom is nine-purple. Nine-purple is associated with the element fire, and if it is situated anywhere else in the house, it will pose a threat associated with fire. However, because the bathroom is where water is plentiful, it is the safest location for nine-purple to be situated, whether it is the Earth Base or Facing Star. The combination that is not suitable for the bathroom is two-black and five-yellow. It forebodes accidents and illness associated with bathing. All other stars and their combinations are neutral for the bathroom.

Utility Room

This room is usually used for storage and for holding utilities such as the washing machine. As such, it is not frequented much.

Therefore, it is best for malevolent stars such as five-yellow and two-black to be situated there. Moreover, if this room has a utility sink and a washing machine, then it is an excellent place for nine-purple. The abundance of water will eliminate the threat of fire associated with nine-purple.

One last consideration remains in interpreting the meaning of the stars of the Nine Palaces for each area of a house. In chapter 14, we discussed the effects of conditional and unconditional numerical interactions in the Facing Palace. Those interactions take priority over the ones that we just discussed. For example, if the living room occupies the square of the Facing Star, or the dining room occupies the Central Palace, the conditional and unconditional interactions are evaluated first, and then the specific conditions particular to that room are considered. If there is a difference, priority is given to the interpretation from the conditional and unconditional interactions.

SUPERIMPOSING THE GEOMANTIC CHART ONTO EACH ROOM

After you have fitted the geomantic chart onto the floor plan of the house, the next step is to superimpose it at the microcosmic level, onto each room. (See Fig. 15.5 for an example.) Here, the squares of the Nine Palaces are fitted onto the rooms, and the numerical meaning of the stars are used to guide the placement of objects within the room. Unless otherwise stated, all references to numerical combinations pertain to the Earth Base and

Facing Star with no specific designation of ordering.

Bedroom

The bed is the most important object in the bedroom. Its placement in the microcosm of the bedroom affects the health of the individuals sleeping in that room. Two positions need to be considered when you place a bed:

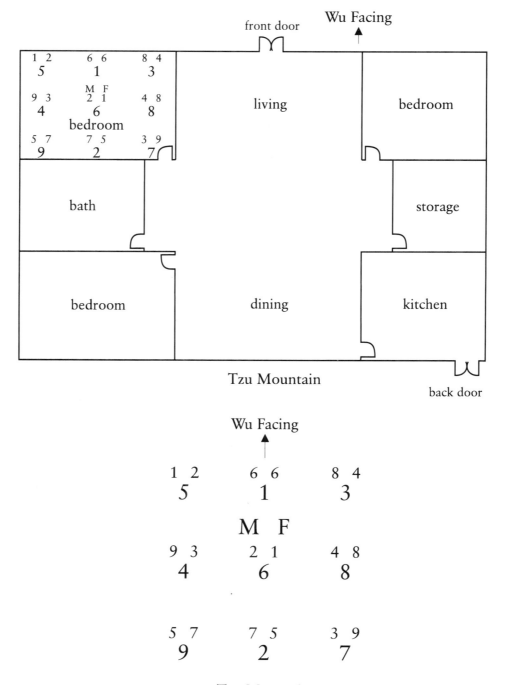

Fig. 15.5 The Nine Palaces superimposed onto a room.

where the bed is actually placed, and where you get off the bed.

The best stars in these two locations are combinations of one-white, six-white, and eight-white. These are stars of health and longevity, and are optimal for bed and bedside locations. Next best is any of the above with four-green. The worst stars are combinations of two-black and five-yellow, and of seven-red and nine-purple. Specifically, a combination of two-black and five-yellow in those locations means that illness will befall a woman who sleeps in that bedroom. A combination of seven-red and nine-purple means that the head of the family will meet with severe illness that may lead to death. A combination of three-jade and eight-white means that the children will have health problems.

In general, do not place a bed under an exposed beam. The person who sleeps under the beam will be "crushed" physically in accidents or psychologically by stressful situations. Mirrors should not face the bed. In fact, you should not be able to see your own image while you are on the bed. Mirrors are said to take away life energy, especially while the individual is asleep. If you have blinds in a bedroom, make sure that the blades are oriented horizontally. Vertical blinds are like knives, cutting into the room and the individuals sleeping in it.

Fireplaces should not occupy the position of nine-purple, because that star belongs to the element fire. A fireplace or wood-burning stove in that position in a bedroom forebodes that the occupants of the room will be injured by fire. If the combination is nine-purple and seven-red or nine-purple and two-black, and the Mountain Star is five-yellow, it forebodes that a person who occupies that room will die by fire.

Finally, the position of the door of the bed-room is also an important consideration. Doorways color the energy entering the room, and malevolent stars like two-black, five-yellow, and nine-purple ideally should not occupy the square where the door is situated.

Family Room

The most important things in the family room are furniture that the family uses a lot. These include couches, recreation equipment (such as video-game machines and computers), pianos, and playpens. Again, it is not desirable to place these objects in locations where there are combinations of two-black, five-yellow, seven-red, and nine-purple. As you have probably noticed, these stars are associated with illness, accidents, injuries, and death.

If the fireplace or wood stove is situated where there is a combination of nine-purple and seven-red or nine-purple and two-black, there will be an enhanced risk of fire. If these stars are coupled with five-yellow in the Mountain Star, then the fire will lead to injury or death.

As in the bedroom, the entrance to the family room should ideally be located in a square where there are benevolent stars, such as one-white, four-green, six-white, and eight-white. It should not be located in a square where there are combinations of two-black, five-yellow, and nine-purple.

Living Room

If you use the living room to receive and entertain formal guests and discuss business matters, the best combination of Earth Base and Facing Star for the entrance to the room is six-white and eight-white. A combination of two-black and three-jade in the doorway to the living room means quarrels among business partners.

Again, the fireplace should not be in a location where there is a combination of nine-purple with seven-red or with two-black. It forebodes that the business will be damaged by fire.

Kitchen

The two most important objects in the kitchen are the stove and the dining table. The stove is where food is cooked, and the dining table is where food is consumed. Both are associated with health and livelihood. Therefore, it is extremely dangerous to have the stove or the dining table located in a square where there are combinations of two-black and five-yellow. Specifically, a combination of five-yellow and five-yellow means severe illness associated with food. A combination of two-black and five-yellow means minor but annoying problems with food and eating.

Do not place the dining table under an exposed beam. It means that the occupants of the house will be "crushed" economically and will not have enough to eat. The placement of the dining table in the dining room follows the same principles as the placement of the table in the kitchen.

If the stove is located where there is a combination of nine-purple with either seven-red or two-black, there will be a high risk of fire in the kitchen.

Study or Home Office

The most important piece of furniture in a study or home office is the desk. Here, the location of the desk as well as the square it faces should be considered. If the desk is used by a student, the ideal combination for the location of the desk is one-white and four-green because it predicts success in academics. If the desk is used for activities associated with a business, then the best combination is six-white and eight-white because this predicts success in business enterprises. The square facing the desk should ideally have a combination of one-white and six-white. If this is not possible, then the desk can face a window, or a square with a neutral combination. Do not have the desk face combinations of two-black and three-jade or seven-red and six-white. These combinations predict competition, obstacles, and robbery through deceit. The ideal combination for the door to the study is one-white and six-white. Academic and business success are enhanced if the desk faces the door and the door's location has this combination.

Do not place the desk under an exposed beam. It means that the user at the desk will be "crushed" by failures in school and in business.

SPECIAL CONSIDERATIONS FOR COMMERCIAL SITES

In general, the principles that govern the location of a home office apply to a commercial site. Here are some guidelines for superimposing a geomantic chart onto a business suite. If a numerical combination is mentioned, it refers to the Earth Base and Facing Star with no specific designation of order.

The most important area of the business suite or shop is the front entrance. The most favorable combinations for the entrance to your unit are six-white and eight-white, one-white and six-white, and six-white and eight-white. These are stars of wealth, prosperity, and fortune. The worst combination is two-black and three-jade. It forebodes disharmony between business partners, between employer and employees, and among employees. A combination of seven-red and six-white means loss of income through deceit and robbery. A combination of three-jade and seven-red means that the business will have many legal hassles. A combination of five-yellow and five-yellow or two-black and five-yellow means that those working in the site will have health problems connected with the building. If these combinations are accompanied by nine-purple as the Mountain Star, then the health problems may become fatal.

Within the site, the next most important area is the office of the highest-level executive working there. In the macrocosm of the site, this room is best located in the square with a combination of six-white and eight-white. Next preference is any combination of one-white, four-green, six-white, and eight-white. Within the microcosm of the office itself, the placement of the desk follows the same principles as the placement of the desk in the home office. If the commercial site is a retail shop,

then the location of the cash register follows the same guidelines as the location of the executive's desk.

The conference room is the next area that requires consideration. Usually, this is the room where business deals and decisions are made. Within the macrocosm of the suite, the best combination for this room is six-white and eight-white. It predicts successful business ventures and good decisions. The worst combination is two-black and three-jade. It forebodes quarrels among the decision makers and inability to come to agreement. A combination of seven-red and six-white means bad decisions leading to loss of business income and possible bankruptcy.

Finally, for a business suite, the reception area is also important, because this is where the visitors are met. Many business connections are forged by the first impression of the company made at the reception area. Make sure that the combinations two-black and three-yellow, and seven-red and six-white, are not present. Two-black combined with three-yellow forebodes failure to make a good impression on potential customers or clientele. The combination of seven-red and six-white means a risk of revealing company and trade secrets in casual conversations.

CHOOSING A GEOMANTIC CHART

How would you choose a house or business site with the best geomantic chart? Surely, you cannot have auspicious stars in all the Nine Palaces. Because there are three sets of nine numbers in each square of the geomantic chart, and their combinations are restrained by the cycle in which the house is built, the range of your choices is not that wide. The following is a set of rules of thumb that I use

for myself and when I advise others.

The most important consideration for any occupants of a building is health. If the inhabitants are ill or meet with accidents frequently, then no matter how much wealth you have, you cannot enjoy it. Therefore, my first priority is to select a geomantic chart that has no fatal combinations in any square of the Nine Palaces.

My next consideration is to make sure that the front door, or the most frequently used door, does not have combinations of five-yellow, two-black, and nine-purple. I also do not like to have combinations of stars that forebode fire at the front door. If you travel frequently, then you need to look at the stars at the position of the stairs, to make sure that no malevolent combinations are there.

My next step is to examine the bedrooms, making sure that again the combinations of five-yellow and two-black and nine-purple do not constitute the Earth Base and the Facing Star. After that, I check the kitchen, to ensure that the combinations of stars associated with illness and fire do not occupy that area of the house.

I would then look at the family room. Again, I want no combinations of stars that forebode illness, death, accidents, and quarrels. If the stars in the family room are not favorable, and if you are left with no other alternatives, then I would suggest that you use the kitchen area for family activities and frequent the "family room" less. (See chapter 18 for ways of dealing with aversive circumstances.)

Next, I would examine the stars for the study. Again, if they are not ideal, you can easily do homework or home accounting at the kitchen table or dining room table, or even place a desk in the bedroom. I do not advise people to maximize the stars for the home office to obtain business success at the expense of the health of the family. I have seen too many people do that and end up losing family members through illness, accidents, quarrels, and divorces.

Then I would look at the living room. If the stars are not favorable, I would advise people to use that room less. You can always meet business partners in the study or even the family room, if need be.

Finally, I would examine the utility room and the bathrooms, just to make sure that there are no combinations of fatal stars.

When I am evaluating the geomantic chart for the feng-shui of a business, again my priority is health and harmony for the people who work in the building. Of course, for businesses, the next priority is success in business ventures. Thus, I would examine the location of the executive's office, the conference room, and the reception area. Make sure that there are no stars of business failures, disharmony, deceit, and legal hassles in these areas.

This concludes the discussion of superimposing the geomantic chart onto a floor plan. At this point in a feng-shui reading, you will have gotten a general feel for the energy flowing in the Nine Palaces in a site. However, fitting the geomantic chart onto a floor plan only tells you that something is likely to happen or not likely to happen while you live there or do business at the site. It does not tell you when the events will occur. To get this kind of information, we need to look at the flow of energy that changes with the years and months, and this is what we shall turn to in the next chapter.

16

The Influence
of the Yearly and Monthly Cycles

Movement of energy through the universe changes with the year and the months. In this chapter, you will learn how these changes in the movement of energy can affect a dwelling and its inhabitants.

When evaluating the general feng-shui of a place, the stars in the Nine Palaces of the geomantic chart carry the greatest weight in determining the fortunes of the occupants of the building. Next in importance is the influence of the yearly cycle, and then the monthly cycle. Some feng-shui practitioners routinely calculate the daily and hourly cycles as well, but personally, I think that such detail need only be heeded for very special circumstances

such as lowering a casket, cutting the ribbon in an opening ceremony, moving into a house, pouring the foundations of a building (or setting up the cornerstone), dedicating a temple, and ordaining clergy. If you read Chinese, you can find the auspicious days and hours for these events by consulting the Chinese almanac (the *tung-shu*). Toward the end of the almanac there is a section that resembles a calendar. Here the days and hours are noted as to whether they are auspicious for the above events. If you do not read Chinese and you need this information, I would suggest that you ask a professional feng-shui practitioner for help.

THE YEARLY INFLUENCE

Each year has a Ruling Star. The Ruling Star of the year is the star (or number) that occupies the center of the Nine Palaces for that year. Most people work out the yearly influence just before the current year's end so that they can make plans for the placement of countermeasures and enhancers for the next year. (See chapter 18 for a discussion of the placement of these artifacts.) The Ruling Star of the year comes in effect on the first day of the Lunar New Year or the day of the Coming of Spring, whichever is first. You can find these days by looking at a Chinese calendar or by asking a proprietor of a Chinese restaurant or grocery store.

Again, if you read Chinese, the best way to find the Ruling Star of the year is through the tung-shu, the Chinese almanac. Look for the picture of the plowboy and the water buffalo toward the front of the almanac. Immediately following this page you should see an eight-sided boxlike figure. In the center of the octagon are Chinese characters that identify the Ruling Star of the year. The almanac also tells you the Ruling Star of the following year. This information is usually found on the last page of the almanac.

If you do not read Chinese, you will have to figure out the Ruling Star of the year yourself. The procedures for doing this and for figuring out the influence of the yearly movement of energy are very simple. Here are the steps.

1. First, you need to know the Era (Upper, Middle, or Lower) the current year is in. Recall from chapter 6 that the sixty years of the Sexagenary Cycle make up an Era. The Lower Era started in 1984. The sixty years that started with 1984 therefore belong to the Lower Era. Thus, the years between 1996 and 2043 are all in the Lower Era. The Upper Era begins again with 2044.

2. Second, find out the Ruling Star for the year you wish to work out its influence. The table in figure 16.1 gives you the Ruling Stars for the years in the Lower Era. Now set up the Nine Palaces for the year by placing the Ruling Star in the center square. For example, from the table, you see that the Ruling Star for 1996 is four-green. Following the pattern of the clockwise movement of the numbers of the Nine Palaces, place five-yellow in the lower right-hand corner, and so on, giving you the configuration shown in figure 16.2. This is the Nine Palaces of the yearly stars for 1996, with the Ruling Star, four-green, in the center.

3. Third, superimpose the Nine Palaces of the year onto the Nine Palaces of the geomantic chart of the house. An example is shown in figure 16.3. Make sure that the two Nine Palaces grids are oriented in the same direction, especially when the Facing Palace is located in a corner square.

4. Now you are ready to find out the influence of the yearly cycle of stars in the Nine Palaces on the house. Examine the interaction of the yearly star with the Earth Base Star and the Facing Star in each of the nine squares. This will give you the yearly projection of events that may happen in each area of the

Fig. 16.1 (opposite) Table showing the ruling star of the year and the ruling star for the first lunar month of that year for the Chinese and Western calendars. For example, the ruling star of 1990 is one-white, and the ruling star of the first lunar month of that year is eight-white. To get the ruling star of successive months, simply count down from the number of the ruling star of the first lunar month, in the second column at the left. In this example, the ruling star of the second lunar month is therefore seven-red.

Ruling Star of the Year	Ruling Star of First Lunar Month	Years in Chinese and Western Systems
one-white	eight-white	keng-wu (1990), chi-mao (1999), wu-tzu (2008), ting-yu (2017), ping-wu (2226), i-mao (2235)
nine-purple	five-yellow	hsin-wei (1991), keng-ch'en (2000), chi-ch'ou (2009), wu-hsü (2018), ting-wei (2227), ping-ch'en (2236)
eight-white	two-black	jen-shen (1992), hsin-ssu (2001), keng-yin (2010), chi-hai (2019), wu-shen (2228), ting-ssu (2237)
seven-red	eight-white	chia-tzu (1984), kuei-yu (1993), jen-wu (2002), hsin-mao (2011), keng-tzu (2220), chi-yu (2229), wu-wu (2238)
six-white	five-yellow	i-ch'ou (1985), chia-hsü (1994), kuei-wei (2003), jen-ch'en (2012), hsin-ch'ou (2221), keng-hsü (2230), chi-wei (2239)
five-yellow	two-black	ping-yin (1986), i-hai (1995), chia-shen (2004), kuei-ssu (2013), jen-yin (2222), hsin-hai (2231), keng-shen (2240)
four-green	eight-white	ting-mao (1987), ping-tzu (1996), i-yu (2005), chia-wu (2014), kuei-mao (2223), jen-tzu (2232), hsin-yu (2241)
three-jade	five-yellow	wu-ch'en (1988), ting-ch'ou (1997), ping-hsü (2006), i-wei (2015), chia-ch'en (2224), kuei-ch'ou (2233), jen-hsü (2242)
two-black	two-black	chi-ssu (1989), wu-yin (1998), ting-hai (2007), ping-shen (2016), i-ssu (2225), chia-yin (2234), kuei-hai (2243)

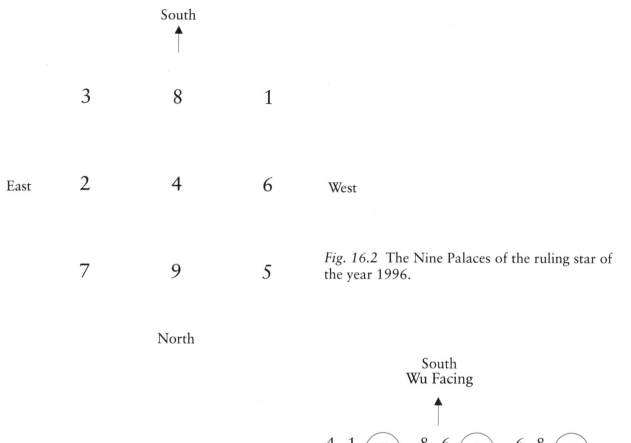

South

3	8	1

East   2   4   6   West

7   9   5

North

Fig. 16.2 The Nine Palaces of the ruling star of the year 1996.

South
Wu Facing

$4\ 1$ (7) $8\ 6$ (3) $6\ 8$ (5)
6 2 4
bedroom   living room   bedroom

M F

$5\ 9$ (6) $3\ 2$ (8) $1\ 4$ (1)
5 7 9
bathroom   living room   study
and
storeroom

$9\ 5$ (2) $7\ 7$ (4) $2\ 3$ (9)
1 3 8
atrium   dining room   kitchen

East   West

Tzu Mountain
North

Fig. 16.3 The Nine Palaces of the ruling star of the year 1996 superimposed onto a geomantic chart for a house. The yearly stars are circled.

house. The interactions are interpreted using the information contained in the sections that evaluate the influence of the stars of the geomantic chart on each room of the house. You can find them in chapter 15, starting on page 207. For example, when a bedroom with two-black as the Earth Base is "visited" by the yearly star five-yellow, the interaction is interpreted as a two-black / five-yellow combination, meaning that persons sleeping in that room are likely to be ill that year.

THE MONTHLY INFLUENCE

Each lunar month also has a Ruling Star. Again, the Ruling Star of the month occupies the center square of the Nine Palaces for the month.

The procedure for evaluating the monthly influence of the stars of the Nine Palace for a site is also very simple.

1. First, using the table in figure 16.1, find out the Ruling Star for the first lunar month of the year. For example, in the year 1996, the Ruling Star of the first month is eight-white. Eight-white will therefore be the number in the center of the Nine Palaces for the first lunar month. (Again, note that the Ruling Star of the first month of the lunar year comes in effect on the first lunar day or the day of the Coming of Spring. For the rest of the year, the Ruling Star for the month is effective on the first lunar day of that month.) Now, following the clockwise sequence of the movement of numbers in the Nine Palaces, fill in the rest of the nine squares by placing nine-purple in the lower right-hand corner, and so on.

2. Second, figure out the stars of the Nine Palaces for the rest of the twelve months in the following way. The Ruling Stars for the subsequent months are determined by counting backward from the number of the Ruling Star of the first lunar month. If eight-white is the Ruling Star of the first month, then seven-red is the Ruling Star of the second month, six-white is the Ruling Star of the third month, and so on. These stars will occupy the center square of the subsequent months respectively. Panel A of figure 16.4 shows you the arrangement of the stars of the Nine Palaces for the first four lunar months of the year in 1996. Note that the order of the numbers in the Nine Palaces for these months follows a forward sequence.

After the summer solstice, the placement of the numbers in the Nine Palaces of each month follows a reverse order. For example, if summer solstice falls on the fifth lunar month, and if the Ruling Star of that month is four-green, then three-jade goes into the lower right-hand corner for the Nine Palaces of the fifth month. This ordering applies to all months after the summer solstice, until the beginning of the next year. Panel B of figure 16.4 shows the arrangement of the stars of the Nine Palaces for four months after the summer solstice for 1996.

3. Third, superimpose each month's Nine Palaces onto the geomantic chart of the house.

4. Now you are ready to find out the influence of the stars of each month. Look at the interactions between the monthly stars in the Nine Palaces and the Earth Base and the Facing Star for each area of the house. Again, the interactions are interpreted using the information from the sections on evaluating the

South ↑

4 7 6 5	9 3 2 1	2 5 4 3
3 6 5 4	5 8 7 6	7 1 9 8
8 2 1 9	1 4 3 2	6 9 8 7

A

South ↑

8 5 6 7	3 9 1 2	1 7 8 9
9 6 7 8	7 4 5 6	5 2 3 4
4 1 2 3	2 8 9 1	6 3 4 5

B

influence of the stars of the geomantic chart on each room. This information is found in chapter 15, starting on page 207. For example, if the Facing Star for the kitchen is nine-purple, and the month's "visiting" star is seven-red, then there is a risk of fire in the kitchen in that month.

With the conclusion of this chapter, you have learned the part of feng-shui that is typically covered in the traditional Landscape School and the Compass School of the geomantic arts. The next three chapters—"Matching the Occupants to the Dwelling," "Setting Up Countermeasures and Enhancers," and "Sweeping the Karma of the Building"—deal with information and techniques that have developed in more recent times. In traditional China, the principles of feng-shui have evolved along the lines of avoiding sha-ch'i, or destructive energy, and taking advantage of benevolent energy. In a place and time where land was plentiful and ordinances regulating land use were almost nonexistent, there were not many constrictions in choosing a place to live or bury the dead. However, in our times we do not have such luxury of choices. Feng-shui in modern times therefore needed to develop techniques that deal with what happens when you have no choice.

These newer techniques reflect a more active approach to feng-shui. They suggest that human intervention, if done properly, can work with the forces of nature to create or improve environments for harmonious living. It is these techniques that we will turn to in the next three chapters.

Fig. 16.4 The Nine Palaces of the monthly ruling stars. (A) The numbers follow a forward sequence before the summer solstice. (B) The numbers follow a reverse sequence after the summer solstice.

17

Matching the Occupants to the Dwelling

*I*n the Taoist universe, all things emerge from the primordial energy of the Tao. Through division and differentiation, things acquire their individuality and identity, but underneath their transient nature, all things share an underlying structure. Just as life in nature is sustained by shade and light, yin and yang, our own existence is maintained by exhalation and inhalation, the cyclical movement of yin and yang, in our bodies. Just as five elements—metal, wood, water, fire, and earth—are present in nature, these elements are a part of us.

In the Chinese divination arts, it is said that each of us is born under the guardianship of one of the five elements. When our guardian element is nourished, we will enjoy good health and good fortune. When our guardian element is weak, our health and fortune will be poor. When our guardian element is destroyed, we also will be destroyed by illness and misfortune. It follows that the conditions that benefit our guardian element will also benefit us, and conditions that are destructive to our guardian element will also be destructive to us.

The year of our birth determines which element is our guardian element. The simplest way to get this information is through a table. For persons born in the Upper Era (1864 through 1923), use the table in figure 17.1; for persons born in the Middle Era (1924 through 1983), use the table in figure 17.2; for persons born in the Lower Era (1984 through 2043), use the table in figure 17.3.

You will notice in the tables that each element is paired with a star of the Nine Palaces. In fact, it is the sequencing of numbers of the Nine Palaces through the Sexagenary Cycle that provides the match between an individual's birthday and an element. Recall from chapter 8 that each star of the Nine Palaces is associated with an element. Therefore, we are each born under the guardianship of both a

UPPER ERA (1864 through 1923)

Star	Element	Male	Female
one-white	water	1864, 1873, 1882, 1891 1900, 1909, 1918	1869, 1878, 1887, 1896 1905, 1914, 1923
nine-purple	fire	1865, 1874, 1883, 1892 1901, 1910, 1919	1868, 1877, 1886, 1895 1904, 1913, 1922
eight-white	earth	1866, 1875, 1884, 1893 1902, 1911, 1920	1867, 1876, 1885, 1894 1903, 1912, 1921
seven-red	metal	1867, 1876, 1885, 1894 1903, 1912, 1921	1866, 1875, 1884, 1893 1902, 1911, 1920
six-white	metal	1868, 1877, 1886, 1895 1904, 1913, 1922	1865, 1874, 1883, 1892 1901, 1910, 1919
five-yellow	earth	1869, 1878, 1887, 1896 1905, 1914, 1923	1864, 1873, 1882, 1891 1900, 1909, 1918
four-green	wood	1870, 1879, 1886, 1847 1906, 1915	1872, 1881, 1890, 1899 1908, 1917
three-jade	wood	1871, 1880, 1889, 1898 1907, 1916	1871, 1880, 1889, 1898 1907, 1916
two-black	earth	1872, 1881, 1890, 1899 1908, 1917	1877, 1879, 1888, 1897 1906, 1915

Fig. 17.1 Guardian stars and elements for males and females born in the Upper Era.

Palace star and an element. The next thing that you will notice in the tables is that the element earth is associated with three Palace stars, and metal and wood have two Palace stars each. There is only one star for water and for fire.

Where there is more than one star to an element, the quality of the elements is different for each star. Earth in five-yellow is explosive and volatile. In two-black it is stable, and in eight-white it is malleable. In their order of strengths, five-yellow is strongest, followed by two-black and eight-white. Metal in six-white is soft, and metal in seven-red is hardened. Therefore, seven-red is a stronger metal than six-white. Wood in four-green is soft, like the leaves of a tree, and wood in three-jade is hard, like the trunk and roots of a tree. Three-jade is therefore a stronger wood than four-green.

The nourishing, destructive, and weakening effects that the elements have on one another form the basis of matching the occupants to a dwelling. Therefore, in learning

MIDDLE ERA (1924 through 1983)

Star	Element	Male	Female
one-white	water	1927, 1936, 1945, 1954 1963, 1972, 1981	1932, 1941, 1950, 1959 1968, 1977
nine-purple	fire	1928, 1937, 1946, 1955 1964, 1973, 1982	1931, 1940, 1949, 1958 1967, 1976
eight-white	earth	1929, 1938, 1947, 1956 1965, 1974, 1983	1930, 1939, 1948, 1957 1966, 1975
seven-red	metal	1930, 1939, 1948, 1957 1966, 1975	1929, 1938, 1947, 1956 1965, 1974, 1983
six-white	metal	1931, 1940, 1949, 1958 1967, 1976	1928, 1937, 1946, 1955 1964, 1973, 1982
five-yellow	earth	1932, 1941, 1950, 1959 1968, 1977	1927, 1936, 1945, 1954 1963, 1972, 1981
four-green	wood	1924, 1933, 1942, 1951 1960, 1969, 1978	1926, 1935, 1944, 1953 1962, 1971, 1980
three-jade	wood	1925, 1934, 1943, 1952 1961, 1970, 1979	1925, 1934, 1943, 1952 1961, 1970, 1979
two-black	earth	1926, 1935, 1944, 1953 1962, 1971, 1980	1924, 1933, 1942, 1951 1960, 1969, 1978

Fig. 17.2 Guardian stars and elements for males and females born in the Middle Era.

how to match individuals to a dwelling, you need to be familiar with the relationship of the five elements in their nourishing and destructive cycles.

In the nourishing cycle, metal strengthens water, water strengthens wood, wood feeds fire, fire feeds earth, and earth nourishes metal. In the destructive cycle, metal cuts wood, wood dominates earth, earth obstructs water, water quenches fire, and fire melts metal. The elements can also weaken each other by drawing energy from another ele-

ment. In the nourishing cycle, the element providing the nourishment is weakened because its energy is absorbed by the recipient. In the destructive cycle, the element destroying another element is weakened, because energy is used in the act of destruction. Thus, when metal nourishes water, water takes energy from metal and weakens it. Similarly, water is weakened by wood, and so on. For your convenience, a summary of these relationships is shown in figure 17.4.

Some stars (and their elements) are by na-

LOWER ERA (1984 through 2043)

Star	Element	Male	Female
one-white	water	1990, 1999, 2008, 2017 2026, 2035	1986, 1995, 2004, 2013 2022, 2031, 2040
nine-purple	fire	1991, 2000, 2009, 2018 2027, 2036	1985, 1994, 2003, 2012 2021, 2030, 2039
eight-white	earth	1992, 2001, 2010, 2019 2028, 2037	1984, 1993, 2002, 2011 2020, 2029, 2038
seven-red	metal	1984, 1993, 2002, 2011 2020, 2029, 2038	1992, 2001, 2010, 2019 2028, 2037
six-white	metal	1985, 1994, 2003, 2012 2021, 2030, 2039	1991, 2000, 2009, 2018 2027, 2036
five-yellow	earth	1986, 1995, 2004, 2013 2022, 2031, 2040	1990, 1999, 2008, 2017 2026, 2035
four-green	wood	1987, 1996, 2005, 2014 2023, 2032, 2041	1989, 1998, 2007, 2016 2025, 2034, 2043
three-jade	wood	1988, 1997, 2006, 2015 2024, 2033, 2042	1988, 1997, 2006, 2015 2024, 2033, 2042
two-black	earth	1989, 1998, 2007, 2016 2025, 2034, 2043	1987, 1996, 2005, 2014 2023, 2032, 2041

Fig. 17.3 Guardian stars and elements for males and females born in the Lower Era.

ture stronger than others. A strong element can better withstand destruction and weakening, and will benefit more from strengthening effects. The strong stars (and their elements) are two-black (earth), five-yellow (earth), and nine-purple (fire). The moderate stars are three-jade (wood), four-green (wood), and seven-red (metal). The weakest stars are one-white (water), six-white (metal), and eight-white (earth). The strengths of the stars and their elements are important considerations when we design countermeasures and en-

hancers in the next chapter.

We are now ready to look at how occupants are matched to a dwelling. We are going to use an example to illustrate the procedure.

First, find out the elements and birth stars of the occupants. You can do this by referring to the tables in figures 17.1, 17.2, and 17.3. For example, in a family of four, the birth star and element for the husband is one-white (water), for the wife it is five-yellow (earth), for a male child it is seven-red (metal), and for a maternal grandparent it is nine-purple (fire).

RECIPIENT ELEMENT

Acting Element	Metal	Wood	Water	Fire	Earth
metal	NE	WD	WN	D	N
wood	D	NE	N	WN	WD
water	N	WN	NE	WD	D
fire	WD	N	D	NE	WN
earth	WN	D	WD	N	NE

Fig. 17.4 Relationships among the five elements. N = nourishing. D = destructive. WN = weaken by nourishing. WD = weaken by destroying. NE = no effect.

Next, examine the interaction between the element of the head(s) of the family and the Earth Base number in the Palace where the front door is located. This interaction tells you how effective the head of the family will be in providing support for the family. The head of the family is the person who earns the income to support the entire family. In our example, let us say that both the husband and the wife provide equal support. Figure 17.5 shows the geomantic chart for this family's home. The Earth Base number at the front door is two-black and its element is earth. Now figure out whether the two individuals' guardian elements are helped, hindered, or unaffected by this Earth Base star. In our example, the element of the male head of family is water (one-white). The relationship between earth and water is one of destruction (refer to fig. 17.4). Therefore, the male head of family will meet with obstacles in employ-

ment and will not be an effective breadwinner. The element of the female head of family is earth (five-yellow). The relationship between her element and the element of the Earth Base star at the front door is neutral. Therefore, her career may not have obstacles, but it will not be extremely prosperous.

Now we shall look at which are the best bedrooms for each individual in the family. In

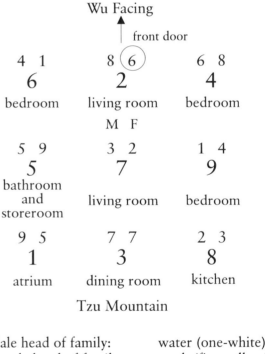

Fig. 17.5 Geomantic chart of the example used in the text. The guardian stars and elements of the occupants of the house in the example are also shown.

our example, figure 17.5 shows three bed-rooms, with six-white, four-green, and nine-purple as Earth Base stars. The elements for the husband and wife are water (one-white) and earth (five-yellow) respectively. Let us examine the bedroom with four-green (wood) as the Earth Base. Wood dominates earth, so the room is not good for the wife. Water is weakened to nourish wood, so this room is not suitable for the husband either. In the room with six-white (metal) as the Earth Base, the husband's element will be nourished and the wife's element will be weakened because it is used to nourish metal. Now consider the bedroom where nine-purple (fire) is the Earth Base. Fire nourishes earth, so this room is good for the wife but is bad for the husband, because water loses energy when it is used to quench fire. However, because five-yellow (earth) by nature is stronger than one-white (water), the woman's guardian element will not be weakened by nourishing the metal of six-white as the man's guardian element would be in quenching the fire of nine-purple. Therefore, the bedroom with six-white as the Earth Base is the best choice for the couple.

Now let us see which bedroom is best for the child. The guardian star and element for the child is seven-red (metal). The room with nine-purple as the Earth Base is clearly not suitable, since the fire of nine-purple will destroy the metal of seven-red. The room with six-white is neutral because both six-white and seven-red are metal. The room with four-green as the Earth Base star is at first glance not very suitable for the child because metal is weakened when it destroys wood. In this situation, I would put the child with the parents if he is young. When the child is older, he can use the room with the four-green in the Earth Base if countermeasures are set up to neutralize or weaken the four-green. Since four-green (wood) is only moderate in strength, its effect can easily be countered with placement of artifacts (see the next chapter).

Finally, in the example, the guardian element of the maternal grandparent is fire (nine-purple). The room with six-white (metal) as the Earth Base will not be suitable since fire is weakened in destroying metal. The room with four-green as the Earth Base is excellent for her because wood nourishes fire. The room with nine-purple as the Earth Base is neutral toward her. Since the nine-purple room is harmful for everybody else and is neutral to her, this is the most suitable room for her. Another alternative is to let her have the four-green room when the child is young, and then move to the nine-purple room when the boy is old enough to have a room for himself.

As you go through the procedure of matching the occupants to a house, you will notice that in the example, the effects of the Earth Base stars on all the occupants are considered before a final decision is made. The situation in this example is not uncommon. It is a rare case when all the occupants can find a bedroom with an Earth Base star that nourishes their element. Sometimes, when none of the rooms are suitable, it will be up to the feng-shui practitioner to figure out how to use countermeasures and enhancers to make the rooms suitable for habitation.

18

Setting Up Countermeasures and Enhancers

*I*deal feng-shui conditions are rare, and most of the time we have to live with what we can get or improve on what we have. The art and science of setting up countermeasures to deal with aversive conditions and installing enhancers to improve on existing conditions have become a very important part of a modern feng-shui practitioner's knowledge. Nowadays it is almost impossible not to use countermeasures and enhancers when working with the feng-shui of a building. Even if you have optimal positions in the Nine Palaces in the geomantic chart, the stars of the yearly and monthly cycles change, and you may have to use countermeasures to lessen the impact of destructive effects and enhancers to bolster beneficial influences.

COUNTERMEASURES

Countermeasures deal with aversive conditions. They are designed to help us avoid, dissolve, weaken, or remove destructive energy. Countermeasures can be used to work with the external environment, internal environment, the stars of the Nine Palaces of the geomantic chart, the cyclical change of energy in the years and months, and the guardian elements of the occupants.

Countermeasures That Deal with the External Environment

PROTECTION

You will recall from chapter 11 that protection is a very important factor in the feng-shui of a place. If there is no existing protection from natural landforms or human-made structures, you will have to build your own.

For protection at the back, a row of trees can be an effective Black Tortoise. If planting trees is not feasible, a fence or a wall with vines or ivy crawling on it can serve the purpose. Bushes, preferably evergreen, will make an effective Green Dragon, and a white stone wall can be a viable White Tiger. If you need to build a Red Raven structure for protection in the front, a low red-brick wall or a low redwood fence are good choices.

HARMFUL STRUCTURES AND OBJECTS

You will also recall from chapter 11 that it is not desirable to have harmful structures and objects near your building, especially if they are directed at your house. Harmful structures and objects include:

- Harsh and sharp objects (natural or human-made). These include large structures such as rocky escarpments, knife-edge rock slabs, buildings with irregular and sharp edges, and smaller objects such as tree branches, antennas, sculpture, and power transformers. Included also are objects that cut horizontally, like wires and clotheslines. Objects of destruction or their images are also in this category. These include guns, cannons, and jet fighters.
- Precarious, falling, or colliding objects. These include large boulders balanced precariously, a slope with loose gravel, and a road or driveway pointing at your house.
- Reflecting objects. These include satellite dishes and all objects and structures with shiny surfaces.

Harsh and Sharp Structures and Objects. You can protect a building and its inhabitants from the destructive effects of these types of

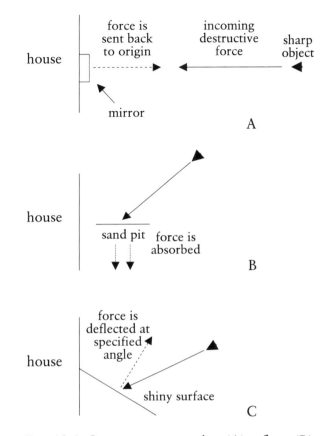

Fig. 18.1 Countermeasures that (A) reflect, (B) absorb, and (C) deflect.

structures and objects by placing artifacts that will reflect, absorb, deflect, bounce, block, or destroy in strategic places (see figs. 18.1–18.2). Typically, the larger the structure that you are countering, the larger should be the countermeasure artifacts. Size and quantity are interchangeable; if it is not viable to install a large artifact, you can set up several smaller ones.

REFLECTORS. A countermeasure that reflects will send the destructive effect back at the pointing object, thus preventing it from entering your house. For example, if you find

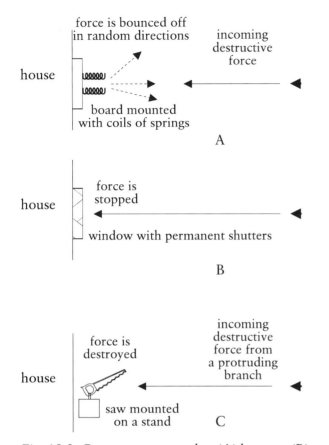

Fig. 18.2 Countermeasures that (A) bounce, (B) block, and (C) destroy.

that sharp points of a TV antenna are pointing at your bedroom, you can use a mirror to counter its harmful effects. When you place a reflector, make sure that the object or structure that you want to ward off is fully imaged on the reflector. Thus, while you can reflect small objects with a small mirror, you may need a large mirror to reflect a large structure. Mirrors, glass, a large piece of foil or an aluminum surface, and a basin of water can function as reflectors. In other words, anything that produces a reflection visually will work as a reflective countermeasure. Reflectors are the most commonly used artifacts to counter

sharp and harsh objects that point at a building.

ABSORBERS. A countermeasure that absorbs will "eat up" the destructive effect of the pointing object and prevent it from spreading. An absorbing object or structure "attracts" the destructive effect of the pointed object to it so that its harm cannot be directed to anything else. It is like pushing a needle into a pincushion, or absorbing the impact of a stone with a bed of cotton wool. Examples of absorption-type countermeasures are a sand pit or sandbox and a large pile of cedar chips. For the absorber to work, it must be placed in the angle at which the sharp structure or object is pointing. Therefore, the absorption-type of countermeasure is typically used when the harmful object is higher than the house. For example, a sand pit can be placed in the backyard of a house to counter the effect of a transmission antenna that is pointing down from a hilltop.

DEFLECTORS. A countermeasure that deflects will redirect the path of the destructive energy so that it avoids your house or room. A system of reflective surfaces can be used as a deflector if their angles are adjusted so that the reflection is directed at another place rather than the source of the incoming destructive energy. Deflectors are tricky to set up, and it is recommended that novice feng-shui practitioners not do this. An error in the placement of the deflecting structures could send destructive energy to a neighboring house.

BOUNCERS. A countermeasure that bounces the effect of a harmful structure will send the forces away from the building to a random location. This kind of countermeasure should only be used if there are no neighboring buildings or structures that can be harmed. I have used objects such as coils of springs, and even an effigy of a baseball player with a bat.

BLOCKERS. A countermeasure that blocks will prevent the effect of the harmful forces from entering a building by stopping it. This countermeasure works like a closed door. In fact, a boarded-up window or a window with permanent shutters is the most common kind of blocking-type countermeasure.

DESTRUCTORS. A countermeasure that destroys the incoming harmful energy is an object that can overcome that force. Typically, the countermeasure is an object of destruction itself. Moreover, for the countermeasure to work, it must be stronger than the structure it is designed to destroy. For example, if the harmful object is a protruding branch pointing at your house, the countering object might be a saw. If it is from a sculpture with pointed arrows, then it might be a gun.

Precarious, Falling, or Colliding Objects. Against objects such as large boulders that overlook your building, slopes with loose rocks, driveways or roads that point at your house, and traffic movement that is directed at your house, the best countermeasures are reflectors, deflectors, bouncers, and blockers. Reflectors are especially effective against driveways, roads, and moving traffic. See the above sections on how to place these countermeasures.

Reflecting Objects. The optimal countermeasure against shiny objects directed at your house is a larger reflecting object, a system of deflectors, or a blocker. Do not use bouncers or destructors, as your countermeasure will be reflected back to you. Absorbers simply do not work against reflecting objects. Again, see the above sections on how to place the countermeasures.

Countermeasures That Deal with the Internal Environment

The internal environment includes the floor plan, the interior structures, and the interaction between the geomantic chart and these factors.

FLOOR PLAN

When the geomantic chart is superimposed onto a floor plan and is found untenable, the position of the Nine Palaces in the rooms can be altered by "stretching" the geomantic chart. For example, figure 18.3 shows how an undesirable situation for the living room can be rescued by stretching the geomantic chart and putting in some artifacts. In panel A you can see that the combination of nine-purple in the Earth Base with seven-red as the Facing Star forebodes fire. This hazard is heightened because in the microcosm of the living room, the fireplace is located in this position. Panel B shows a possible solution to the problem. An atrium or covered garden is added to the side of the house, thus stretching the geomantic chart when it is superimposed on the new floor plan. The fireplace is removed and a door is put in its place, opening into the covered garden. In the new location of the nine-purple / seven-red combination (in both the macrocosms of the house and the microcosms of the atrium), a fountain is installed. The presence of water neutralizes the threat of fire from the combination of the stars of the Nine Palaces in that area.

Another way of stretching the geomantic chart to avoid having undesirable stars in cer-

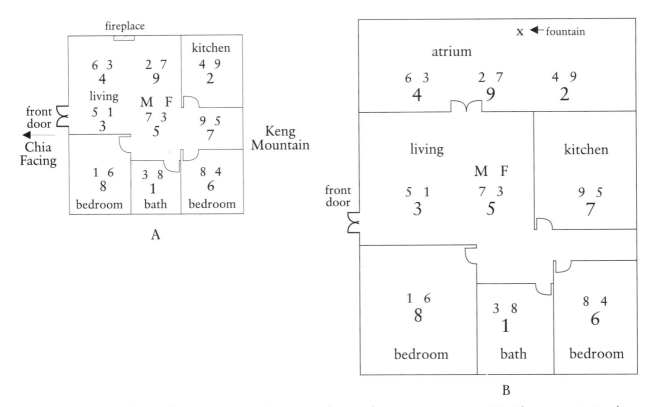

Fig. 18.3 Stretching the geomantic chart as a form of countermeasure. (A) The geomantic chart superimposed onto the original floor plan. (B) By adding an atrium to the side of the house, the geomantic chart is stretched in the new floor plan.

tain areas of the house is to remove some parts of the house so that the squares with the malevolent stars fall outside the building.

Yet another way to deal with a problematic floor plan and its geomantic chart is to change the partitions of the rooms, or change the location of the front entrance. If the renovations occur in a different cycle than when the house was built, then a new and possibly more favorable geomantic chart can be drawn up for the renovated house.

INTERIOR STRUCTURES

Interior structures that require countermeasures are fireplaces, woodstoves, cooking stoves, and ovens. These are objects of fire that, if not neutralized, may increase the strength of this element in the building and add to the fire hazard. The countermeasure for objects associated with fire is water. They can be the physical presence of water, as in a fountain, a water tank, or a humidifier, or they can be a picture of water images such as waterfalls and waves. Pictures of stagnant or still water will not work. The countermeasure artifact should be placed close to the object of fire. Thus, you can hang a picture of a waterfall above the fireplace. If there is a sink in the same room as the oven and cooking stove, then the threat of fire is neutralized. However, if the oven and stove are located in an area where nine-purple is located, then the presence of water needs to be strengthened by placing a tank filled with water, or a picture of moving water, in that area.

Countermeasures That Deal with the Stars and Elements of the Nine Palaces

You will recall from chapter 9 that some stars of the Nine Palaces are malevolent and some are benevolent. Furthermore, in chapters 14, 15, and 16, you saw how the interaction of the stars of the Nine Palaces in the geomantic chart can affect the fortunes and health of the inhabitants of a house, depending on their positions in the building.

There are two ways to counter the harmful effects of malevolent stars: avoidance and intervention.

Avoidance is based on the principle that an effect on a location is heightened if there is movement in that area, and is lessened if there is no movement. Therefore, the best way to deal with malevolent stars or dangerous combinations of the Earth Base and Facing Stars is not to frequent the rooms where they are located. If an especially harmful combination, like five-yellow and two-black, is located in a room, see if you can arrange to have the room used as a storeroom. If a destructive combination occurs in your bedroom during a yearly or monthly cycle, you can avoid the room by temporarily moving into another room until the "visiting" malevolent star has left.

A destructive effect is minimized if you do not put moving objects in that place. Moving objects include fans, clocks, video-tape players, televisions, and computers. Stereo equipment is also considered a moving object since there is rotary movement in turntables, compact disk players, and tape players. In fact, anything that runs on electricity is a moving object. These moving objects should not be placed in areas where malevolent stars are present, unless the object is used as a countermeasure.

Intervention involves countering the malevolent stars by neutralizing the element associated with them. Using the knowledge of how the elements nourish, weaken, and destroy each other, it is possible to place objects or artifacts in strategic locations to counter the effects of malevolent stars. (See fig. 17.4 on page 227 for a review of the relationships among the five elements.) The artifacts are carriers of elemental energy, and can be used to lessen or even eliminate the harmful effects brought on by the star's element.

Feng-shui masters have figured out the best countermeasures for certain combinations that have specific harmful effects that need immediate attention. The following list gives artifacts that are commonly used by feng-shui practitioners to counter the effects of specific combinations of the stars of the Nine Palace.

- To counter the effect of a combination of five-yellow and two-black, the stars of illness, use a chiming clock or a set of metal wind chimes. These two items belong to the element metal. Their presence, sound, and movement will draw energy from the earth elements in five-yellow and two-black, thus weakening their strength.
- To counter the effect of a combination of seven-red and two-black, or of nine-purple and seven-red, the stars of fire and burning, place artifacts of water in the area of these stars. A fountain, a fish tank, or even a bowl of water can serve

the purpose. Alternatively, images of water, like pictures of a waterfall or waves on a beach, would also work.

- To counter the effect of a combination of two-black and three-jade, the stars of disharmony, use a strong light. A standing lamp or a spotlight mounted on the wall will suit the purpose. The strong light is a manifestation of the element fire, and the fire will draw energy from the wood of three-jade, thus weakening it.

- To counter the effect of a combination of seven-red and six-white, the stars of robbery and treachery, place six moving objects in a bowl of water in the area where the combination is located. Water drains energy from metal (both six-white and seven-red) because metal nourishes water. Therefore, water is the ideal element to counter a combination of seven-red and six-white. Since movement increases the strength of energy, having something that moves in the water will increase the strength of water to counter metal. The moving objects can be animate, like fish swimming in a tank, or mechanical objects. If you use fish, do not use colorful ones. Red-colored fish are especially inappropriate because red is associated with fire, and having fire in water will weaken the effectiveness of water. Dark-colored fish are preferred.

- If the combination of five-yellow and two-black is accompanied by nine-purple, place water artifacts in addition to the chiming clocks. Water counters the fire of nine-purple, while the metal of the chiming clocks will draw energy from the earth elements of five-yellow and two-black.

In addition to countering special combinations of stars that are especially harmful, there are times when you may want to weaken or remove the effects of an element associated with a certain star. The most likely situation is when a malevolent star of the Nine Palaces is in the location of certain rooms that will be harmful to you. Another condition is when a malevolent star of the Nine Palaces is "visiting" certain rooms in its yearly or monthly cycle.

The following is a set of guidelines in using the five elements to build effective countermeasures. Recall that an element can be neutralized by being destroyed by its antagonist, by being drained of energy by nourishing another element, or by being "used up" by having it destroy another element.

The first method, that of destruction, is based on countering force with force. The most effective way of removing an element is to use its antagonist to destroy it. However, this method is risky, because if the antagonist is not strong enough, it can be destroyed, and with it the element or the individual that it is designed to protect. Therefore, when you use this method, you will need to make sure that the antagonist element is bolstered. This method is most effective against a strong element like fire.

The second method is based on dissipating the energy of an element by channeling its usage to nourish another element. This is the safest way of countering an element, because it does not use force against force. It tames the destructive energy by directing it toward a creative or nourishing activity. This method is more effective against malleable elements such as water, earth, wood, and metal.

The third method is based on directing an element toward destroying another element, so that its energy is used up in the process.

This is not as safe as channeling the element's energy toward nourishing another element, but it is safer than the method of destruction. Rather than fighting force with force, we are providing a condition where the element's energy can be vented at another element, thereby dissipating its force. This method is not very effective against fire, but it is effective against water, earth, wood, and earth.

The following is a set of guidelines of how to use the five elements to counter each other.

FIRE

Fire is dominated by water. It is drained when it is used to nourish earth, and it is dissolved when it is used to destroy metal. Fire is a very strong element, and is best countered by a strong antagonist, such as water. To counter the threat coming from the fire element (nine-purple), place artifacts that are carriers of the element water in that location. These include pictures of moving water, objects of the color blue and green, and of course, the physical presence of water itself. For example, when nine-purple is a "visiting" yearly or monthly star in a position where the Earth Base and Facing Stars cannot neutralize its influence, you can place a blue or green spread or cushions on a couch in that area. Make sure you do not have red objects where nine-purple is located. These include drapes, curtains, Venetian blinds, couch covers, cushions, vases, and so on. Finally, if possible, try not to use that area.

You can also counter fire by having it nourish earth. Here, you need to place artifacts of earth, such as ceramics, in the area of nine-purple. However, fire is a strong element, and its strength will not be drained easily by giving it something to nourish. If you also place a metal object there to weaken fire by letting it expend energy in destroying it, there is better chance for neutralizing its destructive effect. Normally, I use water against fire, along with either metal or earth as a supplement.

EARTH

Earth is destroyed by wood. It is drained when it is used to nourish metal, and it is dissolved when it is used to destroy water.

To counter the threat of earth, you can use metal to dissipate its strength. Place a clock or a metal wind chime in the areas where you want to neutralize the effect of earth. The effectiveness of these artifacts is increased if they move. Thus, if the chimes are blown by wind, or the clock has a swinging pendulum, their strength is enhanced.

You can also counter earth with its antagonist, wood. Plants, especially small trees, are good carriers of wood energy and can be effective against earth. Carved wooden objects will also work, but living plants are preferred because growth is a form of movement, and movement enhances the strength of the artifact.

Yet another way to counter earth is to have its strength drained by giving it an object to destroy. Since water is the antagonist of earth, its presence can be used to dissipate earth's energy. Again, a bowl of water or a picture with water images will serve the purpose.

I find that flowers in a glass vase filled with water are the optimal choice. This is because flowers are growing plants and are carriers of wood energy; glass, which has a visual resemblance to ice, is a carrier of water energy; and the physical presence of water is in the vase.

WOOD

Wood is destroyed by metal. It is drained when it is used to nourish fire, and it is dissolved when it is used to destroy earth.

To counter the destructive effect of wood, you can use its antagonist, metal. Metal objects such as sculptures, tools, pewterware, and clocks with a swinging metal pendulum are good choices. I once advised a sculptor friend to place a small bronze statue of a logger swinging an ax as a countermeasure against the threat from a wood element.

You can also use the presence of fire to dissipate the energy of wood. Red objects are associated with fire, so you can place a painting with red images, or red-colored cushions and couch covers, to create the presence of fire. Strong lights are also carriers of fire, so it is also feasible to use a lamp or a ceiling light to counter wood. In fact, a ceiling light with a moving fan is a good countermeasure, since the movement of the fan will enhance the strength of the light.

The effects of wood can be weakened by having it destroy earth. Ceramic objects are carriers of earth energy and can be used for this purpose. However, from experience, I feel that ceramic objects are not strong enough, and wood is best countered by its antagonist metal and its beneficiary fire.

METAL

Metal is destroyed by fire. It is drained when used to nourish water, and it is dissolved when it is used to destroy wood.

To counter the threat of metal, you can use its antagonist, fire. Red objects and strong lights are carriers of fire.

You can also weaken the effects of metal by placing objects or images of water to dissipate the strength of metal when it is used to nourish water. Again, pictures of water images or a bowl of water will suit the purpose.

You may also place wooden objects to weaken metal by letting it expend its energy in destroying wood. A plant or wooden sculpture are viable objects for this use.

WATER

Water is destroyed by earth. It is drained when it is used to nourish wood, and it is dissolved when it is used in destroying fire.

To counter the threat of water, you can use its antagonist, earth, by placing earthen objects like ceramics in the position of water.

If you wish to neutralize the effect of water, you may have it nourish wood by placing wooden objects in the area of water.

Finally, you may also remove the effect of water by placing objects that are carriers of fire.

Countermeasures That Work with the Guardian Elements of the Occupants

In chapter 17, you learned that each person is born under the guardianship of a star of the Nine Palaces and its element. Some individuals are more suited to certain rooms because their guardian element has a harmonious relationship with the Earth Base star of the room. If the situation is such that it is not viable to get a perfect match between individuals and rooms, you may need to neutralize the influence of the Earth Base element in a room so that individuals with incompatible guardian elements can use it and not be harmed. There are several ways of doing this.

• You can neutralize the incompatible Earth Base element by destroying it with an antagonist element, draining it by having it nourish another element, or dissolving it by using it to destroy another element. In this method, you follow the same procedures described in the section above on how to counter the effects of malevolent stars of the Nine Palaces and their elements.

- You can strengthen the guardian element of the individual by placing artifacts that are carriers of the element that nourishes the individual's guardian element. Thus, you would place metal objects in a room to strengthen someone's water element against the room's Earth Base star nine-purple. In fact, metal is ideal here because it both strengthens the individual's guardian element and weakens the Earth Base element.

Using the Stars of the Nine Palaces as Natural Countermeasures

Sometimes the stars of the Nine Palaces in the geomantic chart can neutralize each other. For example, an Earth Base star of nine-purple (fire) can be neutralized by the presence of one-white (water), if the latter is the Facing Star of that square of the Nine Palaces. Thus, the presence of the stars themselves (and their elements) in the Nine Palaces can destroy, drain, and dissolve other elements, as described above.

In general, the element in the Facing Star is strongest, followed by that in the Earth Base, and finally the Mountain Star. The malevolent effects of a Mountain Star can usually be neutralized by the elements of either the Facing Star or the Earth Base star. The destructive effect of an Earth Base star can be neutralized by the element of the Facing Star alone. The malevolent effect of a Facing Star can be neutralized by a combination of the elements of the Earth Base star and Mountain Star. If you are doubtful about whether the stars in the

Palace can dissolve the destructive effect from the malevolent star, install a countermeasure artifact as well.

Special Objects

You will notice that in the discussion above on countermeasures, we have used ordinary objects as countermeasures. There are some special objects of power that can ward off destructive influences regardless of the nature of the incoming destruction. Here are some examples of such objects.

Figure 18.4 shows the images of two door guardians. When placed on both sides of the door, these guardians will ward off any destructive forces that may enter through the front door. They can be used against a driveway pointing at your house, incoming traffic from a road leading straight to your house, and a malevolent yearly star that occupies the position of the front door.

Another power object is the pa-k'ua mirror (fig. 18.5). This is a plaque with a mirror in the center surrounded by the trigrams of the pa-k'ua. The pa-k'ua mirror is generally used to ward off the effects of pointing objects, falling objects, reflecting objects, and traffic and driveways that are directed at your house.

The door guardian and pa-k'ua mirror plaques may be obtained in Chinese grocery stores in large Chinatowns and in Buddhist and Taoist temple supply stores in Hong Kong, Taiwan, or any Asian city with a large Chinese population.

Another object of power is the talisman. Talismans are words of power woven into a special script. The script calls on the guardians of the cosmos to help ward off destructive forces. Figure 18.6 shows a talisman that is designed to protect the occupants of a house from harm. Placement of this talisman at the

Fig. 18.4 Door guardians placed on the left (A) and right (B) sides of the door. The pa-k'ua mirror on top of the picture of the guardians adds strength to this artifact. (C) Placement of the two door guardians and the pa-k'ua mirror on a front door.

front entrance or living room will serve the same function as the pa-k'ua mirror and the door guardians. The talisman must be hand-written in red ink on yellow paper by an adept in that art. If you wish to use this method, you should seek the services of someone who practices Talismanic Taoism. Such persons are most likely found in Taoist temples. The talismans reprinted in this book are used as illustrations only. Do not attempt to copy the talismans printed in this book and place them yourself. They will not work, and may draw anger from the guardian deities if they are improperly written or placed.

C

Fig. 18.5 A pa-k'ua mirror. Most of these mirrors come with a hook, indicating the top orientation of the mirror. Should you get one without a hook, be sure that the segment with the three solid lines is oriented on top when you place this artifact.

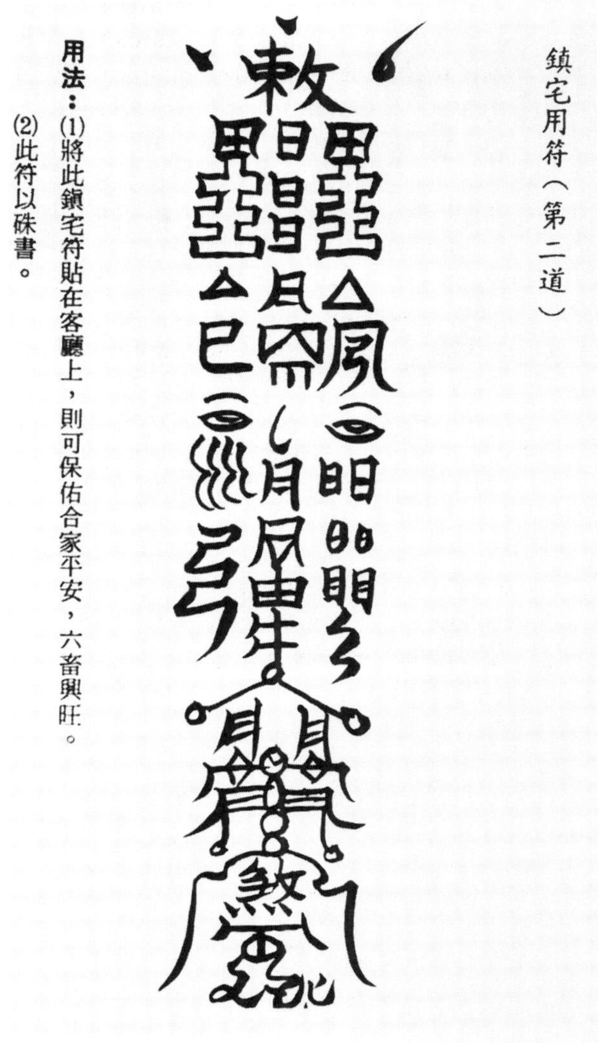

Fig. 18.6 A talisman of protection.

鎮宅用符（第二道）

用法：(1)將此鎮宅符貼在客廳上，則可保佑合家平安，六畜興旺。

(2)此符以硃書。

ENHANCERS

While countermeasures are used to neutralize undesirable effects, enhancers are designed to increase desirable effects. Typically, an enhancer is placed in an area to strengthen the element associated with a benevolent star or to increase the strength of an individual's guardian element.

Enhancers work in the opposite direction of countermeasures. Therefore, in installing enhancers, you will be using elements to nourish each other. Therefore, metal enhances water, water enhances wood, wood enhances fire, fire enhances earth, and earth enhances metal.

The following are scenarios in which enhancers are generally used.

- When you wish to increase the strength of a benevolent star and its element so that their effect on the occupants is increased. For example, if you wish to increase the effect of one-white (water), a star of health and longevity, you can place a metal object in the area where one-white is located.
- When you wish to enhance the effect of the element of one star so that it can counter the element of another star more effectively. For example, you can increase the effect of one-white (water) over nine-purple (fire) by placing a metal object in the area where one-white is located.
- When you wish to strengthen an individual's guardian element (see chapter 17) so that he or she can be protected from harmful elements. For example, if an individual's guardian element is wood, and if the individual is sleeping in a room with nine-purple (fire) as the Earth Base, you can strengthen the individual's element by placing objects associated with water in the room.

The art of placing countermeasures and enhancers is one of the most difficult skills of modern feng-shui. To excel in it requires experience, intuition, and creativity. But above all, it requires a deep understanding and an intimate relationship with the five elements and the stars of the Nine Palaces. For in working with countermeasures and enhancers, the feng-shui practitioner is truly a master of wind and water, and of the substances that make up the universe and the energy that swirl in it.

19

Sweeping the Karma of a Building

Why are some houses said to be haunted? Why do some buildings have a creepy feel to them? Why do successive businesses in the same building go bankrupt despite change of ownership or management? In feng-shui, we attribute such phenomena to the karma of the building. The relationship between humanity and the environment is reciprocal. As the forces of nature affect us, so our actions make an impact on the natural world, which in turn affects our lives. In the web of the universe, all things are interwoven with each other, and our world is tied to the world of the deities as well as the world of dead spirits.

Buildings are affected by their inhabitants and the activities that go on inside them. Houses have been described as "old and tired," "strange and eerie," or "warm and friendly." In feng-shui, we recognize that each building carries its own karma, which is the effects caused by activity that went on in the building in the past. Even when the inhabitants had vacated the house, these effects remain and will affect the fortunes of the new occupants.

Some buildings have good karma, some have bad karma, and some are neutral. Buildings that have good karma are those that have been occupied by honest and prosperous individuals, happy and harmonious families, and virtuous and honorable persons. In these houses, none of the inhabitants have met with untimely or accidental deaths, and none have committed crimes against humanity, nature, and the deities. Good karma in these buildings will linger to benefit the subsequent occupants. When a building has good karma, unfavorable factors in the geomantic chart, the internal environment, and the external environment will be lessened. Favorable factors will be enhanced. However, the good karma of a building can be destroyed if the current occupants become dishonorable or dishonest, or become involved with unethical or criminal activities.

Buildings with neutral karma are those that have been occupied by people whose fortunes did not rise dramatically and whose actions did not cause large effects. Such buildings will have very little effect on what is determined by the geomantic chart, the internal environment, and the external environment. In other words, the karma of the building is not a moderating factor.

Buildings that have bad karma are those that are associated with death, violence, crime, and illness. Bad karma of a building may neutralize favorable factors in the geomantic chart, the internal environment, and the external environment, and will increase the severity of the unfavorable factors.

When you select a house, you should therefore find out why the previous occupants moved out of the building, what kind of people they were, and what activities went on inside the building. Some karmic repercussions are so strong that even after the building has been torn down, the land still carries the effects of previous usage. In Hong Kong, a movie theater was built on a lot where a funeral parlor once stood. The patrons of the theater reported hearing voices and seeing ghostly figures walking in the aisle. Sometimes, instead of hearing dialogue in the films, the audience would hear "complaints" of how someone had died an untimely death.

The owners of the theater finally invited both Buddhist and Taoist priests to conduct several days of chanting to make peace with the deceased spirits. After that, the ghostly phenomena never occurred again.

If you discover that your building has bad karma, you need not move out. There are ways to sweep the karma of the building so that the causes in its past do not carry effects into the present. The following are conditions when the karma of the building need to be swept.

1. When the building is on an ancient burial ground.
2. When the building is on ground where executions, mass killings, or other deaths have taken place. Examples include battlefields, sites of massacres, and concentration camps.
3. When the building is on land where these types of buildings once stood: slaughterhouse or butchery, funeral parlor, prison with an execution chamber, hospital, hospice, morgue.
4. When the building was once used as one of the categories listed in (3).
5. When a person has been murdered in the building.
6. When an occupant of the building has died an untimely or accidental death.
7. When the building was vacated due to bankruptcy or foreclosure.

METHODS OF SWEEPING THE KARMA OF A BUILDING

The best way to sweep the karma of a building is to invite people who are adept in methods of calming the spirits of the deceased and removing mischievous spirits to restore peace and well-being to the place. The Buddhists and Taoists have developed very specialized techniques for these purposes, and you can obtain their services by contacting their temples. If you choose this method, then you should expect ceremonies and chanting sessions. Most of these ceremonies require altars and paraphernalia associated with the event. The Buddhist or Taoist temple will generally provide the trappings and special objects for the altar, but you may need to build the altar or buy the fruit offerings and incense required for the ceremonies.

Typical Buddhist ceremonies involve invoking the names of the Buddha, or chanting a sutra of the bodhisattva Kuan-yin (the Compassionate One) or the bodhisattva Kshitigarbha (or Ti-ts'ang, the Deliverer of Tormented Souls). Typical Taoist ceremonies ask the guardians of heaven and earth to purify the environment and purge the place of malevolent spirits.

If you cannot engage Buddhists or Taoists to perform these rituals, and you still wish to follow an Eastern method of washing away bad karma, you may perform the following simple ritual. On a table, place incense in a burner. Stand at the table, preferably accompanied by two or three others, and chant the Buddhist mantra known as the Great Dharani. This mantra invokes the names of the bodhisattva Kuan-yin, and in chanting it, the restless spirits may be calmed. A phonetic version of this chant, translated from the original Sanskrit, appears in appendix E. After chanting this mantra three times, make some offer-

ings. If you live in a city where there are Chinese grocery stores, you can see if the store carries "paper money for the dead." Get a packet of this item and burn it. In your mind, sincerely ask the spirits to vacate the place and be at peace. This procedure is to be used only if you cannot get the services of Buddhist or Taoist adepts to sweep the karma of the building. If the karmic forces of the building are strong, then this technique may not work, because you may not have enough personal power to ask the spirits to leave.

Another technique in sweeping the karma of a building is to put up talismans. Figure 19.1 shows talismans designed to purify the land and its surrounding environment. Should you decide to use this method, you need to obtain one from a Taoist temple. The talismans shown here are for illustrative purposes only. Do not copy and place them yourself.

If you wish to seek help in sweeping the karma of the building, you may ask practitioners from wisdom traditions other than Buddhist or Taoist. Native American, Celtic, and many indigenous shamanic cultures have equivalent ceremonies for this purpose. The philosophy of feng-shui is compatible with all spiritual traditions, and you should feel comfortable in using an approach from the spiritual tradition of your preference.

CARRYING GOOD KARMA FROM ONE BUILDING TO ANOTHER

Many Chinese families keep the house where they made their fortune even when they can afford a newer and larger home. If they do move into a new house, the old one is kept as a future home for the children or as a guest house. I know several millionaires in Hong Kong who continue to rent their old apart-

ments even when they have built large mansions. It is also a traditional practice for Chinese businesses to keep the building where the business became successful. The owners may open a new branch on larger premises, but the old location is kept as an office or a secondary storefront. These practices are based on the

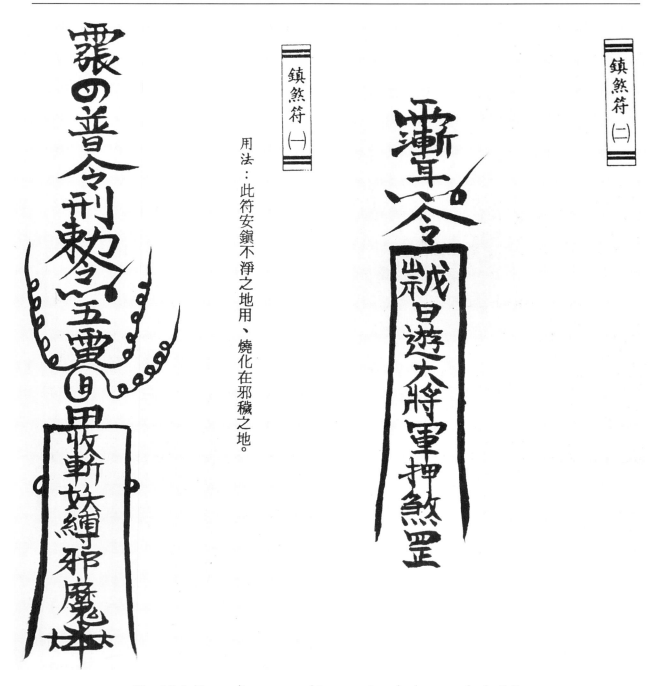

Fig. 19.1 Two talismans used in sweeping the karma of a building.

belief that good karma accumulated in a building can be carried to another building, if the old one is kept. You may wish to keep this in mind should you decide to move into another building when you expand your business or when you have resources for a bigger house.

With the end of this chapter, you should have completed an introductory course in feng-shui. You have been exposed to the history and theory of feng-shui, and you have learned how to practice the rudiments of the art. All the materials covered in this book came from my experience as an apprentice and a practitioner of feng-shui. When I learned this art from my granduncle, I did not have the luxury of a textbook or a manual. Information was not necessarily organized; knowledge came now and then, and in bits and pieces. I hope that this book will help you to learn a very complex art in an easy way. In any case, you will have the security of having the book to refer to when you need it. Thanks to many modern developments, like publishing, photography, computer graphics, and word processing, it is now possible to learn the basics of feng-shui from a book. When I was an apprentice in this art, I had to commit all the information covered in this book, and more, to memory. While it made me appreciate the scope of feng-shui and the challenge of mastering it, looking back, I would have liked to have a textbook when I was struggling with the intricacies of an art that has over three thousand years of development in history.

—

H I D I N G
A N D   R E V E A L I N G
T H E   U N I V E R S E

—

White clouds close behind when I look back.
Green mists disappear when I enter.
Earth patterns change at the middle peak.
Shade and light are different in every valley.

—WANG WEI, Chinese poet of the T'ang dynasty

Guard the Mysteries!
Constantly reveal Them!

—LEW WELCH, American poet

20

An Ancient Wisdom for Modern Times

The universe hides and reveals. To some people, once something is known or explained in a particular way, the door to that part of the world is closed. To others, the universe constantly reveals its wonder and mystery, and the more they see, the more there is to see.

Feng-shui has been studied by anthropologists and Sinologists from the perspective of a so-called detached observer who analyzes and collates information. Unfortunately, this attitude is precisely opposite to that which is required to understand this art. The images in feng-shui are rooted in encounters with the spirit of the land, and to the practitioner of feng-shui, the land is a living entity.

When feng-shui is experienced from the perspective of a practitioner, it offers us a different way of seeing the world. It sensitizes us to aspects of reality that we never would have known, and reorients us to interact with the land and the environment in a harmonious

rather than destructive way. The universe becomes an interplay of dynamic forces and changes rather than a collection of objects to be dissected, manipulated, and exploited.

Although feng-shui is founded on the Taoist vision and experience of nature, the idea that the land is filled with energy, life, and power is not unique to Taoism. In his book *The Ancient Science of Geomancy,* Nigel Pennick says, "The practice of geomancy, which may roughly be defined as the science of putting human habitats and activities into harmony with the visible and the invisible world around us, was at one time universal."[1]

All indigenous peoples share a sense of appreciation and harmony with the world around them, and believe that humanity has been charged with the responsibility of preserving this harmony. At a conference on the

[1] Nigel Pennick, *The Ancient Science of Geomancy* (London: Thames and Hudson, 1979), p. 7.

249

world religions, I met Burton Pretty-on-Top, spiritual leader of the Crow people. We talked about the Taoist and the Native American views of the environment and discovered many similarities between these two traditions.

If our own existence is to involve a constructive relationship with the world around us, it follows that there are "correct" ways of living. "Correct" living is harmonious living, and to live harmoniously with the environment is to be attuned to the energies that flow in the universe. It also means that we build dwellings that do not disrupt the flow of these energies. Respect the environment, and the environment will nourish you. This is what partnership and interdependency with the land are all about. The point is eloquently stated by a Tibetan spiritual leader, the Twelfth Tai Situpa; "Your surroundings should be chosen according to [subtle] energy currents, and the most favorable sites are those that receive and make the most of the beneficial energies available. . . . The science of geomancy is a study of the effects of environmental energies, the operating principles of these energies, and the steps that can be taken to improve circumstances by harmonizing environmental forces and incorporating the environment's inconspicuous forces into architectural and landscape design."[2]

The awareness of energy or power flowing through the land is hardly restricted to Asiatic cultures. In the Celtic tradition, the earth is diffused with spirit, and its power is present in the rocks, caves, hills, springs, rivers, wells, and trees. When energy moves, it travels through the ley lines, or the Old Straight Tracks. When it is still, it is concentrated in grottoes, springs, and groves. The ancient peoples of Europe experienced these energies directly and understood that they were the source of power that renewed the earth. If the places of power were damaged or destroyed, then life on earth would not be renewed and everything would wither and die.

The sense that there is power in nature was central to the ancient Greeks as well. From the poetry of Hesiod we get the impression that nature is alive and that this power is "generous." It gives freely to nourish all things intertwined with it, and its power is primarily concentrated in caves, streams, and mountains. Even when the Celts and the Greeks settled in towns, the architecture that was built in places of power was a linkage between earth spirit and human existence. Any incorrectness in orienting such structures or error in selecting the site would bring uncontrollable disaster.

If the intimate relationship between humanity and the environment was so deep-rooted in both Eastern and Western cultures, then why did the Western philosopher Martin Heidegger lament that environment and dwelling have lost their meaning in modern society? In *Poetry, Language, and Thought,* he says, "The real dwelling plight lies in this, that mortals ever search anew for the nature of dwelling, that they must ever learn to dwell."[3] Heidegger is referring to the alienation between the natural and the built and to the loss of the sense of wonder at nature in our time. The land has become real estate that can be bought and sold, and is no longer felt as a source of energy and nourishment. More-

[2] The Twelfth Tai Situpa, *Relative World, Ultimate Mind* (Boston: Shambhala Publications, 1992), pp. 109–10.

[3] Martin Heidegger, *Poetry, Language, and Thought,* translated by Albert Hofstadter. (New York: Harper and Row, 1971), p. 161.

over, our modern temperament has a tendency to dismiss the indigenous and ancient views of the environment as primitive and the product of illiterate minds, just as many "objective" and "detached" observers have regarded feng-shui as a bunch of superstitious beliefs.

To recover the meaning of the environment, we need to "see" the land in a radically different way. Some geographers and ecologists have already called for a change in our geographical experience of the environment to include "the entire realm of feelings, [and the] acts and experiences of individuals in which they apprehend themselves in a distinct relationship with their environment." There is a "need to conceive the environment as a network of potential places capable of inviting and sustaining a complex of physical, emotional, intellectual, and spiritual interactions." In these ecologically centered approaches to the environment, "landscapes, therefore, take on the very character of human existence. They can be full of life, deathly dull, exhilarating, sad, joyful or pleasant."[4] As a theory and practice, feng-shui can help us recover this experience of nature.

To experience the power of the land, we need to set aside our view that nature is composed of inanimate objects. In the world of feng-shui, the land is alive and filled with energy. It breathes, it feeds, it sleeps, and it frolics. It is sometimes playful, sometimes mischievous, and at times it can even be malicious and angry. When you look at rocks, trees, and rivers, what do you see? Do you see obstacles along the trail? Do you see objects that will

make a good photograph? Are you only concerned with the activity of walking and never notice what's around you? Or do you see landscapes smiling, grimacing, contemplating, chatting to each other, chuckling to themselves, or even trying to attract your attention, as if saying, "Hey, look at me!"?

Look at the areas of the photographs enclosed in boxes in figures 20.1 through 20.3. These are rocks that doze, watch, and feed. They are just a few examples of the spirit in nature. I saw these spirit rocks on casual walks in the foothills near where I live. You can see such things too if you allow yourself to be open to the spirit in nature. If you wish to experience the totality of the world and catch a glimpse of the energy that flows through the universe, you must let the land invite you to interact and participate in its secrets. This is the essence of feng-shui.

Even if we have cultivated a sense of openness to nature, we still need to work on the relationship between the natural landscape and the structures we build on it. When we build our dwellings in the environment, we need to ensure that a harmonious relationship exists between the natural and the built. Again, feng-shui can give us guidance. Some buildings blend with the environment, while others clash with it. In feng-shui, buildings with irregular shapes and sharp features are not conducive to both people and environment. Buildings that have long, dark corridors stifle those who inhabit them because they shut out the yang energy of the sun. These age-old guidelines from feng-shui are surprisingly similar to the ecologically oriented approaches in modern architecture. One of the most prominent American architects of our time, Christopher Alexander, came to similar conclusions about shapes of buildings, ceiling design, and placement of windows. I was un-

[4]David Seamon and Robert Mugerauer, eds., *Dwelling, Place, and Environment* (New York: Columbia University Press, Morningside Edition, 1985), pp. 20, 191, 23.

Fig. 20.1 A mountain in the form of a frog lying in repose.

aware of Alexander's work until I had almost completed this book. As I read his book *A Pattern Language,* I am fascinated by the similarities between the feng-shui of external and internal environments and Alexander's vision of environmental planning and architectural design.[5]

Alexander writes, "People are by nature phototropic—they move toward light, and when stationary, they orient themselves toward the light."[6] He goes on to recommend that buildings should not have long, dark corridors, and that windows or skylights will make passageways more comfortable and inviting. Of dark, long, and winding corridors, he says, "The movement between rooms is as important as the rooms themselves. In a building where the movement is mean, the passages are dark and narrow—rooms open off them as dead ends; you spend your time entering the building, or moving between rooms, like a crab scuttling in the dark."[7]

[5] C. Alexander, S. Ishikawa, and M. Silverstein, *A Pattern Language* (New York: Oxford University Press, 1977). I am indebted to Jonathan Green of Shambhala Publications for steering me toward this book.

[6] Ibid., p. 645.
[7] Ibid., p. 628.

Fig. 20.2 A rock in the form of a head with eyes, nose, mouth, and a large forehead. This figure is watching the river flowing by.

Alexander also warns against ceilings that slope or have irregular surfaces, and of high-rise buildings with sharp and pointed features. He says, "High buildings make people crazy. High buildings have no genuine advantages, except in speculative gains for banks and land owners. They are not cheaper, they do not help create open space, they destroy the townscape, they destroy social life, they promote crime, they make life difficult for children, they are expensive to maintain; they wreck the open spaces near them, and they damage light and air and view."[8] In feng-shui,

tall buildings with sharp features disturb the flow of energy, create vortices of malevolent forces, and block the yang energy of the sun from the streets. When yang energy diminishes, dark or destructive energy rises. Where destructive energies gather, crime and violence will be enhanced.

What kinds of buildings are harmonious with the environment and what kinds are not? From the perspective of feng-shui, buildings that intrude into the environment or do not blend with the surroundings are inharmonious with the land. Such buildings appear as if they want to stand out and show themselves rather than be a part of their environment. It

[8] Ibid., p. 115.

Fig. 20.3 A rock with an open mouth, about to feed on the branches of a tree.

is as if they want to feel more important than everything around them. This idea is reflected in a remarkably similar view from ecologically sensitive philosophers of environment design. "It will no longer be quite so ridiculous to think of buildings as narcissistic—as self-absorbed images forever performing before the camera without giving much attention to the living needs of the inhabitants and passersby. A great deal of recent architecture, including interior design, has often managed to perform admirably before the camera without giving much aid or comfort to inhabitants."[9] This was what the philosopher Hei-

[9] Seamon et al., p. 221.

degger meant when he raised the issue that modern humanity has lost its touch with the meaning of "dwelling." When the primary function of a house ceases to be a dwelling, the harmony between the built and the natural, the house and the environment, is broken.

Both feng-shui and Western ecology agree that the dwellings of indigenous peoples and "common" houses turn out to be the ones that are most harmonious with the environment. The pueblos of the American Southwest, the cave dwellings of the Anazazi, the mobile dwellings of nomadic peoples of the world, the log cabins of homesteaders, the European cottage, the farmhouse of the American Midwest, and even the typical house of an average family in the United States do not exert an intrusive presence in the environment. This is because these dwellings were built not for show, but to be lived in. These buildings do not sport designs from the latest architectural and design fads, and were built for one very simple but important function: to be inhabited by people. These houses are not just buildings; they are truly dwellings.

Finally, feng-shui can help us rediscover our sensitivity to the world, to see all that is infinite, powerful, wondrous, and mysterious. It creates for us what the French philosopher Gaston Bachelard calls a "poetics of space."[10] For Bachelard, the mysteries of the universe are revealed in reverie, dream, imagination, and poetics. The mind of a feng-shui practitioner is also a mind that is open to the mysteries of the universe. By cultivating intuition and sensitivity to the environment, we can become aware of the energy that flows through the universe and catch a glimpse of the fleeting moments of transformations and the underlying reality of all things.

Far from being a product of a superstitious mind or a system of explanations that fail the test of scientific scrutiny, feng-shui reveals the hidden mysteries of the universe and provides us with a way of living harmoniously with them. When we practice feng-shui, we are indeed the guardians and caretakers of the environment, for through it we make ourselves and others aware of the vast immensity of the world around us and the interdependency of all things.

---

[10] Gaston Bachelard, *The Poetics of Space,* translated by Maria Jolas. (Boston: Beacon Press, 1964).

THE DYNASTIES OF CHINA

Dates for the Chinese dynasties are those adopted by textbooks of Chinese history published in Hong Kong. Note that the dynasties of China did not always occupy the same geographical regions. Some dynasties overlap in time, and there were periods of political chaos where no ruling house was in control.

Hsia	2205–1765 BCE
Shang	1766–1121 BCE
Chou	1122–225 BCE
Western Chou	1122–770 BCE
Eastern Chou	770–221 BCE
Spring and Autumn Period	770–476 BCE
Warring States Period	475–221 BCE
Ch'in	221–221 BCE
Han	206 BCE–219 CE
Western Han	206 BCE–8 CE
Eastern Han	25 CE–220 CE
Three Kingdoms	229–265 CE
Wei	220–265 CE
Shu	221–263 CE
Wu	222–280 CE

Chin	265–420 CE
Western Chin	265–316 CE
Eastern Chin	317–420 CE
Six Dynasties	420–589 CE
Sui	589–618 CE
T'ang	618–906 CE
Five Dynasties and Ten Kingdoms	907–960 CE
Sung	960–1129 CE
Northern Sung	960–1126 CE
Southern Sung	1127–1279 CE
Yüan	1271–1368 CE
Ming	1368–1644 CE
Ch'ing	1644–1911 CE

The Dynastic Era Ends

Republic of China	1911–1949 CE
People's Republic of China	1949–

STEPS IN DOING A FENG-SHUI READING

1. Evaluate the external environment (chap. 11).

a. Examine the general layout of the land. Look at the pattern of mountains, waters, rivers, roads, and vegetation. Determine whether these environments are beneficial or destructive.

b. Look for harmful objects and structures. If these cannot be dealt with by countermeasures (chap. 18), then this is sufficient reason to reject the building.

c. Look for beneficial objects and structures. These are not necessities but will add to the beneficial effects.

2. Evaluate the internal environment (chap. 12).

a. Look at the shape of the house. If the shape is unfavorable, then this is sufficient reason to reject the building.

b. Look at the positions of the driveway and garage in relationship to the house.

c. Examine the interior structure and building materials.

d. Examine the general layout of the floor plan and look for undesirable features.

3. Take the geomantic compass reading to obtain the Front and Mountain Directions of the house (chap. 13).

a. Figure out the front facing of the house.

b. Take the readings of the Front and Mountain Directions. For those using a regular compass instead of a geomantic compass, use the template provided in chapter 13 or Appendix D to covert degrees to the Twenty-four Directions.

4. Set up the geomantic chart for the house (chap. 14).

a. Find out when the house was built to determine its Earth Base.

b. Using information about Front and Mountain Directions in conjunction with the

Nine Cycles charts, set up the Earth Base, the Mountain Stars, and the Facing Stars of the Nine Palaces of the geomantic chart.

c. Identify the Facing Palace and interpret the conditional interaction between the Earth Base number and the Facing Star number.

d. Identify the Central Palace and interpret the unconditional interaction between the Earth Base number and the Facing Star number.

e. Special geomantic charts like the Three Combinations and the Combination of Ten have unique interpretations.

f. You will need to set up multiple charts if the house has undergone major renovations in a cycle different from the one it was built in.

5. Superimpose the geomantic chart onto the floor plan (chap. 15).

a. Identify the Facing Palace of the geomantic chart, and reorient the chart if the Facing Palace occupies a corner position of the Nine Palaces.

b. If necessary, stretch the geomantic chart to fit the floor plan.

c. Interpret the meaning of the numbers of the Earth Base, Facing Star, and Mountain Star for each area of the building. Pay attention to the stars at the front door, the back door (if it is used frequently), and the hallways and stairs. Examine the effects of the stars for all the rooms in the house.

d. Superimpose the Nine Palaces onto the microcosms of each room, and interpret the meaning of the Earth Base, Facing Star, and Mountain Star for areas in the room.

e. Using information from (d), decide where to place furniture.

6. Determine the influence of the yearly and monthly ruling stars (chap. 16).

a. Find out the era (upper, middle, or lower) of the year you wish to work out the ruling star's influence.

b. Set up the yearly stars of the Nine Palaces, and superimpose the grid onto the geomantic chart.

c. Interpret the interaction of the yearly star with the Earth Base and Facing Star in each of the Nine Palaces.

d. Find out the ruling star for each month of the year. The first lunar month begins on the first day of spring or the first day of the lunar new year, whichever occurs first. Remember that the movement of the numbers in the Nine Palaces changes to the reverse sequence after the summer solstice.

e. Superimpose the monthly stars of the Nine Palaces onto the geomantic chart for each month.

f. Interpret the interaction of the monthly stars with the Earth Base and the Facing Star in each of the Nine Palaces for every month.

7. Match the occupants to the building (chap. 17).

a. Find out the dates of birth of the occupants, and determine their guardian star and element.

b. Examine the interaction between the element of the head(s) of the family and the Earth Base star in the Palace where the front door is located.

c. Look at how each individual's guardian element interacts with the Earth Base stars in the bedrooms, and get the best fit for everyone.

8. Set up countermeasures and enhancers (chap. 18).

a. Install countermeasures against harmful objects and structures in the external environment.

b. Plan the projects on implementing the

countermeasures needed to change the floor plan and other internal structures.

c. Place artifacts to neutralize harmful effects of objects.

d. Plan usage of rooms to avoid malevolent stars in the geomantic chart.

e. Place artifacts to neutralize harmful effects from the stars of the Nine Palaces in the geomantic chart.

f. Place artifacts to neutralize harmful effects of "visiting" yearly and monthly stars.

g. Place artifacts to neutralize harmful effects of stars on individuals' guardian elements.

h. Place enhancers to increase benevolent effects of the stars of the geomantic chart and the "visiting" stars.

9. Sweep the karma of the building, if necessary (chap. 19).

a. Find out about the building and its previous occupants.

b. Decide if the karma needs to be swept.

c. Choose the method, and plan for the event.

WHERE TO FIND KEY INFORMATION

Information is listed in the sequence that it will be needed to do a feng-shui reading.

APPENDIX D

TEMPLATE OF THE TWENTY-FOUR DIRECTIONS RING

Photocopy or cut out this template for use in making your own geomantic compass according to the instructions beginning on page 175.

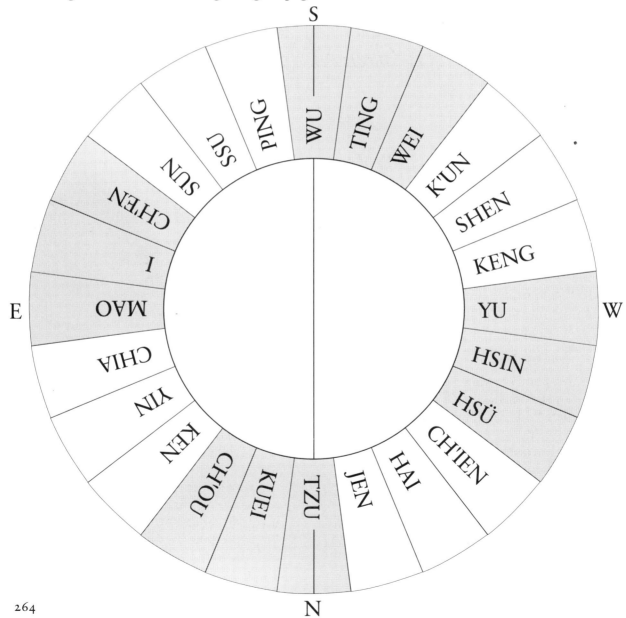

THE GREAT DHARANI

This is a phonetic version of the Chinese chant of the names of the Boddhisattva of Compassion, translated from the original Sanskrit.

1. Nam mo hor la dan na doh la yair yair
2. Nam mo aw lay yair
3. Poh low ghee dee cho bo la yair
4. Poh tai sza doh por yair
5. Mor hor sza doh por yair
6. Mor hor ga lo leh ga yair
7. Aan
8. Sza pun la fa yair
9. So dan nor dan sair
10. Nam mor see ghee le do yee min aw lay yair
11. Po lo ghee de see fu la ling tor por
12. Nam mo nor la gheen chee
13. See le mor hor pun doh sza meh
14. Sza po aw dor dao sue pong
15. Aw see yin
16. Sza po sza do na mor po sza do na mo po kair
17. Mor fa dan dao
18. Dan jee ta
19. Aan aw po lo see
20. Lor ga dai
21. Ga lo dai
22. Ye sze lee
23. Mor hor po tai sza dor
24. Sza po sza po
25. Mo la mo la
26. Mo see mo see le tor yair
27. Kui lo kui lo gay mong
28. Doh loh doh loh fa sair yair day
29. Mor hor fa sair yair day
30. Tor loh tor loh
31. Day ley lay
32. See fu la yair
33. Tsair la tsair la
34. Moh moh fa moh la
35. Moe day dee
36. Ye sze ye sze

37. Sze lo sze lo
38. Aw la aum fu la tsair leh
39. Fa sa fa sum
40. Fu la szair yair
41. Fu lo fu lo mor la
42. Fu lo fu lo sze lee
43. Soh la soh la
44. See lee see lee
45. Soh lo soh lo
46. Po tai yair po tai yair
47. Poh tor yair poh tor yair
48. Lay dee lay yair
49. Lor la gheen chee
50. Day lay see lay lor
51. Poh yair mor lay
52. Sor por hor
53. See tor yair
54. Sor por hor
55. Mo hor see tor yair
56. Sor por hor
57. Shee tor yee tee
58. See pung la yair
59. Sor por hor
60. Lor la gheen chee

61. Sor por hor
62. Mo la law la
63. Sor por hor
64. See la sum aw mo kair yair
65. Sor por hor
66. Sor por mo hor aw see tor yair
67. Sor por hor
68. Jair ghee la aw see tor yair
69. Sor por hor
70. Bor tor moh ghee see tor yair
71. Sor por hor
72. Nor la ghee chee pung kair lay yair
73. Sor por hor
74. Mo por leh sing ghair la yair
75. Sor por hor
76. Nam mor hor la dan la dor la yair yair
77. Nam mor aw leh yair
78. Po lo ghee dee
79. Chor bo la yair
80. Sor por hor
81. Aan see deen doh
82. Wan dor la
83. Butt tor yair
84. Sor por hor

SELECTED REFERENCES IN CHINESE

For those of you who read Chinese and would like to look at some traditional Chinese texts of feng-shui, here is a selected bibliography.

ALMANAC AND CALENDAR

通勝/通書

新編萬年曆

REFERENCES ON TALISMANS

崑崙符法總解

符咒妙術全書

FENG-SHUI REFERENCES

羅經透解

地理四秘全書

青囊海角經

圖解地理辨龍指要

地理集成

地理砂水穴法

圖解地理點穴宝鑑—水龍經

圖解風水本義

地理龍穴判斷

風水形勢理氣篇

平陽全書

地學

地理人子須知

堪輿學原理

唐宋陰陽五行論集

玄空大五行眞傳口訣

易經地理陽宅眞機

陽宅眞訣

沈氏玄空學說

沈氏玄空秘藏

孔氏玄空宝鑑

易經三元羅經透解

挨星闡微

葬書

INDEX

Page numbers for figures and tables are in italics.